NO LONGER A
MUSLIM

BY JAMAL ZAYANI

NO LONGER A MUSLIM

For information, contact Comfort Publishing at P.O. Box 6265, Concord, NC 28027.

First printing

Book cover design
by Reed Karriker

ISBN: 978-1-938388-01-9
Published by Comfort Publishing, LLC
www.comfortpublishing.com

Printed in the United States of America

To my beautiful daughter Zeineb,
Whom I wish one day will discover the true Jesus

FOREWORD

Had people asked me a year ago if I believed in Allah, I would have laughed and probably said, "Are you kidding me?" If they persisted and went a step further to ask, "Do you think Muhammad is a true prophet?" I would have, very likely, answered with a fist to their jaw.

But many things have changed since then. After 11 months in the Gulf region, I was transformed from being a slave into a free man. Call me an atheist — or better, a *ronin* — but never label me with the name of Muslim again. I would rather throw myself to the wolves than wake up one day with the mark of the beast on my forehead. I think anyone who reads my story will understand why.

I remember that almost no one missed the opportunity to take part in the yearly pilgrimage to the holy land of Mecca to pray for Allah's forgiveness upon the mountain of Arafat. Most of my fellow teachers returned home with a renewed devotion to *salat* (prayer). Some of them even became fundamental Salafists.

My teaching experience in Oman was a blessing in disguise. It freed me from the fetters of the so-called sacred, and opened my eyes to a bitter truth. We Muslims have been fooled for more than 14 centuries.

It hurts a lot when you spend a whole life believing in something that turns out to be a fallacy. It makes you lose hope at first, but then, sometimes your eyes are opened and you choose to be free. I was fortunate to have had a friend like Hazem while on my journey to genuinely know the truth.

My story is true and the things revealed in this book are most probably shared for the first time. It might shock some, but I think it is time that the truth should be told to everyone. I know I am taking a big risk with my life, but I think it is a cheap price for the freedom I have been given.

However, let me start at the beginning.

CHAPTER 1

Two weeks before I was born, my father, Hedi, who at that time was working deep in the desert of *Sebha* — south of Libya — had a vision. It was before the time that people could foretell the gender of a child. He was so happy and excited that he called my mum at my Uncle Jilani's home. My uncle was the only person my mum knew, who had a telephone at that time. He told her that she was going to give birth to a male child and she should name him Jamal.

My father's job was to neutralize mines dating from the First World War. It required that he be gone from Algeria, and his family, for long periods of time. In fact, for the first 12 years of my life my father only spent one month every year at home. This particular time he had left before my mum even knew that she was pregnant.

"How do you know this?" my mum asked my father.

"I saw Sidi Ahmad al Tijani, *Khatam Al Awliaa* (seal of the saints) in a dream and he told me I would have a son and I was to call him Jamal," he explained.

"You must go and slaughter an *alloush* (lamb)," he added. "I will send you some money."

Mum was very happy because I was the fourth pregnancy after three successive female births. However, my eldest sister told me many years later that they had almost nothing to eat at that time. They had been eating *gilya* (roasted wheat) for three months. And, unfortunately, the money order Father sent took two weeks to reach her in Algeria, so Mum managed to borrow a few *dinars* from the neighbors and bought a thin old chicken from the market.

Then, just as my father had predicted, I was born on a hot August day at dawn. Blida, where I was born, was hot and dry in summer, but very cold in winter, with icy winds coming from the Atlas Mountains. Much of the year, this created a blanket of snow all around the small city. My mum was very young at that time, and very beautiful. Her skin had an olive complexion, and her eyes were large and hazel. Her hair, tucked most of the time under a *hijab,* was black and thick. When she smiled, the world stopped turning. She was that beautiful. My father, Hedi, was fair-skinned with black hair, and looked like the famous Egyptian actor, Omar Sharif.

When I was young, I would go with Mum to the market, or, after long hours of beseeching, she would agree to take me to the beach. In each place, I could see the hungry eyes of men devouring her, and as young as I was, I would clench my little fingers and glare at them with every bit of my might. My mum never looked at them or gave them the least chance to come close. She loved my father and was very faithful to him.

One day, I remember she was accosted by a drunken vagrant while we were in the market. My mum told him to stay away, but he kept trying to talk and impress her. Suddenly, she took a big stone and threw it at the man's head. The people gathered around the man, who was almost dead. It is needless to say that men feared her from that day on. That very day, I knew why my father loved my mum so dearly.

We were very poor because my father had spent most of his youth as a soldier in the French army. After the liberation of Algeria on the 18th of march 1962, most of the *fellagas* (freedom fighters) were able to learn new trades, but my father lacked social skills and the desire to learn. All he wanted was to spend his time in the company of my mum and me. The pension he received from France (service of 'Anciens Combattants') was scarce and not enough to provide for a relatively large family like ours.

"Had I been injured, I would have been very rich," my father would say at times of financial hardship, when he was struggling to provide for his family.

Indeed, he had spent no less than five years in Indochina and came back unharmed — not even a scratch. A friend of his who had lost his hand received disability payments that were at least 20 times more than his. In 1954, Father joined FLN — the National Liberation Front. He fought with Mujahedeen, or 'sacred freedom fighters,' in the mountains against the very French he had defended in what later would be called Vietnam. Unfortunately, Father did not receive any money from our government, for he lost every document that proved he was a veteran.

My sisters never enjoyed the same love and warmth that I was given from my father and mother. They were simply my servants. Even though I was the youngest, I was a man and I could order them to do anything. I was the only one who ate sweets if there were some, the only one who wore new clothes during *Eid* (the Muslim celebration that follows the fasting month of Ramadan) and the only one who was given some pocket money from time to time.

My sisters developed a certain amount of cunning out of this unjust situation, however. As a case in point, they would eat my pudding and then smear my mouth. Sometimes they would steal my money or convince me that 10 *millimes* (cents) had more value than 100 *millimes*. They would buy my 100 *millimes* with a brand new 10 *millimes* coin.

I lived almost all my childhood years without a father. My mother was, in fact, my father, my closest sister and my friend. My sister recounted that my father never thought about investing his money in any business, as most of his friends did. Had he done that, we would have been better off. Instead, my poor father would return home once a year and when the money was gone, he would decide to return to Libya.

My sister always told me — while laughing until tears welled in her eyes — that Father would trim his moustache and only take with him his old plastic bag, two things that he thought brought him good luck. He would give Mum two *dinars* — the price of a lantern — and leave. We were forced to borrow all we needed from Am Ibrahim — the general grocer — and Am Mihoub, the green grocer who sold fruits and vegetables. Then, at the end of the year, Father would come back and pay them. We couldn't afford to be sick, or to desire anything above the necessary. Most of the people at that time were poor. Inside that poor neighborhood where we lived, except for very few, nobody was better off than anyone else. Consequently we did not know how poor we were and we did not care.

I was 12 when Father decided to leave his dangerous job and come to Algiers to settle down with us for good. He had spent more than a decade working in the large desert of Sebha, Libya. Normally, a male child is circumcised very young. In my case, I was 12 years old when Father decided it was time to have this celebration. At that time there were so few doctors that it cost a significant amount of money to bring a doctor to your home. So people continued with their traditional circumcisers, who most of them worked as barbers, and were dexterous in using scissors. I remember that Hajj Ali — the only barber in our neighborhood — refused to do the circumcision because of my age.

"*Astagfirullah,* I ask forgiveness from Allah; he is already a man — are you crazy?" he asked. My father and my uncles spent a long time trying to persuade the old man. At last he agreed and cut my skin very ruthlessly. For weeks afterwards I suffered both from the pain of the operation and the stigma of everyone knowing my condition. Even the new pair of jeans that my father bought me for the occasion offered no solace for my situation.

A few weeks after my circumcision, Father received a letter of appointment for a job as an *imam* in Omar Ibn Abi Al khattab Mosque. His job was to conduct the five prayers every day and to read a *Khotba* (a sermon) every Friday. Our financial situation became much better after that and my life became relatively normal.

All in all, I lived a happy life. Compared to my neighbors, my family was neither poor nor rich — we simply managed. I would spend most of my time at school or in the public library. I always dreamed of being a writer, to be able to write a great book that made all the Christian *koffar* (infidels) become followers of what I thought was the righteous path.

Since the age of seven, I had never missed a prayer. Then after my father was appointed *imam*, I would always go to the mosque with him. On Ramadan, my father would pray *tarawih* (extra congregational prayers performed by Muslims at night in the Islamic month of Ramadan). As an *imam*, he had the duty to lead the prayer and recite from memory all the Qur'an in 30 nights. Every night he would recite two *hisbz* (chapters) for about two and a half hours after *isha* (night prayers). As young as I was, they allowed me to pray in the first rank, just behind my father. Whenever he made a mistake, I would correct him. He was so proud of me and I followed eagerly as he led me deeper into the faith.

Like anyone from a pious Muslim background, I was taught that Islam was the only true religion and that Muslims were the chosen people. The Jews were the grandchildren of pigs and monkeys and the more one hated them, the more one got closer to Allah. Christians were polytheists and worshipped Isa Ibn Mariam (the son of Mary), who was nothing but a prophet, like the hundreds of prophets God had sent before choosing Mohammed, his beloved messenger, and conveying on him a special seal of prophet hood.

At the age of 16, I became infatuated with the Muslim brotherhood. A few years after the Iranian revolution, led by Khomeini in 1979, that provoked a storm around the Arab world, Muslim parties mushroomed everywhere. In Algeria alone, there were more than a dozen. Some influenced by the Islamic party in Turkey that was slowly destroying Ataturk's infidel secular nation-state and advocated the *stepwise* application of Sharia. Others were influenced by Muhammad Ibn Abdul Wahhab's hardline views. He was the founder of the dominant religious movement in Saudi Arabia. I was influenced by the young *Ittijah Islami,* the movement of Islamic tendency that began in neighboring Tunisia.

We would meet secretly in mosques and learn about true Islam and the benefits of living in a Muslim theocracy. Later, when the government put the majority of our leaders in prison and closed the mosques after prayers, most of us opted for caution. Little by little, Islamic revival lost some of its appeal to me. By now my teenage years were over and I was faced with the dilemma of what to study at university.

When Reagan sent his planes to bombard Libya — a Muslim country, though governed by a mad dictator — I felt Allah wanted me to opt for English literature, translation and civilization. I made a vow at that time that one day I would write a book that would be published in USA — the land where the devil thrived. On that day I envisioned those *Koffar* (infidels) would kneel down to Allah and recognize the supremacy of his messenger.

I opted for English and American literature and received a rude awakening during my first year at university. We Arabs thought that nobody could write poetry better than our poets. I changed my mind when I first read Ezra Pound, Dickenson, Robert Frost and Shakespeare's sonnets. I realized that the people I read about in novels like *Huckleberry Finn* and *Moby Dick* were honest and innocent people who fought injustice, loved sincerely, felt pain and feared death just as we Arabs did. They had scumbags and righteous men, heroes and cowards, very ambitious and very lazy people, just like us.

Sometimes I even thought that they were better than us because very rarely did I read about hatred against Arabs or

Muslims in general, as our books, written in Arabic, portrayed people who have different faith. I kept those thoughts to myself, though, and reasoned that there must be a large difference between reality and fiction.

In spite of myself, I began to love the United States of America when I read about its history. Until then, I had never realized that the land where Shaitan (Iblis or the devil) lived was, in fact, not only the land of the oppressed, but also the land to which everyone in the world desired to go. I saw the opportunities it offered for the people suffering in so many parts of the world, to escape their own bondage and achieve dreams for their children not possible where they lived. The story of the Pilgrim Fathers and the Mayflower held a special place in my heart.

Then I was further introduced to what the French call *un chock culturel* (culture shock)! After finishing two years at university, the government sent us to England for linguistic training. We had to attend courses in English as a foreign language and then end our training program with a research paper.

The people were so nice, compared to Muslims, who were supposed to be the best people ever born. Most of the people I met were honest, helpful and frank. My male friends treated me with respect and included me, as if I were one of them. We played Snooker, Baby Foot and Badminton together. We drank together, chased women and even shared together, the few pounds we had. They were white-faced and blue-eyed, but I never felt that I was an outsider. We were all just a bunch of young guys, having fun, who at that time, never thought about where our individual paths would take us after we left school.

With the fair sex, I discovered that I had great success. My Algerian friends, who were lighter skinned than I was, were very jealous. My olive Mediterranean complexion seemed to appeal to women there. It felt good to me that women desired to date me, and I really enjoyed the disbelief and envy I saw in my male friends' eyes.

After several miscommunications, I discovered that if an English woman liked you, she said it plainly and without fear. In our Arab world, almost everyone had two faces. I lied to my new English friends, and they believed every single word I said. I stole their food and they did not suspect or judge. On reflection, they probably knew what I was doing but chose to look the other way. This culture and the people were an enigma to me. They were so different from what I had been taught, and at that moment I wanted to remain there forever.

I remember that, once, I got drunk with an English friend named Martin who was head over heels in love with an Algerian student who came with us in the training program. The Algerian girl played with his virgin heart and he invited me that night for a drink in order to tell me his sad story. By the time he finished it was late at night and we were both ready for bed except that I was too drunk to even walk. Actually, he literally carried me to his room. When I woke up, I found that I was sleeping on his bed and he was sleeping on the floor.

Another night, I decided to see how far I could go in such a strange world that seemed to me at that time so limitless. At two o'clock in the morning, I decided to play the role of a traffic officer. I stood in the middle of the highway and started organizing the traffic. People laughed and thought it was funny. Then a man with his wife stopped their car and took me to a nearby pub. They invited me for a beer and took me to the student headquarters at the University of East Anglia, Norwich. Those English were always surprising me with their kindness.

I spent six months in England studying English and American literature. Rather, I should say I spent six months on an English pleasure trip that included getting to know every pretty girl who would talk with me. For a boy who had grown up in abject poverty, this trip had surely become a life-changing event. For the first time, I experienced true freedom and I reveled in it.

I wanted to remain there so much that I married a girl on

a whim in order to bring my plan to completion. She was only 17 and worked as a maid, cleaning the dormitory where I lived. Her parents seemed willing to accept me, but our marriage only lasted a month before I was required to return home once again with the other students.

By the time we were on the plane back home, every Algerian thought that these English were such good people, that were they ever to pronounce *shahada* (there is no god but Allah, and Mohammed is his messenger), they would go to Paradise before the best of our theologians.

At home I went to the consulate and tried to obtain a visa. I thought that my marriage certificate would help, but unfortunately I had not taken it to the home office in England for approval, and consequently, the fat man with glasses at the embassy was more than happy to deny me entry on the grounds that my marriage was not genuinely motivated. So, that event triggered the end of my short-lived marriage. I never saw her again. She divorced me soon after I returned home.

I soon realized that the path of Allah was to be different for me. I returned to prayers and being two-faced. I played the pious role nicely in front of my family and neighbors, but each time I found the chance, I sinned to the fullest. I had many rich friends who were my colleagues at university. We would organize one of those red orgies spoken about in *One Thousand and a Night*.

I was able to work my way through school by selling time-shares for a company that later went out of business, leaving the unsuspecting buyers without their money or a place to vacation once a year. All in all, I had very few aspirations for my life, beyond having a good time and graduating from university.

On reflection, I think I was quite satisfied with the simplistic reasoning that we Muslims deserve *jannah* (Heaven) because we are the only true monotheists. According to Islamic eschatology, after death one will reside in the grave until the appointed resurrection. Muslims believe that the treatment of the individual in the life of the grave will be according to his or her deeds in the worldly life. But on the other hand, everything one longs for in this world will be there in Paradise. When faced with the question: Why are they (the people in the United States) so blessed, then, if Allah hated them that much? My answer would be the answer of the prophet who was sleeping one day upon an old rug. Omar, the second caliphate and one of his closest companions approached him. "Pray to Allah that He makes us live in comfort like the Romans who are *Koffar*," Omar said.

"Those people are given their paradise on Earth, for they have no place for it in the hereafter. Do you want to exchange the eternal for the ephemeral?" the messenger asked.

After graduation in 1992, I tried, once more, to return to England but could not obtain a visa. My brother-in-law saw my discouragement and felt sorry for me, I guess. He gave me 1,000 *dinars* and told me to go travel. I thought that Sweden did not have any visa requirements, so I decided that was where I wanted to go. It was another experience that I will never forget.

My first impression of Sweden was that it looked like a cold diamond, which had been expertly cut from the splendid *jannah* we Muslims have been promised in the Qur'an. I heard a Moroccan who stood next to me tell his friend, "I swear by Allah these beautiful Barbie girls exceed in their beauty, the *hoor al Ayn* (beautiful women reserved for Muslims as a reward in heaven) described by Mohammad, peace be upon him." I smiled at the idea, and then muttered a shy *Astagfirullah*. I was asking pardon from Allah because my thoughts were the same as his.

As we were standing in line to go through Customs, we were informed that the Swedish authorities now followed the path of other European countries and required a visa for any North African wishing to enter its territory.

"This is bad luck," an Algerian exclaimed, then swore under his breath. All the North Africans who passed through Customs were asked to wait in a separate section as soon they saw our passports. It simply meant deportation. No matter how much they kept shouting "tourist-tourist!" No matter how heartbreaking their cases were, nobody listened and no one cared.

As I reached a blue-eyed, slightly heavyset woman, I decided to play my last card. I gave her my best smile and said, "Excuse me, mum, but I think you have the most beautiful eyes in the world." The woman smiled back at me and a very robust man behind her shifted in his seat. "I'm sorry," I interjected. "You both just seem to make a perfect couple to my mind." The man smiled and, with a gesture of his head, allowed her to let me through. It had worked, and most probably I helped break the ice between the man and the woman.

It was two o'clock in the morning when I left the airport, thinking that it was not 50 kilometers away from the city center. I stopped a taxi. The man driving it was a Mexican. "Where do you want to go?" he asked in broken English after he had tried his broken Swedish. I told him to take me to any youth hostel.

"Don't you know anyone here?" he asked.

"No," I answered. The driver gave me a curious look, but kept silent. After a while he simply turned off the meter and lit a cigarette.

As we reached the youth hostel, which was actually a big old wooden ship, he told me not to give him a penny. "You remind me of my first day when I came here," he said. "Good luck. You're going to need it."

I did not understand what he meant by his statement, but I thanked him and went inside. The man behind the desk was half asleep. He gave me an application form to fill out, took my passport and put it inside a safe. Then, after paying 20 coronas, he led me to a big room where some blacks and North Africans slept. At that moment I knew I made a big mistake, and the country that used to be a haven for people like us had become our nemesis.

I do not blame the Swedish, though, because many of the people who were welcomed with open arms during the '70s and '80s did not behave as expected. Most of them married and then mistreated their Swedish wives; most of them were not law-abiding, and a few did some heinous crimes.

Two Moroccans who seemed friendly enough started a conversation and brought me back to reality. "I wouldn't leave my luggage here in this place," one of them said to me. I was immediately taken in by what I thought was a genuine concern for me.

"Why not?" I asked.

"Because this place is full of thieves and the moment you turn your back they will steal everything you own," the other man replied.

"Then where do you recommend I put my things so they won't get stolen?" I asked.

"The central train station has lockers," he said very nonchalantly. "Most people who stay here use the lockers."

I was totally taken in by these smooth-talking men and did not realize at the time that, in fact, they were the very thieves who were planning to steal my money and my few possessions. They did it so deftly, by performing a popular scam called key exchange. They simply changed the key behind my back and then subsequently disappeared, anticipating that I would not notice the changed locker number until it was too late.

So after only one week I found myself without money in a very beautiful but cold neighborhood called Slussen. At night I hid from police inspection and slept in a cemetery. I smoked cigarette stubs and waited for the supermarket to open. I shoplifted something to eat and a packet of cigarettes then went out thinking about what I would do next. As I sat on a wooden bench, a black African came and sat by my side.

"Hi," he said. "Your face is not familiar. You must be a newcomer."

"Yes," I said absentmindedly.

"Hard country, isn't it?"

"The people are different from the English. They hate us."

"They have become the most racist country in the world," he continued. "Gone are the days when women used to wait for us in the airport."

I heaved a sigh and swore under my breath.

"Are you okay, brother?" the perfectly white-toothed black man asked.

I thought for a while, and then told him my story. He laughed at my stupidity, and subsequently surprised me by the following question.

"Have you been in prison back home?" He waited for a long moment, then continued. "If you want to work I can introduce you to some people. They need a trustworthy man and I believe you are trustworthy."

"What kind of work?" I asked. He related to me the nature of his illegal activities. I explained that I was a student back home and not the kind of person he thought, but I thanked him and told him to take care. I do not know why, but he felt compassion for me.

"Let me give you some advice before I go," he said. "You can go to the police and apply for a refuge. Tell them any story and you will get at least six months stay here. You will have enough time to find a Swedish woman and get married." I welcomed his suggestion with open arms and entered the first police station I came across. I was afraid at first and lied to the police officer, but he seemed willing to accept everything I said to him. I gave him a wrong name, the name of a famous wanted Islamist in Tunisia. I told him I had no passport and just escaped off of a big Norwegian ship. The man simply recorded my statements and then shortly afterwards I was taken to a refugee camp on the outskirts of the capital.

My first impression was that I had traveled back in time at

least 200 years. Most of the refugees were either from Somalia, Sudan or Iraq, but there were a few North Africans, some Eastern Europeans who were mostly from Czechoslovakia, and even some Cubans. Actually, I shared the room with two Cuban nuclear scientists who had escaped from Russia.

My stay in Sweden had turned out to be very different from what I had expected, but at least I had something to eat and a warm bed. After the first two weeks I discovered that my case was helpless. There were people who truly deserved a refuge, I thought. After my second interview I knew I was going to be deported very soon, so my young mind decided to fabricate something before it was too late. I hit my face and ransacked the small room I shared with those two scientists and then pretended I was a victim of an assault by two government agents. As a result, I was transferred to a high-security camp in Nortalia. Then, after two weeks, I was sent to a bigger camp about 130 kilometers away from the capital.

There I met several very unforgettable individuals. *Wahsh,* which means monster, was a huge Lebanese man who said he had escaped a death sentence by Hezbollah activists in Tripoli. Another man who called himself Mosalli was a Syrian opposition activist to Ha'fed Al Asad, the former father of President Bashar. He was a real character. He told me that he had killed five men in Eastern Europe and I believed him because I noticed that every night he read his past criminal exploits, which he had carefully recorded in a large old copybook. Needless to say, I kept my distance as much as possible.

I also met a Tunisian man who soon became my friend. He said that he was a deserter from the Tunisian army, but I did not ask him about it and he did not ask me about why I was at the camp. We just seemed to silently agree that it was better not to know too much about each other. We became friends and soon shared the same goal, which was to find women we could marry. It was the only way to guarantee a permanent residency in Sweden. One day we started dating two Chilean refugees. I still remember that we had no money to buy our dates flowers so he took me to a nearby cemetery and suggested that we take the flowers from the gravesites.

"After all," he said, "they are dead and their families will bring more flowers another day." On reflection, I saw no harm in it and chose a pretty arrangement. Though I felt bad about it, I could not explain why.

After one week of talking, mostly by sign language and a mixture of Spanish, Svenska and rudimentary English, Rosa, my date, invited me to her house — a small apartment in an old building inhabited mostly by foreigners. After the first night, all the reserve and the caution I had seen originally in her green eyes dissipated and she simply gave me a copy of her keys. We spoke about marriage and she was willing to get married to me if my asylum application did not succeed. I spent the following two months in a better shape, especially psychologically. I called Mum for the first time and told her I was alright and very soon I would be able to work and send her some money.

I remember that in those days, while I was still living at the camp, I felt we were like spiritual guinea pigs. Evangelizers would come and speak about the love of Christ, the true Son of God. We would shun Shaitan and wonder how such intelligent people could believe such nonsense. Jehovah's Witnesses would then appear as soon as the evangelizers retreated. They would say that Jesus was not God, but would refuse to admit that Mohammad was a prophet from God. Then, from time to time, a long-bearded Afghani or Pakistani would appear and speak secretly about *Jihad*. At that time most of us did not care about religion; we simply wanted to live a better life. Although getting a residency was the ultimate goal, no Muslim was ready to renounce his religion for it.

After two months or so I received a letter from the Swedish government asking me to come to the police station in Nortalia.

My friend thought it might be good news and I thought they might even have swallowed my story and decided to give me a Swedish passport. After all, I thought to myself, I'm better than those illiterate Iraqis or long-bearded Mujahideen, who were given a nationality as soon they had their first interview. As soon as I went inside the police station they asked me a few questions about my real identity and then put me into solitary detention. I was there for a week before a female police officer accompanied by two tough-looking male officers dashed into my room. The female officer was literally fuming with rage. "You told us you have no passport — am I right?

I weighed my options and decided to stick to my stupid, fabricated story. The woman appeared to me out of her mind with anger. She reached into her left pocket and produced my old passport and held it like a gun. She must have used all the expletives she knew in her native language, but I kept calm because, due to the language barrier, I simply could not understand what she was actually saying to me.

As her anger seemed to subside, I asked her, "Are you happy now?" She said yes and left the room.

The next day, two very strong Swedish men wearing suits took me to the airport and did not leave me until I was in Huwari Bumadien Airport, in Algiers. I remember that as we flew over Stockholm at early dawn and saw the dazzling lights of that perfectly cut cold diamond, I thought, I will never go back to Sweden unless it would be to receive the Nobel prize for literature.

When I returned home, my life settled down and I got a job teaching English in a secondary school. My students were children ranging from 12 to 18 years old. Some of them were very bright but the overwhelming majority was very weak at a language they consider less Important than French. All In all I was decided to start anew and be satisfied with my lot as they always say in Algeria. But my passion for seeing more of the world would not die and as soon as I finished the required 10 years of teaching, I applied for a job in the Gulf, and the Omani Ministry of Education accepted my application after two long years of waiting. My mum was very happy and proud of me, and if the truth be told, I was excited too. Finally, I thought, I would have the opportunity to have enough money to buy or build a house and visit the most holy place (Mecca).

"They say pilgrimage is very cheap from there," my mum rushed to point out.

It is said that there are events in one's life that become pivotal points, where your direction changes ever so subtly that you barely notice it. For me this was one of those times. I could never have imagined how much my life would be forever changed from the moment I set foot on Omani soil.

CHAPTER 2

The day my feet stepped off the airplane upon arrival at Abu Dhabi airport, I felt as if I was walking into the realm of Shaitan (Satan). This impression was probably due to the unbearable heat, the women shrouded in black from head to toe, and the full beards — dyed sometimes with red or black *hannae* — which the Sunna followers wore proudly.

My discomfort soon dissipated with the first blast of air-conditioning inside the luxurious airport, and when my friend — an Algerian teacher like me — motioned for me to see the display of Bacco Rabani perfumes.

We were part of a group of 70 teachers, who were being sent to the Kingdom of Oman in a technical cooperation. The Sultanate of Oman borders Saudi Arabia to the west, the United Arab Emirates to the north, the Gulf of Oman to the east and Yemen to its south. We taught English — a language difficult to learn there — or music, still considered *haram,* which means forbidden by Sharia law. The men taught English and music and the women taught sports to the women in the Gulf. I discovered later, the women there rarely participate in sports, for fear they might lose their virginity. They believed that participating in gymnastic exercises would harm them.

"I swear by Allah, this country is better than USA!" my colleague, Ahmed, said. His face showed more than its usual twitch of enthusiasm.

"Have you been there?" I asked. My question caught him unprepared. He narrowed his eyes and then cleared his throat.

"No, but I know. Trust me," he replied.

Ahmed was thin and bald. There was nothing exceptional about him except the eyes. They were mouse-like, hard and uncompromising. I countered with a short smile and chewed at my under lip.

The airport was full of people-mostly Indians and Europeans — but from time to time we could see a resident dressed in a white *dishdasha*, or a woman staggering under the darkness of an *abaya*. The United Arab Emirates was a country without people, who had a king who ruled over a cloud, I thought.

"Look at the watches, see the price?" Ahmed snatched me back to reality. His bushy eyebrows frowned as we checked the price. My eyes locked onto a Breitling. "It costs 270,000 dirhams (approximately $75,000)!" He shouted. I squinted to study the watch closely. It was my way of evaluating things. I could not take my gaze off of it.

"Just two watches like these," Ahmed said, "and I wouldn't need to remain here in the Gulf anymore. With just one I could finish my house, and with the second I could buy a brand new Golf 5 (Volkswagen) and get married." Ahmed laughed while I pondered how it might feel to have a seventy-five-thousand Breitling around one's wrist.

"We took a one-and-a-half-hour transit here from Houari Boumediene, Algiers. Next we will take the plane to Muscat, right?" Ahmed asked. I nodded in agreement.

I remember that a strange idea dawned on me at that time. I asked Ahmed, "Why is it that all the women in the Gulf are dressed in black and the men are dressed in white?" A burst of anger rippled across Ahmed's face. "You want them half-naked like our girls in Algeria?" He responded.

"I read somewhere that women who worked as prostitutes in *jahilia* (during the period before Islam) would dress like this so that their profession was not evident." Ahmed's face appeared strained and his eyes squinted. I could tell by his expression that he was considering whether or not he should enter into a confrontation.

"You believe that nonsense?" He finally said. "Come on, Jamal! You are a teacher — someone who is supposed to be a model. These Omanis are truly rich. This is the only place around the world where Europeans come as workers and not as tourists," Ahmed acknowledged, changing the subject.

Flashes of fearful *shaitans* (demons) flickered in my head, but I knew he was right. After all, they were truly rich. Money seemed to flow without cessation. The petro dollar; the innumerable business transactions from the East and the West; and the laundered money from the scumbags around the world, all came together in this one God-forsaken place.

"Once we arrive at our destination, I'm going to do some research," I said, reverting to the previous topic of discussion. "I should have more than enough time-and if the information in that article is true, then I'm not sure what I will believe about Sunna, Islamic tradition." Ahmed rolled his eyes. "What article are you talking about?"

"The one about women before Islam," I said.

"You are mad," Ahmed said. "You are wasting time on trivialities. Do you think you are better than our *olama* (theologians)? Are you a Karadhaoui or a Huwini? Are you equal to any of the great men of our faith, who are considered the authorities in matters of religion? Besides, did you come here to think or to work and earn money?"

We stood in edgy silence. The *adhan* was shouted, "Allahu Akbar," and Ahmed left hurriedly for prayers at a small mosque nearby. That fierce, silent anger that had risen in my blood calmed down and I felt the color seep back into my face. I knew that Ahmed's point of view was right. A poor man like me did not have the luxury of time to sort out religious matters. He had to work for his bread and butter.

When I boarded the plane for Muscat and saw how the

Omanis laughed and talked, the mischief in their eyes — shallow, cunning, blatant to every discerning eye — a wave of fear went down my spine. I knew deep down in my soul that I was between the jaws of a beast.

CHAPTER 3

We reached Al Seeb, Oman, late in the afternoon, just after *Maghreb* (sunset prayers). After the ostentatious luxury of Abu Dhabi, the austerity of Sultan Quabous airport was a drastic change. There was nobody to welcome us so we had to spend the night inside the airport. We were so hungry and exhausted that each one of us used his luggage as a mattress and went into a light, jittery sleep.

With the first streaks of dawn, shortly after the *fajr adhan* (dawn prayers), the Omanis, who worked for the ministry of education, together with police officers dressed in sandy uniforms, streamed into the airport.

They put us into two long lines — one for women and one for men. They fingerprinted us and then confiscated our passports. They questioned us about everything, even our hobbies. Then they asked the more serious question: our faith. This time the smiles disappeared from every face. We were all Muslims, but they wanted to know if we were Sunnis, Shiites or Ibadies. To my surprise, my friend Ahmed wrote Ibadhi. Later, I discovered that those who lied about their sect of Islam got the best posts in Muscat or its outskirts.

The Ibadhi faith was first followed by the people who separated themselves from Ali (the idol of all Shiites) and the fourth caliphate during 'Harb Jemal,' or the Camel war against the Sunnies. They were nicknamed at that time khawarij or splitters. Later, most of them would settle in Oman and some of them in Algeria, Tunisia and Libya. In Oman there are three

23

Muslim sects: the Shiites, who are persecuted; the Sunnies, who are treated fairly better; and Ibhadies, who are in power. The Omani government continues to do its best to keep the Ibhadies in the top government positions.

It was more than four hours before we left the airport. I still remember the moment. As soon as the automatic door of H.M. King Quabous International Airport opened, my sunglasses fogged up and my face was hit with full force by the scorching heat. The heat — the simmering, suffocating heat — instantly sapped my energy. It was only 8 o'clock in the morning and the sun was more scorching than the Tabouna (traditional oven) where my mum still bakes her bread. The heat really overwhelmed all of us, except for the few Indian and Bengali passengers. As they squatted on the side walk and hugged their luggage, they smoked cheap cigarettes, which were lodged tightly between their lips. Their eyes crinkled against the smoke. It was obvious that they were acquainted with pain — the real slaves of our modern time, I thought.

The sky seemed full of clouds, but what looked like clouds, was only dust and the swirls of humidity. The crows, the only birds that could resist that heat, nestled in the few palm trees that lined the highway. I remember thinking that Dante Alighieri must have visited this part of the world before traveling deeper and deeper inside the circles of purgatory described in his book, Dante's Inferno.

I had been to the desert south of Algeria; my skin had been scorched by the cruel sun of Sibha, Libya, but if the truth be told, I had never felt heat such as this in all my life.

"There is a heat, then there is a heat," I overheard an Egyptian say between clenched teeth.

"This can't be real!" I mumbled. Yet the intense heat was as painful as a blow on a chin or the stab of an Omani *khanjar* (dagger.) Music cannot transform hearts in this region, I thought, like a good air conditioner can. At least I now know why music is *haram* (forbidden) … because the excruciating heat does not let people taste its beauty, even if they wanted.

"I tell you, Jamal, I'm going to return home — I won't spend more than one week in this place. I swear by Allah!" Nizar, a music teacher said, and pulled me from my daydreams.

Nizar was from Bejaya, the largest city in Kabylia. I met him in the airport of Houwari Boumedian, while waiting for the plane, and we spoke over some beers. He was suffering the aftermath of a devastating divorce and decided to come to Oman to breathe a new air and to decide what to do next. He had two children and wanted to save some *Rials* (Omani currency.)

"I spent a long time asking some of the people here about this region," Nizar had said. If these people consider me a second-degree Muslim, call me a *wafid* (alien), deny me the right to possess land, the right to marry an Omani woman, the right to have an Omani passport regardless of the number of years I will spend serving them, then it is absurd for me to remain here. They even consider music *Haram,* so, according to their fossilized minds, I will go to Hell unless I repent and choose to hate music.

The problem is that I can't do it … music is my life … so here is my decision. Even if Islam is true and I risk Hell or imminent death and am branded a *Mortadd* (a person who leaves Islam for another religion) because of my apostasy, I would not remain a Muslim. I'm ready to become anything: a Buddhist, a Christian or even a Zoroastrian, but never a Muslim anymore. It would be better to go to Hell than spend eternity in the company of such hypocrites."

His words cut straight through my heart, but I thought he was only letting out his anger. I was wrong. An anxious cloud stole over Nizar's face and he gave me a questioning look. I felt my throat becoming dry and I swallowed hard.

"At least they have put you in Sohar, Nizar. They say it's the second biggest city in Oman. You will see. I'm sure you will change your mind," I said, trying my best to make him feel more comfortable.

Nizar looked around the sweltering platform. "These fancy cars do not deserve this," he commented.

"Why do you say that?" I asked.

"I mean, look at that Lamborghini, that Porsche or that beautiful red Mustang burning under a ruthless sun." I looked and observed that, every now and then, those exquisite cars were hit by a blast of sandy wind.

"I swear by Allah … don't they know about underground parking garages?" Nizar asked.

I ignored his question as my eyes locked on a blue Subaru parked under a palm tree. The plush leather seats were powdered with dust while crows perched on its roof. From time to time another blackbird floated through the palm tree branches and joined the flock. I remember that pang of envy within my chest.

"Lucky bastards," I murmured.

"Life's a bitch," Nizar replied.

"Wait until the petrol runs out … By Allah, they will return to their tents and will travel on camels' backs again," I said.

I followed Nizar's gaze and looked over my shoulder toward the moving crowd still lulled by the residual effects of the airport's air conditioner. The non-smokers — free from nicotine addiction and demands, and who had not rushed to go out for a cigarette, were stunned, clutching their luggage and cursing as soon they reached the automatic door. A grin tugged at Nizar's mouth when a Bengali janitor trotted in front of us, happy and satisfied. Omani men exited in front of their women, who seemed unable to move under a dark tent. As they jumped into their cars, they started their air conditioners, gulping in the mechanical fresh air.

Other passengers — mostly pale-faced Europeans, as Nizar described them — seemed to love the heat. One of them, very likely a South African, stretched under its harsh rays like a cat stretches under the warm rays of a spring sun.

"No wonder they have invaded the whole world," Nizar pointed out. I nodded agreement. Nizar smiled and prodded my elbow. "You know what? I think it was the biggest mistake of my life ... what the hell am I doing here?"

"Let me tell you something the consul told us," I said. "The first thing that will come to your mind when your feet hit Omani soil will be to go back home. But he assured us, after two or three weeks, we would like the country and its people and we would never be homesick. He said the Omanis are very nice, the best people in the Gulf. They are very modest, polite and are not conceited like the Kuwaitis or Emiratis, for example.

"He also told us that money is scarce, but the country is inexpensive to live in, compared to Algeria. He also told us that, with some effort, we should be able, in about three years, to pay our debts and maybe even buy a new car. These are two things we wouldn't be able to do back home in ten years."

Nizar listened without assurance and I felt a strange emptiness inside my chest. Later, I discovered that the consul was lying and three years were not nearly enough time to do either of those things.

The crowd of Algerians — waiting for their scheduled journeys to every part in Oman — was getting bigger now. The unlucky would be taken to the desert where people still lived under tents, or to Dhofar, which was located about 1,000 kilometers away from Muscat. Nizar, some Jordanians, a middle-aged Egyptian man, two women and I were some of the lucky few.

After the long hours of standing up, they herded us like sheep into an old Toyota van. We climbed inside the stifling vehicle; the men sat in the front and the two women sat at the back — no doubt they were Egyptians. The seats were very hot. The Omani driver jabbed his key into the ignition, then rushed to turn on the air conditioner. He turned the dial to 'max,' then pushed a button and the window opened a couple of inches.

"Do not worry, I will close it in a while," he said. "Praise be to

Allah that we have AC. Muscat is very hot — you will see Batna Shamal is much better." Beads of perspiration were forming on his forehead. He nervously wiped at them with the back of his hand, then looked into the mirror and tucked a shock of grey hair under his red turban. He backed out of the parking lot and soon the van gathered speed in the middle of a wide highway.

The highway shimmered with mirages every time we looked ahead. The roundabouts were endless and the dust powdered the roadside trees. After Muscat, there was nothing but a flat, parched wasteland. From to time to time, a cluster of some Indian or Bengali laborers whose faces carried the mark of indenture waited under the shade of a meager tree for the arrival of an empty taxi. Behind them, the dust rose in swirls and there was no shade — nowhere to escape the harsh, glaring sun.

"Oman needs rain and some cold gusts of wind," a Jordanian teacher said.

"And a reasonable amount of oxygen," said another.

The perfect place where a *shaitan* could thrive, I thought.

I remember, now, that Nizar refused to relinquish his passport, and when we reached our stop at Sohar, he refused to go with us. Instead, he phoned his brother in Berlin, Germany, and asked him to send him some Euros. I understand that he spent a week in a hotel there and then went back to Algeria.

His decision was the subject of much gossip. Some thought he was not a man: too weak to handle a difficult situation. Others thought he had more courage than we did. On reflection, I think he did not have a money issue. Had he been shackled with a debt, like most of us, he would not have walked away so easily. I remember that during our transit in Abu Dhabi, he spent most of his time with veterans or people who had been to Oman for the second time.

The place in which I was appointed was named Shinas, about 300 kilometers away from the capital. An Egyptian who had come to Oman for the second time told me it was like Hell. By that he meant it was mostly Sunni, completely poor and full of crime. Hazem was his name and he was clearly remarkable. His hair was scarcely flecked with grey and his eyes were warm and intelligent. The handsome middle-aged man whispered into my ear, "What makes someone like you, or me, leave his own country to work under the authority of such Bedouins? I tell you, brother, you will see wonders in this country. I guess it's your first time here, right?"

I nodded and then asked a very naive question. "Why have they taken our passports? They have fingerprinted us and have all the information they need. Why on Earth do they have to do the same job twice?"

"What do you mean? Hazem asked.

"In two weeks or so, we will have to stand in line again to get our passports back," I said. Hazem burst into laughter. Even the Omani driver thought it funny.

"I'm sorry, Mr. Jamal. Please forgive me," Hazem said.

"Why do you laugh, then?" I asked, trying hard to keep my tone even.

"You are Algerian. In your country, you are acquainted with Algerian law and the French system. Here, you must forget about human rights. You will see what I mean," Hazem said. I stared at him with blank eyes.

"We will get our passports back next year, during the summer holiday," a slightly bald and fat Jordanian teacher explained.

"But why keep our passports? It's stupid," I exclaimed.

"I know, but think about it — they know we are underpaid, so they confiscate our passports to make sure we remain in our posts," Hazem explained, speaking in broken French.

"But we have signed a contract — no one has twisted our arms," I replied.

"Forget about the terms — just pray to Allah that you will receive half of what they promised you," Hazem said.

"This is inhuman." That remark resulted in a stern look from the driver. "In Israel they do not do it!" I said.

"Welcome to the Gulf," Hazem whispered.

I closed my eyes and took a deep breath. My throat was dry and I was hungry. The frugal meal they gave us on Omani Airways did nothing but boost my appetite. "You know what? As soon as we reach Shinas, I am going to take a long, cold bath," I said.

"Not so quickly," Hazem replied. "We will have to spend at least four hours repeating the same process done here — this time for the police in Sohar. And then I don't think they will send us directly to our rooms." My head spun round and round and my temples throbbed. "No wonder we are the shame of the civilized world," Hazem remarked in his broken French. Then he burst out laughing. Despite the stifling heat, I felt a chill run down my spine.

CHAPTER 4

We spent the first two days, Thursday and Friday in Sohar, the second largest city in Oman and the birthplace of Sultan Quabous' father. The room that had been assigned to Nizar was now occupied by Hazem, the same Egyptian I had met in the airport. Clearly, the man had intelligent eyes and dressed nicely. His head was not bald — contrary to most Egyptians — but cut fashionably and gel-rumpled. Too good for an Egyptian, I thought.

We Algerians do not get along well with Egyptians. I do not know why, but the grudge seems unsurpassable. I thought we were heading towards a conflict. I never realized that I had met a lifetime friend.

We reached Shinas late in the evening. The Omani driver, whose name was Khalfan, gave us the keys to our living quarters and rushed back to his Toyota van. His reaction surprised us, but we assumed that he must have been busy and needed to return quickly.

The neighborhood was mainly inhabited by Bengali salesmen who sold every cheap Chinese item imaginable and Indians, dressed mostly in grey uniforms, with a 'Total' label written in red on their backs. There were also a few black Omani families, with dozens of children crying. Toothless old men smiled under the shade of some short palm trees.

The old brick wall around the *mojamma* (worker's apartments) was uneven in height, some parts of the wall completely hid the place from the outside, but other parts were so low that an old woman wearing his *abaya* could easily hop through to fetch her black hen which had gotten loose. The gate did not give way easily. The rust inside the lock required us to borrow some lubricant from an Indian mechanic who lived nearby. When the key finally turned we still needed to give the old iron door a forceful push. As we stepped inside, a dank odor crept into our nostrils. The courtyard was covered with tiny pebbles and the walls were constructed with brick and mortar. Cobwebs covered the corners and creepy insects of different sizes darted from one hole to another. Despite the dreariness of the view, we were sure the bad smell came from somewhere else.

The *mojamma* consisted of three small flats. The one at the backend was occupied by a Sudani, but we were sure that he was probably in the mosque at that time.

"I wonder how he comes in," I asked.

Hazem thought for a while, and then said, "He doesn't. He climbs the wall … look over there." I followed Hazem's hand. The wall opposite his house was no more than one half a meter high. "Pretty clever or rather simple," Hazem pointed out.

The doors of our houses were open and we discovered that the soggy, awful odor came from the only bathtub, which was outside. I caught my breath as I stepped inside to what I thought was the best house of the remaining two. The walls were covered with dust and dirt, and only splotches of paint showed their original color. The ceiling was dotted with green and brown mold. Dusty cobwebs gathered around the holes. The air smelled of a mixture of rotten eggs, damp heat and dried sweat. The floor was filthy; the sandy paint on the walls of the small bedroom had peeled off. The light bulbs; mounted to the ceiling with no cover were bare and very cheap, and Hazem and I could barely manage to hear each other over the roar of an old air conditioner. The few pieces of furniture were old and falling apart. But the large white wooden bed was in good condition and the nightstand though almost grey with dirt would match the bed once it was cleaned. The rug on the floor was a faded crimson color that, after washing, promised to provide the room's only color.

Hazem said, "You can take the other one, if you like ... but let me tell you something. My third eye tells me it would be better if you stick with this one."

He was right, because his room was far worse than mine. The small kitchen that we were supposed to share was repulsive. Like a Pakistani garage, it was heaped with soiled plates, dirty take-away food containers, empty bottles of juice and water, empty packets of cheap cigarettes and a collection of flags from all over the poor, forgotten world — from places such as India, Bangladesh, Somali, Egypt, Morocco, etc.

"Are you sure this guy from Sudan lives here?" I asked.

"Oh yes, I'm sure ... his door is closed but the lights are on," Hazem replied.

"What a pig!" I countered, but Hazem kept silent. "Why on Earth do they treat us in this way?"

"Because they are scumbags, but things are slowly changing — God bless America, the human rights watch, and all ..."

"If they were true Muslims, they would treat us much better," I cut in. A tiny, but perceptible cloud came over Hazem's face, but he kept silent.

"I think we should have a talk with him. If we are going to live together, we need to help each other," Hazem said.

"And what if he loves disorder and filth?"

"Then we will report him to his superiors. Don't worry, Sudanese people think that coming to Oman is the chance of a lifetime. He will do anything to remain here. Don't worry about that!"

"I hope so," I said, not completely convinced.

Soon afterwards, the tall, thin Sudanese teacher knocked on our door. "Welcome, sir," he kept repeating as we shook hands. "My name is Hafidh. Do you like the place?" He asked.

We glanced at each other.

"How long have you been here?" Hazem asked him.

"About a month or so," he said. Then, without taking a breath, he continued. "You will see it is very calm here. Oman is a very peaceful country ... I guess you are from Egypt, right?"

"Yes ... from Alexandria," Hazem said.

"Ya Allah — that is a beautiful, Mediterranean city." Then he offered a smile that did not reach his eyes, but showed the decayed state of his front teeth. "And you, sir — let me guess. You must be from Morocco?"

"No, Algeria," I answered. If the truth be told, I did not like the man. I could not stand the way the Sudanese *jibbah* in which he was wrapped clung to him, nor the white skullcap on his small head. In addition, I was wary of the mischievous eyes magnified behind the steel-rimmed spectacles. He showed too much *takwa,* or piety, I thought.

"Algeria, ya Allah, is like France or Italy. I sometimes watch television and *al horma* (my wife) becomes jealous." He laughed to himself.

His mouth definitely needed a crew of dentists, I thought.

"Do you have your own bathroom or is that the only one outside?" Hazem asked.

"We have only one, unfortunately, but Mr. Khalfan promised that the ministry will build a new one in every house."

We glanced at each other once more and Hazem, again, took the initiative. "We smelled a bad smell when we came in. What is the cause?"

"Oh, you will get used to it ... unless you are ready to pay a fortune for detergents — you see what I mean?" Hazem stubbed out his cigarette, then immediately lit a new one. A deep sigh whistled through my teeth.

"Where do you live in Sudan?" Hazem asked.

"I'm from Khortoum — from the Janjawid tribe. Actually, my father was a nomad, a camel herder from the South ... we are real Arabs, sir," Hafidh said, as if to defend his heritage.

"Nobody is a true Arab in Africa. We are the offspring of concubines or female loot from war," I snapped.

Amazingly, Hafidh kept his calm. "Yes, you might be right, but the woman is not important for the Nassabin, lineage experts. It's only the man who really matters; name, genes and even character."

It was useless to continue this ignorant talk, I thought. I lit a cigarette and decided to keep silent.

Hazem and Hafidh talked about everything, from the weather in Oman to infibulations of young girls among the different tribes in Sudan. Then they discussed the awkward problem of the Darfur region, the situation of Christians and Muslims who live together there and the role of the USA. Hafidh never looked me in the face during that entire discussion.

"Would you like to come and taste Sudanese food?" Hafidh asked suddenly. The question brought me back to reality. Hazem and I both said, "No thanks," in unison, even though we were hungry. Finally, the tall, thin man left and I felt relieved.

"He talks too much and he doesn't seem to care much about hygiene. It seems to me, he still lives in the 18th century. I don't think he will change. We had better keep our distance and ignore him," I said.

"Yes, we definitely need to stay away from him," Hazem replied, looking me in the eye. "But without offending him, of course."

"You are asking for a miracle," I replied. "The man will stick like a disease."

"I have been here and I know the system — just ask him to lend you some riyals and you won't see his face until dooms day." We laughed and it was at that moment that I realized how much I liked Hazem.

"So, you think we had better rely on ourselves to do the cleaning?" I finally asked.

"Exactly!" Hazem said with a smile.

"The only thing that bothers me is that I don't want to clean the dirt of such a worthless man." I said.

"Look at it from another angle," Hazem said. "We will teach him the beauty of cleanliness till he gets accustomed to it and then, hopefully, he will be transformed."

That remark was the first hint that told me Hazem could not be a Muslim. I thought he must be an atheist because he behaved like most of them back home. Personally, I liked them, but I could not be an atheist because I had been born into a truly conservative family. My father was a Jomoa, Friday sermon *imam*. All my family members were devout Muslims. My mum prayed to Allah day and night, and fasted on Mondays and Thursdays like Dawood-King David in the Qur'an.

"The first thing we need to do is collect all the detergents we come across, and spend the night cleaning and washing," I said, returning from far away thoughts about my mum holding her rosary tightly in her hand and wishing me a good fruitful journey.

"Yes, that's what we shall do, but I think it is too late now. I had better come and sleep in your place, and tomorrow morning we will do it, I mean after school, of course." Hazem said.

"Why do we have to work tomorrow?" I asked.

"These Omanis would take your last drop of blood if they could do it. Do you think they will let you have any rest? They probably won't hold us until two o'clock though-the few students that even show up will probably leave at about 10 in the morning, since it's the first day. But the administration will find any pretext to keep us busy till the noon. Don't worry, though, we will send someone to buy what we need. So let's leave the cleaning until Friday. It is still a holiday here, as I remember," Hazem said.

"I think you are right," I replied. "We need some rest first." One needs to draw upon all the stoicism of a life experience to be able to live in Oman. A pang cut through my heart. I missed Algeria and its lovely Mediterranean weather. I missed the morning smile of my old mum and the taste of her coffee after a breakfast that was fit for a king. Then I recalled that I had spent more than two months in England studying, and had forgotten to phone her. But the allure of England had so much more to offer, than this God forsaken existence that I had contracted for myself.

There are countries where its people, its weather and its atmosphere make you feel as if you were born again. And there are countries that make you hate yourself from the very first day. Oman definitely fit into the latter category for me.

CHAPTER 5

Shinas was the last Omani city before you reached Emirates soil. My first impression was that it resembled Waziristan, that deadly place where one hears about a suicide attack or a car explosion.

The dull, grey morning foreshadowing the rising heat and wet humidity brought the crows out of nowhere. I watched with suppressed resentment the macabre symphony they offered my unwavering eyes. They scampered along electric lines, leapt from house to house, looked me in the eye and then boldly landed on the dry, scorching pebbles a stone's throw from where Hazem and I stood. They seemed to recognize their kingdom and all the foreigners who come and go. I wondered what I was doing in this hellish place that lay on the outskirts of civilization.

I was surprised by the intense heat at such an early time of day. I was even more surprised when I caught a glimpse of a group of women, dressed in their black *abeyas,* some of them wearing Aniquab over their faces; others wore *burqas* that showed only the eyes. They followed a meager herd of goats and strolled about most of the time, breathing what they thought was fresh air.

"I can't believe it, "I said. "It's only seven in the morning and I'm already perspiring. I've never felt such heat."

"You will get used to it. I sometimes pity these people — they do not know what fresh air is."

Never in my life had I experienced such a harsh sun. It scorched the air that was already stifled by humidity. Perspiration glistened on foreheads and sapped the energy of even the sun-toughened Omanis. Only the Indians and Bengalis seemed to be immune and safe. I took off my hat to the heroes who transformed the desert into a habitable place.

Husein Ben Aly School looked like a mosque that was washed the color of sand. There was no one outside except the Bengali janitor who kept smiling as we bid him good morning. A blast of cool, refreshing air-conditioning hit my face when I entered the teacher's room. I was very thankful to the Koreans. God bless their products and those that assembled them, I thought.

From out the window, the palm trees appeared so marvelously slender, and amazingly beautiful. But I began to hate that region, and consequently, I began to hate palm trees.

The long-bearded principle dashed into our room. "*Salamu alaykum*. Time for *tabour*," he said. We went out like a group of soldiers and I noticed the irritation reflected on each forehead.

I overheard an Omani speaking to his friend. "This is a new type of *wathaniya* (paganism)." We stood like Buddhist monks under the lashes of an unmerciful sun. Heat rose from the asphalt courtyard and the shade withdrew quickly. In the Gulf, nature was a real foe, but the sun was the greatest *shaitan* — an *efreet,* if I use a Qur'anic term. It seemed to me that it tried every morning — as early as sunrise — to melt the brains within our skulls. That explains why people of this region wear turbans, I thought.

The air smelled of rotten fish and Toyota exhaust. "Don't worry, it's the ocean … you only smell it in the morning, but your nostrils will become familiar with it," a heavily built Omani colleague explained. "You will see, in two weeks or so you won't even notice it. My name is Mohammad, by the way," he said as he extended his hand. His hold was strong, but honest.

"I'm …" I began to say.

"I know, Jamal from Algeria," he cut in. "In Oman, nothing is hidden. But I'm Blushi– we are different."

"You mean you are not Omani?" I asked.

"In fact, I'm more Omani than anyone around here, but my

ancestors came from Iran. The king's father — Allah, rest his soul — brought them to fight the *imamies*. After victory over the southern forces, he gave us the right to settle here, but we kept our traditions and our tongues," he explained.

Despite the silly *abeya* and the thick turban around his head, he looked all right ... but the fleshy nose and the *thalja* — the gap between his upper front teeth — hindered him from being truly honest, I thought. Ibn Hisham, in his biography, says the prophet Mohammed had a *thalja* and it was a sign of good luck, so I convinced myself that it must be so.

He stood erect when the national hymn started playing, and his compassionate features became cold and hard. All the teachers and the few students closed ranks like professional soldiers and began worshipping his majesty, Sultan Qaboos. For 45 minutes, we glorified him, prayed for his health and implored Allah to make him eternal. Then we listened to some verses from the Qur'an, recited by an Omani student. The young *taleb* (student) wore a beard too long for his age, I thought.

As I was engrossed in these musings, a crow swooped down out of nowhere and nearly touched the reciter's turban. Was it a miracle? I wondered. For, in Islam, we have an uncountable number of stories of animals that loved to listen to *sahaba* — the prophet's companions — when they recite.

It was finally time for the last episode in that painful show — the students' press (a time in which students recite some proverbs and school news.) My feet ached and the sun almost succeeded in its everlasting mission: boiling the brains in our skulls. When the director blew his whistle, I felt as though I was born again. "Ya Allah, every year do they do such an excruciating show?" I asked.

"Every year? You must be kidding," Hazem countered. His face was no longer cheerful.

I swallowed hard. "You mean it's every day?"

"Of course, man ... every day."

"I can't believe it."

"Don't worry, you will get used to it," Hazem said.

"But it's insane!" I exclaimed.

"Just wait, my friend. You haven't seen anything yet." Hazem lamented. One needs to get himself drunk every day to live in this hell, I thought.

Hazem left me and went to his classroom. Under the shade, some of my stamina came back, but his words kept tumbling around in my mind. I hurried, not because I was eager to teach, but because I was anxious to feel the blast of air-conditioning that awaited me inside the classroom.

As soon as I entered, I began to see some of what Hazem meant by his previous remark. The 12th grade students lacked discipline with a capital D. Though big in size, wearing beards that varied from trimmed to out of control, the boys behaved like kids in kindergarten. Big words borrowed from applied linguistics such as 'involvement', 'participation' and 'cultural authenticity' seemed to be completely inapplicable to these Omani students. They needed a baby sitter, not a teacher, I grumbled to myself.

"Teacher, teacher, tell him to give me back my phone," cried a tall, stout pupil.

I stared at the stalk of *siwak* (a teeth cleaning twig) he held between his teeth, which he chewed very impolitely. "Take that thing out of your mouth," I said.

"Teacher it's a *sunna* (prophetic tradition) to keep my teeth clean."

Something tightened within my chest, but I stifled my response and simply asked, "Where is he?"

"Over there, teacher," he said, pointing in the direction of a boy across the room. Without even noticing which boy he singled out, I said, "Come here."

"Just a minute, let me see this *thailandese* shemale," a voice replied. I looked up and saw an olive-skinned, hostile-looking boy glaring back at me. All of a sudden the whole class burst into laughter. Then a boy with *khol* around his eyes and a small mirror in his hand approached me.

"Teacher, let me straighten my *izar*."

"Do it!" I shouted. The classroom burst into laughter again. I later discovered that the Omanis do not wear underwear. They just tie a piece of cloth round their waists and throw a *dishdasha* over it. That piece of cloth is called an *izar*. I let him go out to the toilet while I secretly prayed to Allah to help me to keep my wits about me.

That day, I knew my first impression was right but I needed time to convince my skeptical mind. At two o'clock, I sat beside Hazem in the old Toyota van.

"You know what? This country needs a revolution like the one that happened in Russia against the tsar," I whispered into Hazem's ear.

"From your mouth to Allah's ears," Nazih, the Jordanian teacher said from behind me.

CHAPTER 6

Several weeks had passed when late one night, Hazem knocked on the door of my small bedroom. His whisky breath took me by surprise. "Are you drunk?" I asked.

"Of course — how do you expect me to live in this world?" Hazem replied.

"Is whisky authorized here?" I asked.

"Yes, my friend, but I prefer to buy it from the Indians. It is much cheaper."

"That's rather good news. I thought they were very strict about liquor."

"Nothing is *haram* (forbidden) and everything is *haram* at the same time. This region is based on the famous Shakespearean dichotomy: reality versus fiction. Once you understand this, you can live anywhere in the Gulf."

"You know what? There is no end to surprises in this country," I said as I caught his grin.

Hazem laughed, and then looked me in the eyes. "If you are intelligent, you only need a short time to understand everything. Then, if your heart is still alive, which is something I do not doubt, you will hate the very day when you came here. Actually, you will hate many things and you might even get ... "saved." He stopped to light a cigarette. "Then you will find your own path, or simply will not care anymore. It happened to me and most of the honest colleagues I knew. We Muslims are the scum of the earth, my friend."

The cloud on his face pierced my dignity like a spear. I found myself wondering why he talked in riddles, and then words poured out of my mouth. "Islam is not to blame, if that's what you mean!"

Hazem looked me in the eyes, the same cloud spreading over his face again. "I think Islam is the cause — yes, I'm sure about it." His answer came like splashed water on a freezing morning.

"What are you saying, Hazem? I think you are drunk."

"You know that you do not need to believe me — follow your own path. You will have enough spare time this year — actually, too much time. Go places after work — read books and see for yourself. Watch the Al Hayat channel," Hazem encouraged. I have heard about that channel in Algeria. I heard about Komos Zakaria, an Egyptian priest who exposed what he thought real Islam on the Al Hayat channel. He is described on most Arab religious channels as a *shaitan*.

"There are things that do not need to be questioned, such as Allah, Mohammed, the Sunna," I replied instead.

"Everything is questionable, my friend, and I'm sure you know this. I know that in the heart of your hearts you are not satisfied. I've seen that in your eyes."

Actually, he was right, but I was not ready to admit it. "I can't live without God! Nobody can. We are from the East — you know what I mean?"

"Most of the civilized world lives without God and they manage better than us by far- but I'm a believer, Jamal, and for the first time in my life, I know the God I believe in."

"Are you a Christian? I asked bluntly.

"I can't tell you now — maybe by the end of this year. My sixth sense tells me so. Anyway, you are intelligent and different. I'm sure you will find your own path."

I decided not to give a lot of attention to what he said. He was drunk, after all. My cautious mind opted for a change in the subject.

"I have been to Sohar this evening. I never thought that in this desert they could build such a beautiful city."

"They did not build anything," Hazem corrected me.

"What do you mean?" I asked.

"The entire hard and dirty job was done by Indians or Bengalis. They are the true silent heroes." Hazem angrily waved a mosquito from his left cheek.

I lit a cigarette and puffed on it greedily.

"Welcome to Oman, the land where hearts are black and clothes are as white as snow," Hazem murmured quietly to himself.

"Your first year, I guess?" I questioned.

"No, I've been here before," Hazem answered.

"Why did you return if you don't like the place?"

"You don't have kids, do you?" He asked me, ignoring my question.

"I have a daughter," I said.

"What's her name?"

"Zeineb, which means a beautiful, fragrant tree."

"Beautiful name."

"Many thanks, and you?" I asked.

"Five — three daughters and two sons," Hazem replied.

"A wife?"

"No," Hazem said. He lowered his eyes and fell silent.

"A friend of mine told me that Oman makes you a tougher man," I said.

"Bullshit!" He said.

"I think so," I countered.

"I will tell you something. This country is a heaven to Al Said or the Europeans," Hazem explained.

"I heard they are treated like kings around here."

"You're telling me … You can harm an Omani and get away with it, but not one of them," Hazem pointed out.

"All the human rights are applicable once they are involved … their embassies will make a fuss if one of them has the least problem. I know … it's the same in Algeria."

"Here in Oman and the entire Gulf region, your salary and your status depend upon your passport. They do not ask or care about how good you are, the real question here is where you come from. There are three types of people around here: foreigners, Omanis and then come the *wafideen*. In other words-us," Hazem commented.

"That's racism!" I said, clenching my teeth. "We are supposed to live in a Muslim country, where there is no injustice and all people are alike," I said.

"The true god is the *baisa*, the *dirhem* or the *dinar*. Islam is like a beautiful disguise … or better, like a habit," Hazem said.

I secretly questioned whether Islam really destroyed injustice. Wasn't Koreish, the prophet's tribe, the best tribe among all other tribes? Wasn't the Koreishi Qur'an preserved whereas all the seven other Qur'ans were destroyed? Didn't Mohammed explicitly and implicitly humiliate all the Bedouins who were not city dwellers? The examples gushed out of my mind like a nasty cut.

"I'm going to tell you something you probably don't know. You don't have the right to marry an Omani woman. You don't even have the right to own or open a business on your own," Hazem said.

"In Israel, I have these rights," I blurted out.

"You don't seem to get it, do you? You are a Muslim as long as you fight their war in Afghanistan or Iraq. Or as long as you go to Mecca and pay $5,000 for your pilgrimage, or blow yourself up for El Quds!" Hazem exclaimed.

I fidgeted in my seat and scratched my hair. Hazem smiled and then said "I need some sleep now, my friend." With that he said goodnight and left.

Who was this man that could cause my mind to ponder many things that I had for so long taken for granted? I lay on my bed for a long time listening to the roar of the air conditioning unit. My mind turned his words over and over until I finally fell into a very fitful sleep.

CHAPTER 7

The first thing that surprised me about Oman was that all people were dressed in the same way. Men were dressed in white and women in black. The second was that all junior and high schools were either all boys or all girls. I found it odd, or at least different to what I was used to in Algeria and North Africa in general.

"The weather here is very hot and if we allow them to mix like in Algeria, there will be no virgins left. You see what I mean?" Mansour, who was tall, skinny and dark-faced, explained and then offered a toothless smile.

Suspecting that I was not convinced, he resorted to the holy Qur'an and recited a verse from Al Noor24: 31: "And tell the believing women to lower their gaze (from looking at forbidden things) and protect their private parts (from illegal sexual acts) and not to show off their adornment except only that which is apparent (like both eyes for necessity to see the way, or outer palms of hands) and to draw their veils all over *juyubihinna* (i.e., their bodies, faces, necks and bosoms) and not to reveal their adornment except to their husbands, or their fathers, or their husband's fathers, or their sons, or their husband's sons, or their brothers or their brother's sons, or their sister's sons, or their (Muslim) women (i.e., their sisters in Islam), or the (female) slaves whom their right hands possesses, or old male servants who lack vigor, or small children who have no sense of feminine sex. And let them not stamp their feet so as to reveal what they hide of their adornment. And all of you beg Allah to forgive you all, O believers, that you may be successful."

"But I heard they mix at universities and colleges," I protested. "Actually, they should not, according to Islam. But what shall we do with the Ministry of Education?" Mansour asked. His eyes looked very serious. He did not want — like every Omani — to openly criticize His Majesty Sultan Quaboos' policies. Though all of them, educated or not, required these parathion of sexes and feared educated women and their natural desire to do everything right. Yet as long as the women worked and gave men their salaries, usually to their husbands and their fathers, at the end of each month, they would remain lukewarm about Sharia law.

A *mutawa* (religious man) came in. "These human rights activists are leading us towards perdition. They never stop complaining, as though they have true human rights in the West. But everybody knows it's a worldwide plot against Islam, led by Jews and Americans." He said this as he combed his beard, using the window panels as a mirror.

"This year they want us to raise the salaries of *khadimat* (or house maids) to 120 rials, and the government is helpless. If they endorse this policy, I would go to Iran and have a second wife. It would be cheaper!"

The two Omani laughed, and then looked at each other. I forced a smile as they stared at me. Besides, I was curious and I wanted to know whether the rumors I had heard were true. So I asked, "How is one able to hold himself if he has a beautiful *house maid,* especially those from Indonesia?"

"Don't you worry about that. Most Omanis have their bedrooms near the *house maid's* room. At night you would see them, naked except for their *izars,* I guess, sneaking from one room to another." The two Omanis laughed again and I shook my head in disbelief.

"What if they say no?" I prodded.

"They can't," one of the men replied, as if surprised at the question.

"Yes, but suppose they do," I persisted.

"We always have the sword of *tarhil* (deportation) in our hands. We fire them and bring in a new one," they said in unison.

I surmised that the two men prayed each day, read the Qur'an every dawn and every night, visited Mecca once or twice a year and preached about Islam. The long-bearded *mutawa* found the Islamic answer.

"They are, after all, *malikat yameen* (one's own possession) and the Qur'an is explicit on this subject — we are allowed to have sex with them, but the Sharia says that if they get pregnant, then we should marry them and give the child our name," he said.

"Exactly, but nowadays we have condoms, pills, Allah bless science," Mansour pointed out, and the two men laughed again. I felt rage fuming inside my chest. If it were up to me, I would have put them in jail for a long time. When the bell rang, I hurried into the classroom, cursing under my breath. The students were restless, as usual. They needed an army of legionnaires to contain them, I thought.

"Teacher, teacher, is it true that schools in Algeria are mixed?" One student asked.

"Of course", I said weakly while an excruciating pain in my temples began to throb.

"You mean girls and boys study together?" Another asked.

"Yes, for God's sake," I snapped.

"And do they sit together at the same table?" Asked yet another.

I rolled my eyes and looked at my wrist watch. It was only eleven o'clock. The day dragged on at a snail's pace and seemed to gloat over my pain. I had to suffer for another three long hours. If I only had wings, I fantasized; I would wipe the dust from my feet and fly far away — anywhere except the Gulf region.

CHAPTER 8

Inside the stifling Toyota van, I sat beside Anwar, a short and fat Egyptian in his late 50s. I looked at the grey hair, the wrinkles etched deep upon the forehead and around the eyes. Our Omani driver sat silently while he waited for another rider.

"Have you been here for a long time?" I asked the Egyptian.

"More than 20 years," he replied.

"Normally, you have two passports?" I said.

"What?" He seemed incredulous at my comment.

"I mean, one Omani and one Egyptian. In France, you need 10 years, I think."

Anwar laughed and I was embarrassed. "You are speaking as if the Gulf is like Europe or the civilized world in general. Here, my friend, only the Ibadies sect from Libya, Algeria and Tunisia might be granted a passport and, of course, you know why. Yet they will remain *zotties* (people who have no family roots.) No respectful family would become related by marriage to one of them. For Allah's sake, the Blushi warrior tribe that used to live in the region, extending from Iran to Pakistan, has lived here more than 300 years. And they are still not considered true Omanis."

"So, you wasted your youth here?" I put it bluntly.

A cloud came over Anwar's face. "I won't even have a pension. This is a Muslim country, my friend. That means you have no rights."

"Normally we are Muslims and we are Arabs — I'm astonished," I said.

"Had I been in Israel, I would have had at least my permanent residency and a decent pension," he said, then cursed under his breath.

"They want you to work as a slave and then say *shokran* (thank you)," I concluded.

"Exactly, and don't bother yourself. They won't change, at least as long as they have petrol."

"But we are Muslims; I mean why? They are supposed to treat us like equals — Islam promotes equality."

"There is no good reason. That's the law," Anwar cut in.

"You do not seem to like them," I said intentionally, in order to add salt to the wound.

"I will tell you something — before coming here, I was in the USA. I received my master's degree there. I believe that if the people in that country would say *shahada* (there is no god but Allah, and Muhammad is his messenger), they will go to Heaven before our best sheikhs: Karadahaaui, Awa, Koshk — or anyone you can name."

Anwar looked at his watch and frowned." That *hafidh* you are waiting for must have found a lift," he said, speaking to the driver. The Omani driver ignored him and kept waiting.

"The thing that bothers me most is *tabour*,"I groaned.

"It's a must! We are paid to do every morning. Think of it as ablution, can one perform *salat* without it my friend … you can change anything but *tabour*. Do not worry, you will get used to it," Anwar said without conviction.

"Everyone keeps saying the same thing around here," I replied.

"You will get used to pain," Anwar explained. "And then you will find it impossible to teach without *tabour*."

"Are you aware of what you are saying right now? Do you think I'm a masochist?" I questioned.

"It is better than to be a true worshipper of …... Do you see what I mean?" Asked Nazih from the backseat.

"You have very sharp ears," I pointed out. Anwar smiled knowingly.

"I know," Nazih whispered in my ear. "The people here in the gulf still worship their kings. They think when the sun rises; it's due to the good will of their sovereign. We have dictatorships in our countries, but at least we have some space. Here, the king, the sultan or the emir decides even what you should wear."

"Don't you think you are a bit exaggerating?" I remarked cautiously. Every colleague in the school had advised me to beware of him. They said he reported everything to the principal.

"I hope so. But you will see for yourself," Nazih said.

"What about the kids? Are they aware or not, I mean, will they one day rise up and decide enough is enough? Will they be able to change their future?" I asked.

Anwar laughed again.

"By Allah, you remind me of my first day here," Nazih whispered again in my ear.

"By Allah, if you continue spitting, I'm going to lose my hearing," I said curtly as I wiped my ear.

Nazih smiled and kept silent.

"These kids are not taught to use their brains," Anwar said and stopped to let his words settle. "By the end of the year, no student fails — don't you know this?"

"What?" I asked in disbelief.

"Yes," he said, "and everyone will get a job in the end. They don't need us — we need them. They need the subservient Indians and Bengalis, though. They are lucky."

"Are you sure nobody fails his exam?" I asked, stupidly. I couldn't believe what he was saying to me.

"I've been here for 20 years — that senior teacher we have was one of my pupils, so is the principal. We are here to perform a play — that's all."

Out of the old Toyota window, I stared at a flock of crows that formed like a tiny shawl over the face of the blazing sun. I wondered why those vulture-like birds did not peck at those people who were coming out of a mosque. To me, they were as dead as any food the crows might choose to ingest.

The highway was suddenly filled with people. The swarm of the crowd looked like a big ant hill nestled against the arid land, inside which the Korean genius had built a four-lane track. The faces of the people were engulfed by the early afternoon sun. The sweat glimmered in beads on their foreheads and settled on the long beards and bushy brows. The thick desert dust clung to the damp faces and smeared the white *dishdashas*. Our Omani driver pulled up and jumped out of the bus. I thought it was a serious accident, for accidents in Oman happen every day. An Omani once joked that every day, more people died on the highway than those killed in the strip of Gaza.

"What is it?" I asked.

"His Majesty is passing," Nazih said, his eyes watching the expectant crowd avidly. Anwar rolled down the window and a gust of heat scorched my face. Then, he, too, darted out. Everyone except Hazem and I followed him out.

"What's happening?" I asked.

"When the king passes by he usually throws money from the window of his car. Some lucky few — usually young, handsome teenagers — think they might become millionaires overnight."

Out of the window, I could see some of the kids I taught, gathering in small groups. They were well dressed, with *khol* around their eyes. Each time a car passed they would check out their beardless faces on the car windows. I let out a huge sigh.

"This is Omani bare-faced greed. For 20 *rials* or less, they were ready to become like dogs. Most of them won't get a *baisa* (dime) by the way. But what shall I say? No comment," Hazem said.

"When will these people decide enough is enough- aren't they ashamed of themselves?" I snapped.

"They need a miracle … they need …" Hazem's voice trailed off.

"What?" I asked.

"They need an eye opener, a clean mirror where they can see their true reflections ..."

"What do you mean?" I asked.

"Maybe one day you will understand. See those Indians? They work for slave wages here in Oman and around the entire Gulf region — most of them work in construction. They toil ten hours a day under the blazing sun for 70 *rials* a month, and yet they have dignity. Not one of them would dare hustle and bustle for a few coins thrown in the street by a master they don't even see on TV."

After almost an hour of waiting, the rumor that his Majesty was visiting Al Nahyan in the United Arab Emirates turned out to be false. When the driver jammed his gearshift into drive and pushed his way nervously through the sea of faces, I thanked Allah and let out a big sigh of relief.

CHAPTER 9

After two months at Hasan ben Ali school, I became convinced that the Islamic segregation between boys and girls was more malevolent than beneficent. The all-boys school simply boosted *liwat* (homosexuality). I was horrified when I discovered that every boy had his own *sbay* or *frikh* (a special friend.) In the restrooms I could read expressions such as: Ahmed, I love you till death; Ali, you are the apple of my eye; if you go to the moon, you will find me there, etc. There were also, splashed on the walls in different sizes and colors, phone numbers, very indecent drawings, broken hearts and names inside strings of beads.

These young men's natural attraction to girls was completely distorted. Even the eyes of Omani teachers became brazen with lust when they spoke to white, beardless boys. My observations revealed a phenomenon- no, a disease, called sodomy.

"How do you expect them to behave normally while some of the very teachers who instruct them authorize the same behavior?" Anwar asked instead of explaining.

"What?" I asked in disbelief "You can't be right — pedophilia is an international crime — we no longer live in the 18th century. Where is Interpol, or even the United Nations, protecting human rights?" I asked.

Anwar laughed till I saw his back teeth. "You remind me of my first years here, Jamal. I was in the USA but for religious reasons I decided to leave Uncle Sam's country. At that time I was a devout Muslim. I was filled with big ideals about Islam and Muslim *omma,* nation. I decided to work anywhere in the

59

Muslim world except the *koffar's* kingdom. When I came here, I discovered the horrible truth. We truly live in a dungeon of shit and we still think we are the chosen people of Allah!"

"Have you become a *molhid*? (An atheist)" I asked again.

"If the truth be told, yes, but don't tell anybody ... of course you won't — Algerians are not rats."

"But I saw you in masjid (a small mosque)," I said.

"Of course — do you think I'm stupid? I will tell you something, most of them pray out of habit, not pure conviction. Wait for the petrol to run out and you will see the degree of their devotion."

"Many Muslims have become Christians — did you know that?" Anwar continued. Curiously, I thought about Hazem. "For money, no doubt," he said. "There is nothing beyond the sun, my dear friend. If Islam is wrong, then all religions are wrong." His voice was riddled with sarcasm.

"I want to know for sure — do you understand what I mean?"

"Read *Sirat ibn Hisham,* a biography of Ibn Hisham or *Sira al Halabiya,* and do not neglect the small details. Remember, they say the devil hides in the details. I think they are completely right," Anwar lectured.

"Where can I get one of these books?" I asked.

"Everywhere ... they spend millions every year on them. But try to read unembellished books published before 1952. If not, it does not matter — the dirt is still there — if you see what I mean? The library is over there. If you don't have a lesson, you can go and borrow some."

"I will, thanks," I said.

A cloud passed over Anwar's face. "Time to go, I have a lesson."

I borrowed two thick books from the library and went to the teacher's room. I remember that I was often lightened up in those rare moments when I had no lesson to teach, no pupils to supervise and no teacher's copybook to fill up … and, of course, when the principal was absent. Otherwise, he would have concocted any chore to make sure I did not rest. I should mention here that, whenever an Omani teacher was absent, *wafideen* (foreign teachers) were the substitute teachers.

I immersed myself in the biography of Prophet Mohammed, though the desire to read behind the lines was absent then. As I started reading, I found it extremely difficult to concentrate; my Omani colleagues talked too much and too loudly. I remember that I thought they were quarrelling the first day. Then I became acquainted with their high-pitched conversations. They spoke about aphrodisiacs most of the time, poetry that celebrated the beauty of the desert, or the greatness and the heroism of their kings and emirs. And of course about money: the stock market, the businesses they started overnight — all founded and carried through by submissive law-abiding Indians, or slave-like Bengalis. My colleagues sounded as if they were green with envy about the extraordinary wealth in Qatar and Emirates.

I would listen and smile each time they looked at me. I explained that I was a silent man by nature and, by and by, they got used to it; they even loved me for it. I was not really interested in their discussions. My greatest concern was to finish my hard day at work and go home to bed. But that day, Khaled, a colleague — short, baby-faced and in his late 20s — raised an interesting question.

I heard him ask a *mokbali* teacher from the tribe of Mokbal named Hassan who was fat, small-headed and in his early 30s. "I do not understand these Americans. They elect a *khal* (black person) to govern them … don't they have decent men over there?"

Another man laughed and shook his head in disbelief. "Pray Allah our *khals* do not ask the hands of our girls these days," said Muhammad Ahmad. He was from the tribe of Khozeyma — tall, thin and in his early 20s.

"By Allah, anything may happen these days — these are the signs of *kiyama*" (day of doom,) Khaled interjected.

"And you, Mr. Jamal — what do you think about this new president? You teach English and you are the best one among us who can understand these insane people."

Normally, I would smile and say a few neutral words, but I recollect I felt a very intense need to express myself. "Actually, a black president indicates to my mind two things," I said. "The American democracy is sound and not fake, like our so-called democracies. Second, the USA is a superpower, and as long as Americans respect their democratic system, they would remain so."

I remember that my Omani colleagues looked at each other for a long while. I hastened to add humorously as I caught the frown on their faces, "Do you know that Colonel Gaddafi says that Barak is a variant of Mubarak and even Obama is an Arab name — bou Amama." All of them burst into laughter. "Like Shakespeare ... Sheik Zobeir. He claims that he was an Arab who escaped from Spain, or the Andalusia, of that time." The room burst with laughter once more.

"By Allah, you don't speak too much, Mr. Jamal, but when you speak, it's just a real pleasure to chat with you," someone said to me.

"By Allah, you are right, Ostad Khalid," said another. The bell rang and each one went to his class.

CHAPTER 10

After school was over, we waited for Am Khalfan, the driver, but he did not come. The heat was, as usual, stifling and the sun glared ruthlessly upon our heads. Hazem was absent that day, for he had a meeting in Sohar, and the Egyptians and the other *wafideen* found someone who gave them a lift. My pride forbade me to ask this favor.

I stood by a wall in the coolness of the shade and decided to give the driver another five minutes. But he did not come and the streets became deserted, except for a few Bengalis who rode their bicycles completely at ease in the heat. I was tired and exhausted, and had no choice but to go on foot those two miles to my place. After all, they were just two miles, I thought.

I had traveled only a short distance, when my head began to spin and it seemed to me the *shaitan* I had first feared, and whom I had thought hid in the desert, were about to swallow me up and throw my carcass to his ever-black legions of crows. The sound of gravel crunching under the tires of a car snapped me back to reality.

The woman behind the wheel was dressed in red. When she rolled down the automatic window of her Toyota Camry, a blast of cold air mixed with female perfume wafted towards me. The world stopped turning when she spoke. Her voice was so soft.

"You are crazy to walk in this heat. Don't you realize that you will die of heat and dehydration? Are you sure you don't want a ride?" she asked with a warm smile.

She was not beautiful by any standards, but she was not ugly either. Besides, a woman in Oman was as precious as cleansing rain. A woman in Oman, any woman, was more beautiful in my eyes than the most beautiful movie star. Actually, she was sexy somehow. She had plain, thick features, but judging from the shape of her shoulders she definitely had a nice figure.

"Jump in," she said. No doubt I was dazzled by her special charm, I thought. Was it because she was such an enigma? Was she the only free woman in a country where educated, salaried women still gave the fruit of their labor to their husbands or their parents?

"Okay, but I don't think it's a good idea, mum," I answered, my heart pounding inside my chest.

"My name is Moza, and I don't care about Omanis who gossip when they see me give a lift to a stranger. They are a bunch of wolves anyway," she said as I slammed the door shut.

The color of her skin was a cross between sand and dates when they are ripe. Her hands, which were swathed in henna, were delicate — the hands of a woman who never worked in a kitchen. She had a rich, ringing Muscat accent and her eyes changed color and became dark hazel each time she smiled.

"So, you are the new Algerian teacher?" She said as she flipped the AC of her car to its max.

"How did you know?" I asked, stunned.

"Nothing is hidden in Oman, especially in Shinas ... I like Algerians, and North Africans in general. They behave like Europeans. They are very secretive, not like us Omaniya (Omanis). She smiled and I smiled back. Moza shifted in her seat and checked the buttons of her *abaya*.

"We are four major tribes here, besides the Zotties or those who have no roots, of course." She said the last three words with a frown. I smiled again.

"By the way, you teach one of my sons."

I was quite surprised because she did not look like she was more than 30 years old.

64

"You have a son in secondary school?"

"I even have a son in college. He studies engineering. Besides the boys, I have three banet (girls).

"You don't look that old," I said, then gave her one of my best smiles. She was not impressed.

"I'm a grandmother, I have two married daughters and the third is going to marry this month. Have you seen that tent?" She pointed to a large tent erected in front of a large house.

"That's where the wedding will take place."

"Why do you need a tent? The house is a *Masha'Allah,* God has willed it, so big."

"Oh, this is our *adat* (tradition). We celebrate weddings and also mourn our dead in tents."

"How old are you?" I questioned, and then quickly added, "Sorry, I shouldn't ask."

"Why shouldn't you ask? I'm 37," she said.

"Elsewhere in the Arab world, especially Algeria, women of your age are still unmarried." Moza smiled, but there was scorn in her eyes.

As we reached the *mojamma,* she gave me her phone number and promised to come and take me to Sohar the following evening.

"You will see it's very beautiful. By the way, there are lots of Algerians here. Most of them stay in Lulu Centre, in the French café. You can wait for me there while I finish my shopping," she said and then winked goodbye.

What a beautiful surprise, though incomplete, I thought. It was the first time I didn't understand a woman. Several questions entered my thoughts. Was she divorced? Was she after an adventure? Did she like me? Time would tell, I mused.

I had developed the habit of a nap after a hard day at school. The stench in the bathroom was unbearable, but I needed to douse myself with cold water to take off the sweat and kill the desire for Moza. The water under the tub was so hot that I postponed my shower till late in the evening.

I went into a restless sleep in which Moza was the principle protagonist. Her voice was warm, like a kiss, and her eyes had the darkness of a crimson dream. Was I in love with an Omani woman? Or was the forbidden suddenly attractive, I wondered. I tossed and turned in my bed. The heat and the crippled desire made me feel uncomfortable. She was by all means special. Suffice to say, she was the only woman in Shinas who wore a red scarf. The henna on her hands matched the red lipstick on her lips, and the coal around her eyes cried out for a kiss — or so I thought.

CHAPTER 11

Hazem woke me up at about five. "Who is Moza?" he teased. I lit a cigarette and did not answer. "You kept repeating her name while you were asleep."

"I was hallucinating, most probably." I said.

A grin tugged at his lips and I swallowed. "Sure ... hurry up. We have to buy everything this evening." I remembered the stacked plates, and the long hours of cleaning and scrubbing ahead.

"Could we just bring an Indian to do the job for five rials?" I suggested.

Hazem laughed, "Are you becoming like an Omani now?"

I stifled a sigh and went out after him, cursing under my breath. As we reached the corner and were about to turn right and cross the highway, we saw a scene that took our breath away. We came to a halt, breathless, at the edge of a small crowd. At first, I thought I was hallucinating and rubbed my eyes, but the spectacle was so real. Even Hazem, whose incredible interior peace I had thought nothing could disturb, was filled with swelling anger. I could see the crimson tide that invaded his face, the veins of irritation bulging in his forehead.

The corpse of a Bengali was dangling in the air, hanging on an electric post. The spectacle tore at my heart and made tears fill my eyes. Hazem was swallowing hard — his way of fighting back tears, I suppose. The crowd — mostly sad-eyed Indians and Pakistanis — watched silently, the deceased man who had committed suicide.

A short, thin-skinned Omani talked to the police over his cell phone. "He killed himself a short while ago. I have seen everything. I thought he was repairing a wire or something."

"Why did he do it?" an Indian asked in his typical accent.

"I don't know. I just got here," I answered. I stared at the dark blue corpse.

Another Indian spoke in his mother tongue and his interviewer shook his head — was it the Indian "yes" or an expression of regret?

"What did he say?" I inquired.

"He said the man paid more than 900 *rials* (3,000 U.S. dollars) to his Omani *kafil* (bailsman), but unfortunately, he could not find him a job."

"He was down on his luck. Poor man!" another bystander added.

"Actually, he had a job but he could not pay his *kafil* and the rent," Hazem commented.

"I do not understand," I said.

"He pays at least 20 *rials* to the man who brought him in. If he does not pay, the *kafil* calls the police and he will be deported back home," Hazem pointed out with a grimace on his face.

Living in Shinas revealed the true face of Islam, I thought. Hazem seemed to read my thoughts.

"You see, nobody cares for a poor, helpless Bengali — we Muslims are not good at all," he said.

The Omani, with skin that looked parched by the sun, turned out to be the *kafil,* the true murderer of that poor man, I thought. I remember that I overheard him speaking to one of his friends.

"*Astagfirullah,* I ask pardon from Allah. Suicide is *haram,*" he said.

"He has lost his hereafter," said a stout man as he scratched at his long beard.

At that moment, I recall, another strange idea dawned on me: Islam does not change people's hearts. If it did, the people in the

Gulf would not be enslaved. We finished shopping silently, then went to a dingy Indian restaurant and ate a few mouthfuls of rice. After that, each one of us went to his room. Words seemed futile and we had no desire to talk.

CHAPTER 12

Hazem and I spent the following morning washing and cleaning and scrubbing the dirty walls and floors of our rooms. Our neighbor — the Sudanese man — woke up early and went to the mosque. When he returned, rosary in hand and *siwak* between lips, he greeted us and then went back to sleep.

"This guy makes me furious," I blurted out.

"Let the dead bury their own dead," I heard Hazem saying, almost to himself.

"Who said that?" I asked.

"He is someone who is greater than me or you — someone very special."

His evasive answer aroused my curiosity. "I think I know him, I countered. He is a poet … an American … that's his style. Wait a minute … yes … T.S. Eliot."

Hazem burst into laughter; then I could see he was weighing his options. "No, it is not … one day I will tell you about this man — at least I hope so."

"Well, never mind … but you are right, he is a dead man — useless to speak to someone who is dead," I finally conceded, despite the frustration and the fathering tone I could depict in his words.

We finished cleaning at about 12, and then we ate in the same dingy Indian restaurant. After my usual nap, I heard the distinct horn of Moza's Camry. In the twinkling of an eye, I made myself ready.

That evening she was dressed in a blood-red *hijab* over a black *abeya*. The gloss on her lips made her mouth look like ripe strawberries. But that time she was not alone — her two daughters were sitting in the back seat. One of them, called Amani, was tall and pale-faced. The other whose name was Fatma, looked shorter and more portly, but prettier.

I was slightly embarrassed, for as soon as I hopped into the car they laughed and I heard one of them say, "He is a *khal*." The remark won them some stern looks from their mother. I did not understand what they meant, and if the truth be told, I was too confident with myself and my physique that some women back home used to describe as good-looking.

"What does *khal* mean?" I asked innocently. They laughed instead of answering and Moza shifted in her seat. I forgot about it thinking that they were just kids teasing their mum.

We spoke about our accents and how words we consider completely innocent in one place would probably hurt someone else in another. Then we spoke about the beauty of Oman. I lied my best to her. The rugged, treeless mountains became romantic and inspiring. The hot, ruthless weather became mild and good to the health. The Omani people were no longer greedy or stingy; they were simply the best.

"You are not convinced," Moza said, "but believe me when I tell you that the Omanis are the best Arabs of the Gulf. The Emiratis, Qataris or Kuwaitis are arrogant. They despise the poor and consider *wafideen* as their own slaves."

"What about the Saudis?" I asked.

"You must be joking," she said. A shock of black hair protruded from her *hijab* and she quickly tucked it back inside. "They are cruel and really rude, especially the people of Mecca. The people of Medina are much better. Each time I make an Umrah (pilgrimage that can be taken at any time of the year), I suffer … They really don't deserve that holy place."

We talked, but it seemed to me that Moza only half listened. I realized later that she was leading our discussion towards the supernatural. When we spoke about sorcery and demons, she became all ears. Even the girls stopped their whispered gossip and were completely attentive.

"They say that, in Morocco, there are people who can transform water into milk," she said.

Though I did not believe what she was saying at all, I tried my best to impress her. I spoke about King Solomon and the thousands of demons he had under his service. The more I gave vent to my imagination, the more she corroborated my sayings from verses of the Qur'an. I discovered, to my amazement, that I had not read the book very well.

My throat was dry when we reached the center of Sohar; I never knew I could talk that much. Moza went shopping and I waited for her in the only café where a customer could get a French Espresso and smoke a cigarette. There were many Algerians and Tunisians there as well as some Europeans — mostly from eastern Europe — and an old British couple. I listened for a while to their idle talk, then my mind strayed into the red forbidden world of Moza. No doubt she liked me, I thought to myself. But of course she could not show it blatantly in front of the kids.

We left Sohar at about six in the evening. The setting sun spilled its red nectar like henna on the feet and hands of a Blushi woman. The seafaring city of the famous Sinbad did not say goodbye, but smiled a half-smile, knowing that its visitor would soon be back again. The long highway still shimmered in front of us and created a shadowy painting by a romantic painter.

When we drove through Liwa, the scenery became windswept, barren and wild. The world reverted to its primitive, inhospitable soul. Only the Indians and Bengalis were busy here and there — building, cleansing and cutting off hedge groves.

"These people do not get tired — they really amaze me," I remarked.

"Why should they?" Moza replied. "The small sum they get here makes them very rich in their countries … do not feel sorry for them, they are richer than both of us." She smiled, but I did not smile back.

As we reached the shabby quarters where I lived, I wanted to kiss her but my shy attempt fell on rocky ground. Besides, the kids were behind us and she did not seem to be the least interested. We promised to meet the following weekend and she asked me to call her anytime I needed anything. She drove away and I watched her car disappear in the distance. In reality, I did not need her sympathy nor want her charity. What I wanted was her red lips, but they were the forbidden wine of an Omani vine.

CHAPTER 13

I found Hazem working on his laptop. He was studying various types of *khanjars* (daggers). "Have you seen these?" He asked. Why on earth he was interested in those stupid things, I wondered. They all looked the same in my eyes. I squinted and read the prices twice. "I never realized they were so expensive … 3,000 *rials* (about 10,000 U.S. dollars) can you believe it?"

"You can get one for 200, I think. I do not remember which country, but most probably Yemen," Hazem replied.

"Are they real? I mean, like knives with true blades?"

"Everything sharp is real in the Arab world." Hazem's voice rang with sarcasm.

"Sometimes I wonder if we still live in the 16th century. I mean, sometimes it seems time is relative. Of course Einstein said it, but he did not see its real movement."

"What do you mean?" Hazem asked.

"The more we move west, the faster time becomes, but the more we move east, time becomes lethargic — almost dead," I replied.

Hazem clapped his hands. "Bravo, bravo. I'm impressed. I wonder if you will discover a new theory in physics if you drink this cheap Indian liquor." He pointed to an almost empty bottle that looked like an old ketchup container.

"I prefer not — but these pictures make everyone's mind reel with unanswered questions."

He smiled dryly then let out a big sigh. "We are in the 21st century, but people around here still put arms around their waists when they wish to impress — life is a farce, isn't it?" I continued.

"Or dance with swords like the Saudis. You are most probably right. These people still want to live in the 1st century after the *hijra* (the prophets') migration from Mecca to Medina. Time seems almost in a coma around here." Hazem said.

"By Allah, you are right," I acquiesced. "But why would a man pay such a sum for a *khanjar* like this?" I asked.

"It's like one's dear wife. How much would you pay to keep her young and beautiful?" We both burst into laughter. "A metaphor?" I asked.

"I guess everything around here is metaphoric, but the metaphors are not poetic at all. They are so blunt, so macabre. Do you see what I mean?"

"Do they make use of it when they get angry, like the people in Yemen?" I asked instead of answering.

"Maybe in the past, but I do not think they have courage today. Their king has erased the least trace of manliness from them," Hazem replied.

"Probably you are right, but I think it is part of their nature. They are very polite — too polite, perhaps — but I noticed they are so simple-minded, verging on naivety sometimes. Did you not see that? "I asked. Hazem looked me in the eye and then stared ahead. He had so many things to say but, as usual, he only spoke in riddles.

"Maybe they have two faces," he said. "Maybe we are the gullible and not them. Maybe things are not what they seem. My third eye tells me to never underestimate a man wearing a *dishdasha*."

"Nonsense," I mumbled. Hazem smiled; I think he may have been praying secretly for me to see what he saw. I was a bit embarrassed, but deep in my heart I knew that he was right.

CHAPTER 14

That night, real doubt crept into my mind. I mean Oman or Saudi Arabia or anywhere in the Gulf was to us North Africans, the sacred land of Allah — the real Eden of Islamic justice. I could not forget about that dead Bengali man. When someone kills himself in that manner, because of injustice, and then nobody cares — that is too much, I thought. A suicide like that could have happened anywhere in the world but people's response must have been different, even in Israel where the Arabs of 1948 had their rights — at least far better than in the Gulf.

Hazem appeared to quickly forget about the incident. I even heard him humming a song the following morning. I must admit, I was jealous of him, so jealous that I thought he was insensitive. Maybe he was an atheist after all, I thought. I recall that I woke up late at night and went to his room. He was sound asleep. I nudged him awake.

"You don't look disturbed," I snapped.

Hazem stretched in his bed like a cat stretched under the sun. "What's the matter with you — don't you know how late it is?"

"I can't sleep — can't get the picture of that Bengali out of my head."

Hazem stifled a sigh. "I was here ten years ago, Jamal, when there were no human rights and no Internet — nothing. I had my fill and I developed a thick skin."

"Sometimes I wonder if Allah truly exists," I said.

"Oh! You can be sure, He is always there."

"I mean, we Muslims are really …"

"Heartless," Hazem said.

"Exactly … why are these Europeans, though *kaffir,* better than us? I mean, I was in England and people there — at least most of them — do not exploit you and do not lie to you," I replied.

"They respect your humanity," Hazem said.

"Imagine Saudi Arabia was a superpower like the U.S.A."

"Oh my goodness — blood would be shed — lots of blood, my friend," Hazem said assuredly.

"They would have turned the entire world into *ghilman,* shemales, and *jawari,* or concubines," I pointed out.

"You would have been sold in the market — to the highest bidder. They did it before and most of them wish they could do it again," Hazem added.

"But normally the treatment of Muslims is different from the treatment of Nasara, Christians or *kaffir* (infidels) isn't it?

"You won't pay *jizya* (poll tax), but you will be treated, like now, as a Muslim of a second class."

There was a sudden silence as we stared down at the floor. I had run out of steam and most probably Hazem felt the same way. The air was pregnant with questions — questions that had enormous consequences.

Hazem intrigued me. I thought he was an atheist, but each time he pledged that he believed in God. Could he be a non-devoted Muslim like the millions around the Arab world? He did not appear to be the kind of man who left a job undone. Was he a Buddhist? I wondered.

I never seriously suspected he could be a Christian. I recollect that I had always thought that any person with a modicum of reason would not believe that God could have a son and send him to Earth where he would be humiliated, persecuted and then hung on a cross to die. That it was nonsense was my first reaction when I had initially discussed the question with a Catholic priest from Lebanon.

"Don't you have eyes to see — how can you believe in such a legend?" I had asked indignantly. I remember the priest took hold of my hand and closed his eyes. He had prayed fervently for me that day, but I had laughed and thought he was insane.

"Do you believe in reincarnation?" I suddenly, but deliberately asked Hazem.

He raised his eyebrows. "No. I believe in one chance and in a single lifetime."

"I thought you were a Buddhist."

"No, I'm not," Hazem replied. "I'm glad you asked me. By the way, do you know that some Muslims believe in reincarnation?"

"Sorry, but I don't believe you," I said.

"Have you ever heard of the Druz in Lebanon and Syria?"

"Of course; they are Shiites," I said. "Some of them still live in Iraq, too. They are practicing Muslims except that, as far as I know, they think the angel Gabriel made a mistake and took Mohammed for Ali. But do they pray five times a day and fast the holy month of Ramadan?"

"I told you. They do everything. I don't know exactly by which twist of logic they believe in reincarnation, but they even claim to have their own evidences from the Qur'an. However, they are only far-fetched explanations of some verses," Hazem explained with that typical peace of mind, which I was jealous of now.

"I don't know who originally said it. The more you probe deep into Islam, the more questions arise."

"Questions about what?" Hazem asked.

"Faith," I said.

"Beware, you should be sure about what you believe," Hazem replied.

"Everything is relative, Hazem," I countered.

"Yes, you are right, but in the field of spirituality you either know you are right or you don't."

"I see what you mean and I agree with you. I know that Islam is the only true religion in the world, for example, but don't you have your own doubts sometimes?"

"Doubt means you still don't know. Or maybe you are on the wrong path." He smiled to soften his remark. "But it's a thing you will have to learn by yourself, I suppose. Well … it was a nice talk … you had better let me go back to sleep."

Hazem left me to my own doubts and fears. I stretched out on my bed and tried to sleep, but I tossed and turned for a long time. Then, out of my mind, I produced the image of Moza — eyes as black as sin, lips so thirsty for rain. Her Arabian breasts were so proud and inviting. Crippled desire added salt to the wound and only with the first dawn calling for prayer was my body able to succumb to a few hours of rest.

That very dawn, I had a strange vision. I saw Hazem dressed in white, with a smile over his face that beamed like a sunrise. He was in the company of a man shrouded with light. The man had thorns on his forehead but he did not seem to care. I still don't know by which logic I gathered he was the Messiah (Ibn Maryam, the son of Mary). The man was not that handsome, but his eyes were the most beautiful eyes I had ever seen — they were the color of grass and the sea combined. They were so penetrating and so … caring. I heard him beckon to me. "Come and let the dead bury their dead."

When I woke up, it was only half an hour until seven. I knew the dream was real and that the man's identity — whom Hazem had refused to reveal — was Isa (Jesus.) As a Muslim I had been brought up to believe that Jesus was only a prophet and not the son of God, as the Nasara or Christians claimed. So I knew my vision was true and I felt sorry for Hazem. He was a *mushrik* (polytheist) and his lot was the fires of *Jahannam* (Hell.) But I could not find a satisfying answer to why Jesus would speak to me in that way. Why would he ask me to leave the dead and follow him? At that time, the only answer I could rationalize was that the man full of light was not the real Jesus — he was the devil in disguise.

Similarly, I had been taught that only prophet Mohammed, if he appeared in a dream, was genuine, because he had once said to his companions that anyone who sees him in a dream, he truly saw him, for the reason that he is the only one whom the devil can't use as a disguise. I deduced that since the man in my dream was not prophet Mohammed — the greatest among all prophets — he could only be the devil who was trying to lure me from the righteous path.

The explanation was not that perfect, but it was all I had. I remember that a dangerous idea dawned on me at that time. What if Mohammad was *the devil* himself? I prayed to Allah for forgiveness. The dream vanished with the first morning light, but its unsolved mystery lingered in my head.

CHAPTER 15

The morning's moist heat started sapping my energy earlier than usual. A pang of fear went down my spine as I thought about what I would be like a few hours later. I saw myself exhausted and sweating when the sun reached its peak and the kids, who never seemed to tire or be bored, would shout, quarrel and jabber like demons.

Am Khalfan — as it was his habit every morning — played his Qur'an tape, recited by Sheikh Al Tablawi. As usual, he flipped the volume of his Kenwood tape player to its max.

"Have you noticed the mosques?" I asked Hazem. "They are not like in Algeria. Instead, they are crammed with worshippers. Everyone prays in this country — nobody misses sobh or morning (prayers). Our mosques are becoming empty in Algeria. It is very sad."

"Did you pray while you were home?" Hazem asked.

"I did, but not on a regular basis. And you?"

"I have a legion of demons inside, if my old father was right," Hazem said.

"It's a good opportunity to start here anew," Mustapha, a fat Egyptian teacher said from the seat behind. "The best thing you learn in Oman is how to observe the five prayers at their regular times each day."

I could see that Hazem swallowed the words on the tip of his tongue. He smiled instead and kept silent. Am Khalfan pressed a button and opened the automatic door of his van for the last teacher, then started his engine and sped towards the main road.

The crescents upon minarets seemed to cradle the stars that never needed rest. I had read somewhere that sailors believed that the sight of them preceded storm and death.

As Am Khalfan cleared his way through a herd of goats quarreling over an empty Marlboro cigarette pack, I heard the Jordanian tell his friend, a Sudani, "The Omanis spoil these Indians. In their country, they don't even have anything to eat."

"I will tell you something — never show any respect to an Indian. They are accustomed to the big stick. Once you treat them fairly, they just become rude and disrespectful," Hafidh pointed out.

"Indian Muslims are different — at least they have some dignity," said Jalal, another Egyptian teacher and member of the Egyptian brotherhood. "*Sobhana Allah* (Praise to Allah,) I can tell who is a Muslim and who is a Hindu."

I cursed under my breath while Hazem closed his eyes.

Am Khalfan pulled his old Toyota van to the right side of the road and came to a halt not far away from the school. As usual, students milled restlessly in front of the small iron gate. My heart ached as I remembered Tabour — that long painful hour of standing under the sun praising his majesty the king and then listening to Qur'an.

"After *tabour*, the day is over," Nazih said. He was from Jordan and had been in Oman for more than 15 years. There was nothing special about him except the moustache. It was as thick as Stalin's.

"Teaching here is like performing a play. Nobody cares because nobody fails, after all," Anwar, the Egyptian teacher, added.

Hazem smiled and Am Khalfan — an Omani, but from the Blush tribe — did not care. He laughed and revealed a set of decayed teeth. "Had I some authority, I would have taken these *hamir* (donkeys) to the zoo."

We laughed and begged him to come in time in the afternoon.

For even a minute under the sun after two o'clock meant real pain.

"In *Sha'a Allah* (If Allah wishes)," Am Khalfan said.

"It means he is going to be late again," Anwar pointed out. "Better wait for him inside until he makes a call."

Nerves were taut now. We had a mission, simple and clear. We had to praise His Majesty, the Sultan then, for seven long hours, hold in check wild boys who seemed to me like young horses straining at their reins.

An Omani colleague from the Za'abi tribe asked me if I was from Algeria. "Ya Allah; I love Algerian girls," he said openly.

"Omani girls are beautiful too," I replied.

A slight cloud of irritation went over his face. "Our girls are covered up from head to toe."

"That makes them sexier," I teased.

The veins in his forehead bulged, but he kept his anger under control. "You know what? Last night I watched the Algerian national channel. By Allah, I had to do ghosl (full ablution) to pray night prayers. By the way, do you have any porno films?"

I felt a rush of pity and anger at the same time. The long beard that reached his navel did not reflect his demented mind.

"Are you serious?" I asked. My voice was ringing with sarcasm.

"Last year I had an Algerian friend. He had so many films …"

"Do you have any class now?" I cut in.

"Yes, but I'm going to be absent today. You foreigners are really hard workers. Anyway, it pains my heart to know that you do not have the right to be absent."

"Why is that?" I asked.

"I do not know, but I never saw *an outsider* absent a single day."

"It's because they are afraid — I am not. If I'm sick or do not feel like working, I will take a day off," I said.

"You might lose your job — and you know better than me, the poverty back home."

"Yes, there is poverty, but with my *karama* (dignity), it is better, I think," I said curtly.

"Anyway, you will get used to our system here," he said.

"I don't think so, and I plan to give my resignation by the end of the year."

"That's strange," he said. "Anyway, good luck to you, man."

There was emptiness about Oman in general, and about Shinas in particular. The country lacked beauty, I thought. I imagined the beauty that one might see in a woman's uninhibited smile, while she is wearing a flowered dress that signified she was full of life and hope. Oman was like a drearily clad woman desperate for affection — abundant and unrestricted. It lacked love, and may be Christian love, as one philosopher once put it. The desert killed beauty. Despite the drastic efforts of the government to grow flowers on the pavements of big cities such as Muscat, Sohar, Salalah and Sur, and the stoic effort of Indians and Bengalis to fight the sun and to continue watering the precious plants regardless of any cost, Oman, as every gulf country around the region, would remain a swept-out wilderness.

Petrol could not fight the inhuman nature of the scorching sun. It darkened the hearts of its slaves with jealousy, selfishness, greed and lust. The sun breastfed the desert and the desert killed flowers and flowers remind us of our humanity, I glumly surmised.

In class, where the supposed real job of a teacher was, I gave some tasks and then solved them to a group of naughty pupils who did not speak English. They did not want to speak the language of infidels. In fact, I spent most of my time and energy trying to subdue them.

The play would last until 1:30 p.m. and then I would be free. I would eat some Indian food — most of the time rice — and then slip into a dreamless sleep. The days rolled on so slowly that I began to like its monotony. I started to enjoy living at the far end of a world based on nonsense and excessive politeness. During the weekends, Hazem and I would go to Sohar, have cappuccino in Lulu, or some beers in a cheap Indian pub. Life was easy, almost deadly, but I was determined to finish the year with the least damage possible.

CHAPTER 16

I did not forget about the word *khal*. I was about to ask Hazem but, on reflection, I stopped. I assumed that its meaning wasn't a compliment, and as resourceful as he was, I knew he would quickly find out who said it, and of course to whom it was addressed.

During the break, I asked Khalil, an Omani teacher, short and sad-eyed but very sympathetic.

"What's the meaning of the word *khal?*" I asked. A cloud went over his face. He shook his head back and forth.

"Why do you ask me that question?" He asked, surprised.

I was stunned and did not know what to say. "My color is black but I am sure about the white color of my heart, something they certainly do not have inside." He continued. He was obviously agitated at my innocent question and I noticed his hand made a fist as he spoke.

"I heard an Omani woman say it about me," I explained.

Suddenly, all the anger dissipated from his face. The glaring eyes were now full of compassion and sympathy. "Don't worry about it … these people don't live in the 21st century. I'm an Omani like them, and as you see I have green eyes and white skin and yet they could not forget that one of my grandparents was a *khadem* (a slave.) A normal person would pay 6,000 *rials* for a *horma* (woman) I paid 20,000 *rials* for my wife and her family is still not happy."

"I see it is very derogatory — like saying 'nigger' in English?" I asked. I swallowed hard to suppress the lump developing in my throat.

"More than that, it means you are not allowed to live normally, like the others in this country. Of course the law stipulates the opposite, but you see the *adat* (customs) haven't changed. Anyway, we are still the best and no one can take this feeling away from us," Khalil concluded.

I felt pain, real pain in my mind. I cursed the very day I came to the Gulf, but it was too late. I would have to be patient for another seven months. Everything was clear now and the pieces of the puzzle started coming together. I remembered what Moza said when I had pointed to a black Omani man who was waiting for a taxi. I had commented that he looked like Denzel Washington.

"Denzel who?" she had asked.

"A very famous American actor," I explained.

"Well, in Oman he is nobody. Even if he gave me a million rials, I would never let him marry my daughter."

I didn't understand the bitterness and indignation that rung in her voice at that time. I thought she was exaggerating and that racism was a thing of the past.

I asked her, "How do you know which Omani was a slave? They all look the same to me."

Moza's eyes narrowed to a slit. "I know one as soon as I see him. There are so many clues."

"Enlighten me, then," I challenged.

"You look at the shape of the nose, the thickness of the lips, the quality of the hair, and the size of the hands and feet. No former slave can hide himself forever."

On reflection, I don't believe that Moza ever liked me as a man. She only wanted me to teach her sorcery and witchcraft and help her cast spells at which she thought I was an expert. I rushed to the bathroom and threw up. I was ashamed of myself, of my stupidity and of the tears that started to well up in my eyes. I washed my face over and over again and then looked at my reflection in the mirror. My nose was big. It was the nose of a *khadem* or former slave. My lips were thick and my skin was dark. No doubt, one of my great-great grandparents must have been a thick-lipped slave from Africa, I thought.

If I had learned anything good from boxing and the ring, it was the following: Never show your knockout punch as long as you can hide it. I clenched my teeth and regained my composure. If the truth be told, I had a curious feeling that one day I would avenge myself.

CHAPTER 17

In spite of the discrepancies I saw every day in Oman, I returned, avidly, to Islam. I kept my distance from Hazem, and sometimes I hated him for the internal happiness he seemed to enjoy. He was a Christian, after all — a *mushrik* (an infidel) — whether he accepted it or not. I also kept my distance from Omanis. I thought they did not represent true Islam — the Islam of justice and racial equality. I immersed myself in religious books. I started reading about the people of Jahilia, the period before the advent of Islam. I wanted to know everything from the beginning of this religion.

I was curious how the small library of Hassan ben Ali School held unread, beautiful and intriguing stories — stories that neither *imams* told during Friday sermons nor the preachers spoke of on Muslim television and radio channels.

I was fascinated by the story of four men who had made a pact to reject the widespread idolatry of Mecca, and who had set out on their own spiritual adventure of, in their own words, "finding the true religion,". The four men were called Zayd Ben Amr, Waraka ibn Nawfal, Uthman Ben al-Huwayrith and Ubayd Allah ben Jahsh.

Through this beautiful book, I learned that the pact was made shortly before the birth of the prophet, around 570 C.E. Some claim it took place in Mecca, others in Syria, others say that they do not know where it was made. Regardless, as is the case with all Muslim events, all agreed it came about within the decade before the advent of Islam.

This assumption is based on a more or less known historical fact. Zayd Ben Amr — the only one of the four not to adopt the Christian faith — was, as historians report, "killed during his religious quest." At the same time, the Quraysh tribe — the tribe in which Prophet Mohammed was born — was building the *kaaba* ... five years before the mission, or the first time that the angel Gabriel visited Mohammed in Hira Cave.

Upon making the pact, the four "left to roam the earth." The second one was Waraka the uncle of Khadija — the first wife of the prophet Mohammad. He became a Christian and read the old and new testaments, and some of the Talmudic readings available at that time. He, therefore, amassed a great deal of knowledge about Scripture. Later, he would be the first one in Mecca to believe that the entity that visited Mohammed in Hira Cave was angelic and not satanic, as Mohammed had first thought. Curiously, he died shortly after, and the wahy (revelations) stopped for two years.

As for Uthman Ben al-Huwayrith, he went to Rome and became a Christian. It is recounted that Caesar knew him personally and raised his status from a barbarian to a citizen of Rome. The old books say that he went from the poverty and ignorance of deserted Jazira — the only place in the world that was safe from invasions because of the roughness of its hot weather and the lack of its vegetation — to the civilized comfort of Rome.

The fourth man (Ubayd Allah ben Jahsh) was put into prison in Syria. There he met a monk, who shared his cell. He became a Christian, and as Muslims sources claim, was urged by the monk to return to Mecca to witness the beginning of the mission. Actually, the monk was one of the followers of Arius, a heretic who appeared in the 3rd century and claimed that Jesus was not divine. The church fought him, and most of his followers escaped to Arab Jazira. Ubayd was killed on his return to the land of Judham, which lies between Jordan and Saudi Arabia. That left me to merely conjecture as to whether he would have adopted

Islam or remained a Christian and would have influenced the budding new religion of that time.

The first thing I discovered was that the *jahilia* (ignorance) era was not, in fact, an *epoch of total blindness*. It was actually an enlightenment period where people felt free to adopt any faith. The people who lived at that time made their own spiritual quests and were able to freely choose their faith. They were not ostracized, provided they respected the customs and laws of the Kabila or tribe. In fact, banned heretic Christians, Jews, pagans and Sabians lived in harmony and respected each other back then. There was not one single war at that time that had a religious background. When Islam came, it spread ignorance, fanaticism and death. That was the truth, bare and simple, I glumly deduced.

CHAPTER 18

Islam came to Oman , United Arab Emirates and Bahrain in an amazing and incredible way, and the people of that region had no say in the decision. They simply followed the choice of their two kings, the Al Jalandi brothers, who converted to Islam to preserve their kingdom and spare the blood of their people. Ibn Hazm recounts in his book, Al Faysal (The Arbiter, volume 3, page 124), that Amr bin Al A'as (the shrewd fox), as he was nicknamed, was the orchestrator of the first and last peaceful invasion of a foreign land. The intelligent Amr was well informed about the two brothers who governed Oman at that time. He approached the younger brother, who was the weaker of the two and the most credulous. He expertly bluffed about the true military power of Muslims at that time like a skilled poker player. The young brother swallowed the bait and believed Amr's lies. He was so gullible that he advised Amr about the best strategy to approach his hard-boiled brother. The old brother felt he was being duped and kept postponing meeting with him for three days, to give his final answer to the following letter sent by Mohammad: "Peace be upon the one who follows the right path! I call you to Islam. Accept my call, and you shall be unharmed. I am God's Messenger to mankind, and the word shall be carried out upon the miscreants. If, therefore, you recognize Islam, I shall bestow power upon you. But if you refuse to accept Islam, your power shall vanish, my horses shall camp on the expanse of your territory and my prophecy shall prevail in your kingdom."

Amr grew impatient but played his last card and feigned

anger and bluffed again making him think that Muslims were strong enough to invade him and usurp his throne. In one of the most stupid political moves in history the old brother yielded to the threat and gave authority to Amr to gather the money of zakat or alms from the people of Oman.

The call of the Prophet Mohammed to the Omanis to become Muslims altered the course of history. Had the two brothers said no to unfounded threats, Islam would not have probably gone beyond the borders of Negd *(The Arabic word nejd literally means "upland" and was once applied to a variety of regions within the Arabian Peninsula. However, the most famous of these was the central region of the Peninsula roughly bounded on the west by the mountains of Yemen and to the east by the historical region of Bahrain and to the north by Iraq and Syria).* Unfortunately, the two Omani brother kings succumbed easily to the threats and believed the lies of Amr about the conversion of the major powers of that time to Islam. Having embraced the new religion, they were instrumental in defeating the Persians.

The gracious prophet, as Ibn Hazm points out, then expressed his good wishes for the people of Oman: "God bless the people of *Al Ghubaira* (i.e., the people of Oman), as they believed in me without seeing me."

Amr was a leader in the Muslim force that conquered southwestern Palestine in the 630 AD but gained fame when, on his own initiative, he set out to conquer Egypt, succeeding in 642 AD, after a two-year campaign.

CHAPTER 19

As I began to delve into the life of the prophet himself, questions started to flood my once credulous mind. The more I read, the more I became disgusted.

All historians and every reliable *hadith* (collections of sayings and deeds of Mohammad) agree that at the age of fifty-one Mohammed got married to a six-year-old girl. The *Sira* — the traditional name of biographies of Mohammed — recount that Aisha said she was playing with some other children when her mother took her by the hand, cleaned her up and groomed her for her new husband. The poor girl admitted she did not understand anything at that time. How could a man do this and still claim he was from God? I wondered. 'At that time, girls were riper than now. In other words, a girl aged six looked like a fourteen year-old girl nowadays and it is reported by many that he slept with her when she was nine,' explained a long bearded Muslim theologian on Al Nas TV.

The more I delved into the *Sira,* the more questions multiplied. The *Sira* recounts that he sent men to kill Om Kirfa, a 70-year-old woman, for *hijaa* — a satirical poem that ridiculed the prophet and his so-called divine mission. The *sahaba* tied her legs in opposite ways to two strong camels, and you can imagine the rest. She was torn like an old cloth. Om Kirfa did not deserve that horrible death, I thought. 'She was killed because Islam was in its early days and she wanted to eradicate it before it took root. So Mohammed said that Allah ordered him to cut her in two instead.' Gamil also argued in favor of Islam, but the arguments he continued to present without conviction were weak and raised more questions than answers.

Mohammed forbade *riba* (commodity exchanges in unequal quantities) in his Sharia, but when he died, he had his *diraa* (shield) *marhouna* (mortgaged) to a Jewish man. He once saw his adopted son's wife almost naked and lusted over her. Ibn Hisham and Ibn Ishaq — the most famous biographers of Mohammed — recount that, one day, the prophet passed by the tent of Zayd bin Harithah, his freed slave and adopted son since the age of eight, whom he married to Zaynab bent Jahsh, his cousin. The wind blew the curtain of his son's tent open and the prophet saw the beautiful Zaynab wearing a little shift that exposed her nakedness.

"Praise be to Allah who changes the hearts of men," he kept repeating as his lust grew. The son divorced his wife and offered her to the adoptive father as a new spouse. The marriage was considered, by some, enlightened and Courageous men a scandal for two reasons. The first was because of double standards, she was his fifth wife while everyone else was restricted to four. The second was because he married his adopted son's wife.

The Qur'an quickly revoked adoption and said that, "After Zayd got sexually satisfied with Zaynab, we gave her to you as a wife." Surat Al Ahzab 35:37. It is worth mentioning here that Zayd was the only one of Sahaba whose name is spelled directly in the Qur'an.

There were so many unanswered questions. It seemed to me, Mohammad created more questions than he gave answers. Sometimes the very words spoken by Omar — the third Muslim caliph became part of the *wahy* (revelation.)

Apart from the concubines and the women who offered themselves to him, Mohammed married 16 women: Khadija bint (daughter) of Khuwailid, Aisha bent Abi Bakr, Sawda bint Zama, Zeineb bent Jahsh, Om Salma bent Abi Omaya, Hafsa bint Umar, Om Habiba or Ramla bint Abi Sofian, Juwairia bent Al

Hareth, Safia bint Hoyay, Maymuna bint Al Hareth, Zeineb bent Khozeima, Sharaf bent Khalifa, Alia bint Dhobian, Wasni bint Essalt, Sana bint Asma bint Assalt, and Asma bint Ennouman. The claim that he married them to gather the worrying tribes of that time was simply a lie. I discovered that six of the women were from his own Koreish tribe: Khadija, Aisha, Hafsa, Om Habiba, Om Salma and Sawda belonged to the tribe.

Sometimes I even wondered if the sons and daughters he had had from his wife Khadija were truly his. Had I been wrong, then why did he not have a single baby from other wives apart from Maria who was a concubine and had no social status and therefore could have easily sept with one of the servants? For days I mulled over the idea and wondered about it. Why did I even question it? Was this some satanic reasoning that was being introduced into my thinking, or did it have roots in the various books I had previously read about his life? I concluded that the idea came from both.

During his illness — the last illness, from which he eventually died — Mohammed did not want to drink a syrup brought to him by Om Salma and Maymouna, two Muslim women from Habesha (Ethiopia). But when he passed out, his uncle, Al Abbas, poured the medicine into his mouth. When he woke up, he was told that Al Abbas had given him the very syrup he kept refusing to take. Mohammed ordered that all the people, even Aisha his beloved wife, except for his uncle, who was the one who administered the cure, must drink from the same medicine. Even his beloved Aisha drank of it. Why was he so skeptical? Why was the spoiled Aisha not even trusted? Did Mohammed really die a natural death?

"Why he did not marry a second wife when Khadija was alive?" a long-bearded *mutawa* asked his subservient audience on a Muslim channel. "The answer is very clear. Because he was not lusty, as they try to show on some enemy channels."

I switched off the television and puffed intensely on my

cigarette. To my mind, the real question should have been why he married such a large number of women and broke his Qur'anic four-women law. Why did he start to marry or start his sexual adventures at the age of 51, just after the death of Khadija?

The only explanation that seemed logical to me was that Khadija was not only strong and rich; she probably knew the real source of his prophet hood. She probably realized too late, that he was a false prophet. Therefore, he knew that he could jeopardize his situation if she saw him desiring to sleep with other women.

But *la goutte qui a fait deborder le vase* (the straw that broke the camel's back), as the French say, was the following incident. I read about in Siouti's book, Asbab Ettanzil (Causes of Revelation).

It is mentioned that Abdullah ben Saad bin Abi Sarh was the one who wrote the revelations to the prophet, because Mohammed was illiterate, or so he said about himself. The man had his doubts and used his brains. As Prophet Mohammed dictated the revelation, Abdullah ben Saad bin Abi Sarh would change a word or two, then repeat what he changed in front of Mohammed, who never corrected him.

Abdullah once pointed out the difference. To his surprise, the prophet is quoted as saying, "It is the same; most merciful or most forgiving."

Afterwards, Abdullah ben Saad bin Abi Sarh decided to leave Islam and return to his Koreishi tribe. Each time he was asked why, he would simply say, "If Mohammed received revelations from God; I too have received the same message." The man knew the truth and was not afraid to die as a *kaffir*, or infidel.

CHAPTER 20

Let me say that Hazem, unknowingly, helped me discover the truth about Islam and about Mohammed. I kept asking myself, why would an intelligent person like Hazem leave Islam — the righteous religion — and follow *shaytan, satan* and *koffar*, or infidels' way?

That question ignited the desire inside me to check the validity of what I believed in. With a critical eye I immersed myself in books, and the Al Hayat channel on my television opened doors that I never suspected would ever be opened. Anyone who mentions this Christian channel must speak about Abouna Zakaria — a great man who, alone, fought thousands of Muslim theologians busy embellishing Islam every day.

Abouna literally opened my eyes and released me from the fetters of what Arkoun, the famous Algerian thinker called 'sacred ignorance'. He and, later, Daniel and Doctor Ammari, made me become conscious of the discrepancies in the Qur'an. I felt so deceived that I thought about committing a suicide and die as a Muslim before it was too late. Though I knew without a shred of doubt that I, like all the millions of Muslims around the world, were completely misled, I kept hoping that one day Allah will restore my faith again. But the rain kept pouring.

As a case in point, I felt so sorry for myself and other Muslim believers that the Mecca we forwarded our prayers to five times a day did not exist during the time of Abraham. Then the facts began hitting me full in the face. The Qur'an — the living miracle of Mohammed — was full of errors.

It is said in the Qur'an that Mary, the mother of Jesus, was the sister of *Haroun* (Aaron) and *Mousa* (Moses). In some verses the whole universe was created in six days, but in Surat Fussilat, verses 9 to 12, the number was eight. Some verses in Surat Naml, verses 20 to 44 mention blatant legends such as the legend of the Hodhod, the wild rooster, who led King Soloman to the glamorous Queen of Sheba, which reminded me later of the fabled Jewish Targum of Esther where the legend had first begun. Some verses in Surat al Kahf, verses 83 to 96 describe Alexander the Macedonian or *Dhul-Qarnayn* (Literally he of the two horns) as a divine righteous ruler who built the wall to keep Gog and Magog from attacking the people whom he met on his journey to the end of the world where the sun sets.

The Qur'an claims that the wall he built was made out of iron and copper. Following Islamic eschatology, before the Day of Doom, Gog and Magog would destroy this wall and then ravage the Earth:

"Until, when Gog and Magog are let loose (from their barrier) and they swiftly swarm from every mound. And the true promise (Day of Resurrection) shall draw near [of fulfillment]. Then (when mankind is resurrected from their graves), you shall see the eyes of the unbelievers fixedly stare in horror. (They will say) "Woe to us! We were indeed heedless of this; nay, but we were wrong doers. Qur'an 21: 96-97. (The phrases in parenthesis are translations and not in the Arabic original.)

I was taught that all the various Qur'ans in the world are exactly the same and that our holy book is perfectly preserved and free from any variation. To my surprise, I discovered that there was not a single Qur'an during the prophet's life. There were seven *kira'at* — or readings — all revealed by God.

The question that still remained unanswered in my mind was the following: Why did Uthman — the third Muslim caliphate or commander of the believers, burn all the other versions of the holy book.

651 BCE, 19 years after the death of Mohammed, Uthman commissioned a committee to produce a standard copy of the text of Qur'an. On finishing the so-called true version that resembled most the tongue of the Koreishi tribe of the prophet he ordered the destruction of all the other versions that Mohammad himself claimed to be revealed from Allah. Five of these standard versions were sent to the major Muslim cities of the era, with Uthman keeping one for his own use in Medina, the city to which the prophet migrated to spread Islam. The only surviving copy is said to be held in Topkapi Palace, in Turkey.

How could he do such an unpardonable act such as burning what was supposed to be divine revelations and go unpunished, or even unquestioned? Even today, there are three slightly different versions of the Qur'an: The Al-Madina, which is reported by the Hafs; the *El Maghreb*, which is reported by the Warsh; and the Tunisian one reported through Khaloun.

To better understand this, the reader has to bear in mind that the Qur'an came into Muslim hands from Qur'an experts called "the Readers." They were celebrated reciters of the Qur'an in the early centuries of Islam. The manner in which these men recited the Qur'an was, in earlier times, recorded in textual form by other experts called the "Transmitters."

Consequently, these versions differ in their fundamental letters, diacritical dots and vowels, which, in various instances, change the meaning completely. The different Qur'ans also have a different understanding of the *Basmalah,* or saying that there is no god but Allah and Mohammed is his prophet. Some versions accept it as an intrinsic part of the Qur'an while others do not.

The more I read, the more I discovered the falsity found in the Islam religion. I no longer hated myself or Muslims in general. I had come to Oman as a believer, but little by little, I began to lose faith in the holy land of Allah. This was a very hard period for me because everything lost its meaning and only the joy of the passing moment became the reason for my being alive.

CHAPTER 21

My peace of mind was gone. My shackled brain struggled through the inconsistencies of the sacred and Mohammed. The more I studied the Sira, the more I became disturbed by the information it conveyed. But the mind has its own ways to solve things. My first reaction was to reject the blatant truth and stick to the tranquility enjoyed by those fooled by its deception. Its lull was like that of the ancient Greek Sirens, whose melodious voices lured men to their death on the seas. Consequently, I hid my head like an ostrich inside a big sand dune.

My hatred towards Hazem doubled at that time. I remember that I even turned my satellite dish to the Nile channel and ignored the Al Hayat channel forbidden from every Arab satellite. I threw away Sirat Ibn Hisham and all the books that spoke about *Sira Nabawiya*, the prophetic biography, and decided to follow the sugarcoated sermons of Sheiks and *imams*. After all, they knew better than me — who was I to argue against a fifth of the world population? Who was I to understand Islamic *fiqh* (jurisprudence), things only the *ulama* or Islamic theologians can understand or interpret?

I followed the advice of common sense and Mustapha, that Egyptian colleague who was a member of the Egyptian Muslim Brotherhood. For the first time in Oman, I went to pray the noon prayers. When my colleagues saw me inside the mosque, they cried in unison, "*Allaho Akbar.*"

Actually, I had lost faith, but I was determined to give Islam and myself one last chance. I chose faith over doubt, or better, over the blatant truth. Maybe I was wrong after all, or maybe the truth had many faces and I only clung to the wrong face. Maybe in the Gulf — the birthplace of Islam, I would capture the flame of faith again. All I needed was to immerse myself in *salat,* prayer and fasting, or so I thought.

My heart was heavy, and one evening, over a cold cup of tea, I spoke my mind and gave vent to some of my worries to Mustapha, a devoted Muslim who seemed to me well-learned and not afraid to raise controversial questions related to Islam. He scratched his beard for a long time and then he gave me the Web address of Ahmadiyya which is an Islamic reformist movement founded in British India near the end of the 19th century, originating with the life and teachings of Mirza Ghulam Ahmad (1835 — 1908.) Mirza claimed to have fulfilled the prophecies about the world reformer of the end times as predicted in the traditions of various world religions and to have brought about the final triumph of Islam as a world religion. He claimed that he was the Mujaddid (divine reformer) of the 14th Islamic century, the promised Messiah and Mahdi awaited by Muslims. The followers of the Ahmadiyya movement are referred to as Ahmadis or Ahmadi Muslims.

"Do not follow them, for they think that a certain Mirza is the Messiah … but I like the way they defend Islam, their explanations are very modern. Yet, again, beware because they are not true Muslims. They are heretics … they say that the Prophet Mohammed, peace be upon him, is not the last prophet to come. Some say they are planted by the English in Punjab, India … anyway, just take what they say in their war against Christianity and leave the rest."

At that time, I did not think that in matters of religion there was always a gray area. I did not know that either you are on the right path or not. I was more than eager to find something that killed the burning doubt inside my mind.

I do not know why, but suddenly, Islam became the most beautiful religion — so beautiful that, as I recall now, I was so

proud to be a Muslim. Mohammed preached peace and all the
Jihadi aggressive wars were, in fact, defensive wars. Aisha was
not nine years old when Mohammed married her; she had to
be at least 17. I was dazzled by the charismatic late Mirza Taher
— the fourth caliphate. King Solomon never had real demons at
his service. There was no single legend in the Qur'an, he argued.
The demons were only a metaphor for skilled workers. The ants
were names of ancient Arab tribes, and even the Hodhod was a
metaphor for King Solomon's Special Forces.

I watched their programs on MTA International, Muslim
Ahmadiyya International television. Correction, I devoured
them and even phoned them at their headquarters in England
and spoke to them live. I did not pay a single penny, I recall. They
took care of all the expenses, and that made me proud of them.
After a few weeks I became a devout Ahmadi and I thought
Ahmadis were the only true Muslims.

Yet, in the heart of my hearts, two things kept bothering me
about Ahmadiyya. The first thing was that, in their programs for
Arab speakers, there was always an Indian present at the podium
where they held their debates. Of course the Indian spoke good
Arabic, but what for, unless the Indian leaders in London wanted
him to preserve the Indian hegemony.

The second thing was much more serious. After the death
of Mirza Tahar, Mirza Masroor, another Indian — was elected
caliphate. He had no charisma at all. In fact, I was sure there were
plenty of men who would have been a better choice than him.
As I reviewed the caliphates after Mirza Ahmed, I discovered all
of them were Indians. I did not like the fact that they were all
Indians and not a single one from another race, but I kept it to
myself.

I was about to swear *bayaa* (allegiance) when I turned my
network dish to the Hotbird channel. After weeks of Ahmadi
indoctrination, I had had my fill with arguments and counter-
arguments and felt that the *al Hayat* channel — an Arab Christian

channel that spoke openly about the legends and contradictions in Islam — was no longer a threat.

Curiously, when I turned my dish towards Hotbird, the first channel that came up on the screen was the Al Hayat channel. I found father Zakaria speaking about the origins of legends in the Qur'an.

But suddenly he provoked a storm. He said that all legends were stolen from the Jewish legendary Talmud. He gave the name of the book, the Targum of Esther the second, the chapter and even the page number. I checked the information and it was accurate. Everything I had settled in my mind began to fall apart once more. All the metaphoric explanations were, once again, futile since everything had an older origin: the Mishnah, the old rabbinic legends.

The old doubt came back again, but in even higher waves and with a stronger wind. Mohammed must have heard their legends, copied them and then told his ignorant audience of Aws and Khazraj, it was from Allah. I lost complete faith at that time and no other religion, especially Christianity, could fill the void I felt inside my heart.

I said Christianity because Ahmadiyya had gathered its disciples on the debris of Christianity, or so I thought at that time. It was almost impossible for any Muslim who had my experience with Ahmadiyya doctrine to read the Christian Bible again with the raw credulity necessary to any faith.

I remember I had been taught by ahmadis that Jesus did not die on the cross. The proof, they would argue, was that the Bible said water and blood gushed out when he was speared by one of the Romans. Could normal blood ooze out of a dead corpse? Accordingly, he had simply fainted and his followers knew that, so they came later and bribed the guardians.

Thus, what was said about Jesus in the Qur'an was completely true but also had been completely misunderstood by the *ulama* (Muslim theologians.)

They would also argue that the second coming of Jesus will not be in blood and flesh, as most Christians, and even orthodox Muslims around the world believe. Rather, he will come like Elijah, in the form of John the Baptist. Following that logic, Jesus came in the form of Mirza Ghulam Ahmad, of Kadian. They would lament that almost everyone in the world did not recognize him but paradoxically that was the proof of his true messiahship.

They would show the cruelty of King David, for example, when they defended the Prophet Mohammed.

They would also argue that the Bible was full of lies, or else how could a prophet like David perform adultery with a woman who was not his wife, and then send her husband to his certain death? Could Abraham lie to the Egyptians about his wife and tell them she was only his sister? What would we call such a man, they would ask? They would also demonstrate that Paul was the biggest source of all the lies in the Christian faith.

I congratulated myself for being saved from their intellectual poisons but at that point, I was not ready to believe in anything. After three months of my spiritual quest, I had finally had my fill of any religion and decided to become an atheist. Like Karl Marx, I began to think, "Religion is the opiate of the people." I was satisfied, for the first time, in Oman and could relax without any fear or false hope.

From time to time, I would drink in dank, dingy pubs in Sohar in order to drown my thirst for the divine in cheap Indian wine.

CHAPTER 22

The fact is that I became a modern *ronin* or, like a Bushi Samurai with no lord or master during the feudal period (1185 — 1868) of Japan. This experience had its effect on my personality. Even Hazem noticed that I had become temperamental. I became very selfish, or rather Machiavellian, in my philosophy of life that "the end justifies the means." I worked less at school and spent most of my time joking with the kids or taking part in their idle talk.

Each time I went out with someone, it was him who paid. I played *taqwa* (Muslim piety, the Islamic concept of self-awareness which in a broad sense involves thankfulness and respect for God and his creation.) in front of the Omanis and talked about religion with them. I shared their gossip, their backbiting and even their dreams. I had a free meal at night, free beers or even a free Chinese prostitute. I exploited them and they exploited me in their own way. I had two faces — like most of the people around me, and I began to like Oman. I only needed to wake up early in the morning and go to the nearest mosque and show off my piety.

During *dohr* (early evening prayers) I would pray inside the classroom and my Omani colleagues would be impressed. Soon I began to build a good reputation and cultivate the attentions of rich Omani, who would send their children to my house for private lessons. The money came from every direction and I even bought a new Toyota Yaris. I thought I had forgotten about Moza, but when I saw her waiting outside my house, this time in a four-by-four GMC, my heart skipped a beat.

"*Salamo alaykom*," she said. "I'm glad you are all right. Why didn't you answer my calls?"

"Why didn't you come that weekend?" I asked instead of answering.

"I was in the UAE. My husband was sick and nobody was there to take care of him, so I had to do everything myself."

"You have a husband?" I asked in disbelief.

"Of course! What kind of question is that? How do you think I pay for my expenses?"

"Sorry," I replied. "I just have not seen him."

"Don't worry, my husband is always in Dubai, after *harim*, women from Russia and Uzbekistan," she said with a smile.

"Aren't you jealous?" I teased.

"Why should I be? He is a man."

"So?" I asked.

"Anyway ... as long as he provides for me and his children, there is no problem. At least my husband did not marry a second or a third wife. Pray to Allah he does not meet a Tunisian woman or a Lebanese," she said.

"Lucky him," I teased, but she was not impressed.

"By the way, I was wondering if you could help me ..." Her voice trailed off. Was she shy or simply pretending, I wondered? I saw this as a chance that was presented to me on a golden plate.

"Are you kidding? I will do anything you want," I said.

"Would you like to take a short ride with me?" she asked. I hopped into her car and we went to Sohar.

Sohar was truly beautiful. Unlike Muscat, surrounded by mountains, suffocating and with no prospects, Sohar had vastness, freedom and a bright future. The streets, already shimmering with pregnant mirages under the evening sun, were neat and palm-lined. The pavements were curiously green and decorated with beautiful flowers, flowers of different shapes and colors, constantly irrigated by automated hoses dug every two meters or so.

Omani people, wearing clean, ironed white dishdadas, drove fancy cars. Some of them talked on their mobile telephones. Women in dark malayas drove also — in twos or threes and sometimes alone — but all in peace and harmony. No honking, no swearing, perfectly calm, like robots. Their faces were happy, though, unflappable and placid.

From time to time a black Bengali or Indian would go by on an old bicycle, or on foot, as if to remind the privileged that that entire landscaping miracle was due to the everlasting struggle against a ruthless sun. The struggle was actually and truthfully the fruit of their labor, the work of the calloused hands of those poor, sad-eyed, slave-waged and shunned Asians.

Moza finally admitted why she needed me. She conveyed to me that she had an Emirati boyfriend whom she truly loved, but the man left her as soon she introduced him to her friend Aisha, who was also her neighbor. She concluded that the woman stole her man using some kind of magic, for she thought she was too skinny for him.

"Yes," I agreed. "No doubt you are right. This woman whom you consider your friend has made a *hijab* of *tafrik* — an amulet of separation against you. She made your man drink it and now it is simply impossible for him to return to you." It was a bold-faced lie — but a convincing one — and she believed me.

Moza stifled a sigh, but I could see tears starting to well in her eyes. "Ya Allah," she exclaimed, then wiped her tears with the tip of her veil. "I remember the day that the *sharmouta* (bitch) insisted she make the coffee herself. I think she must have put something in it. It tasted a little strange, I remember ... I never would have thought that she could be that wicked."

"But I think it is you who is to blame," I said, in order to add salt to the wound.

She shook her head and drummed her fingers on the driving wheel. "I'm so stupid," she said at last.

"Yes, you are ... unfortunately. "I knew for sure she had swallowed the bait.

"Can you do something about it?" She finally asked.

"How long has he been away?" I asked feigning genuine concern.

"About three months," she said.

"By Allah, it's too late ... unless ..." I replied.

"Unless what?"

"Forget about it ... it's complicated," I said, continuing to bait her.

"Try me."

"Well ... let me explain it to you first. In a simple seperation spell, the subject remains under its effect no more than two or three days, but your friend has done what is worse, I'm afraid. She slept with him for seven nights, and each night she would make him drink the separation formula. After a week, the distance between you and him became like the distance between the Earth and sky. Do you see what I mean?"

"But you said you could help," she implored.

"Well, yes, but it all depends upon you. You see, to counter such a spell, you need to sleep with another man who knows about magic. Hopefully this man would prepare the right antidote, and each time he would make you drink the same dose for the same period of time — seven nights."

"Or seven days?" she asked.

"Yes ... that doesn't matter. The important thing is that it happens seven times." I continued my glib lie to this naïve woman.

"And do you have this anti-magic potion in your house?"

"I can prepare it any time you want me to." I feigned confidence in my abilities.

"Could you do it tonight?"

"Well ... I can." I said, hesitating for just a moment to create the impression I was considering the prospect.

"Then come at about 12 — the children will be asleep by then," Moza said, sealing the deal.

That was how I made use of the naïve credulity of Moza, and how I spent a week living like a king.

CHAPTER 23

I don't know how — by coincidence or satanic scheme, but my classic scam worked. About ten days after arriving home, she knocked at my door. I was in the last phase of my nap in that semi-metaphysical state between sleep and consciousness. I washed my face, put on a t-shirt and opened my door. Standing in the courtyard beside Moza was Hafidh — the Sudanese teacher — who looked ready to worship at Moza's feet. He stood by her side like a bodyguard, a chair in one hand and a cup of tea in the other. He probably thought she was the mother of one of my students, who had come to ask me to give her son private lessons. My intuition told me he wanted to impress her, or even to convince her that he was a better teacher than me. I smiled at the thought; she thought that I was smiling at her and smiled back.

Moza looked happy and the cloud around her eyes was no longer there. I, too, felt good after the dose of envy — pain inflicted upon Hafidh.I let her in and left Hafidh speechless outside. As I touched her hand and was about to give her a kiss, she stiffened and pushed me back. She smiled to lessen the effect of her rejection, but I could see that the old painful boundary between *khal* or former slave and freewoman had appeared again — in the way she clicked her nails perhaps. I flopped onto my old sofa and lit a cigarette.

"You know — I think you are great. My boyfriend called me yesterday. He told me that he was sorry and this morning we met. Look at what he bought me." Out of her right *abaya* pocket she produced an expensive diamond ring. "He says he loves me and does not know what happened to him."

I was amazed … correction, dumbfounded.

"I told one of my friends about you and she wants to see you, but I told her that I have to ask your permission first." At that moment Hafidh knocked on my door and swiftly invited himself in.

"Please sit down, Mum." Hafidh interjected. "And please try my Sudanese tea. All my Omani colleagues can't resist the temptation of visiting me again, once they have tasted my special tea." He laughed and revealed a set of yellow teeth. "We Sudanese have the same Arab tradition of hospitality. The Algerians are different, they are more affected by the French and the Italians, I suppose."

Look at how cunning and mischievous he is, I thought — trying to dupe me inside of my own house. But I had the *shaitan*, or satan on my side. He had no chance, I thought.

"Nice tea, *shokran* (thanks)," Moza said after a sip that barely touched her lips. But she did not sit on the chair, which he had brought for her, which he kept cleaning with the palm of his hand. Her reaction took Hafidh off-guard. With an open mouth and blank eyes, he watched her and stood breathless.

I decided to play on his jealousy and fragile nerves. "Would you like to come in later, Hafidh?" I asked, knowing that he would jump at the opportunity. As he was about to step outside, I stretched out my hand and shook firmly his hands, then whispered in his ears. "I think she wants to be alone with me — she has something private to discuss, if you know what I mean. You see, these Omani women prefer Algerians because we are like the French." I winked and he swallowed twice to get rid of the lump in his throat. He looked like someone who had just seen a ghost.

I recall that I burst into laughter at the time. Moza laughed with me at first and then looked at me with suspicion. I could hear her thoughts — she was questioning my reaction. Maybe she thought that the *jinni* (or genies — the Quran mentions that Jinn are made of smokeless flame or "scorching fire". Like human beings, the Jinn can also be good, evil, or neutrally benevolent) inside me were laughing. Maybe she thought that people who deal with the supernatural had a special way of looking at life. I could see she chose to remain neutral and wait for me to regain my self-control. But the more I thought about these things, the more I laughed. Finally, I was exhausted and felt tears fill up my eyes.

"Have you been doing this magic for a long time?" she asked.

It was on the tip of my tongue to say never, but my *shaitan*, satan, was still hungry for some more of my magnificent farce. "Since I was born," I said instead.

"How do you do it?" she asked.

"My mother is not a normal woman." I said. "You see, my father was raped by a *jinni* woman who had found him very handsome — remember, the prophet ordered us not to sleep without reading some of the *Qur'an as a hisn* (form of protection)."

"I always read Bakara or Yasin or Kahf surats before I sleep. One is good against the devil, the other against the *dajal* (antichrist), and I think Yasin is good for both," Moza replied.

"You must also put some water in a glass by your side and never sleep on your left side, as Sunna enjoins. When you enter the bathroom, always start with your right foot and say, "Oh Allah, save me from *kabayeth* (toilet *jinnis*)."

"They say they prefer to live there," Moza confirmed.

"Only the *Koffar*," I corrected. "For you see … *jinnies* are like us. Some of them are Muslims, others are Christians or Jews. Muslim *jinnis* like clean places and do not enter houses where music is played or pictures are hung on walls. They help us — the *mo'ominin* (believers) — when we are in trouble. They follow the instruction of Sunna and the Qur'an better than the best among us."

"Do they talk to you? I mean, do you see them?" Moza inquired.

"Of course! I see them now," I lied. "They are sitting around enjoying our company," I said.

Scared, Moza looked left and right, then shunned the *shaitan* and read some of the Holy Qur'an from memory.

"Sometimes they appear to me in the form of normal individuals," I said.

"You mean I too could see them?" Moza asked.

"Of course, and talk to them too." I continued.

"I do not believe you," she said and laughed.

I was still not ready to give up. I had various examples that I could use to convince her and I chose the best. "Do you believe in Prophet Mohammed?" I asked.

"Of course, what a question!" She exclaimed.

"Well, the Angel Gabriel, who governs angels and *jinnies* alike, appeared many times to our prophet in the form of Dahia Kalbi. The companions would speak to him as you speak to me, not knowing that he was the Archangel Gabriel. How dare you not believe what I say?" I arched an eyebrow and offered a condemning look. Poor Moza asked pardon from Allah and then pardon from me. "You have not answered my question," she said.

"What question?" I asked.

"About my friend who needs your help."

"All right, bring her in anytime. I know that I don't need to remind you — you must keep silent. Never speak about these things to anybody, the *jinnies* don't like that." In order to drive home my point, I said it in a just-for-your-sake tone of voice.

"Of course — do you think I am mad?" She produced out of her left *abaya* pocket a wad of notes.

She counted them out100 *rials* — and then handed them over.

"I'm sorry. I know it is not very much — but I will give you more next time." She spoke with a mixture of awe and caution. She was scared. Her incredulous imagination made her suppose the worst scenarios. Had she made me angry, I would have sent one of my *jinnies* to her or to that baby-faced Emirati she loved. I could have even used my so-called magic powers and made her do what was more painful than death: marry a *khal!* Or so she thought. I put the easy money into my pocket and led her outside.

CHAPTER 24

The woman that came with Moza the following day was more than beautiful. She was from the Mokbali tribe, which, in the 17th or 18th century, inhabited the mountains that ringed Muscat. They were invaded by the Portuguese whose muscled Caucasian sailors were generous in leaving their genes behind. She was tall, slim and fair-skinned. Her eyes were the color of the ocean caressed by a breeze. She could be from anywhere in the world but the Gulf, I thought. She was highly educated too. She had her B.S. in science from Sultan Quabous University and then went to Australia for a master's degree in computer science.

This client was different and needed a show of muscle, I thought. I started telling her that all sorcery came from the Jews. Then I spoke about the Jews of al Jazira and how they were able to put a spell over Mohammed himself. The *Sira*, or books about the prophet's biography recount that, for a long time, he did not sleep with his wives. Ibn Hisham said that he forgot about his bed duties for months.

I continued to tell the story about of how the Archangel Gabriel came and told him that he had been the victim of a magic spell. Later the prophet sent Ali — the husband of his daughter Fatma, who was the only surviving child of five, to descend the well where he found the spell hidden under a stone. Of course, the prophet returned to his nine wives and shared equally and fairly his nights with them.

At that point the woman was all ears and the clear blue of her eyes encouraged confessions. I was about to say that Mohammed did not die a natural death. Ibn Hisham recounts that he was poisoned by a Jewish woman who hid the poison in the meat he adored. I dug into a past infatuation with the supernatural and told Moza's friend that, as far as I remembered from the old yellow books I had read years before, Moses was the first person who had the science of *al'hikma* (wisdom). On his stick there was written *taa'with* (spells) that had the power to transform things or govern *efreets,* as it is written in the Qur'an.

The stick and its secrets eventually became part of the belongings to the kings that were born after that time. King Solomon inherited the stick and prayed Allah that he would confer on him a power that nobody would be able to have after him. Allah answered his prayers and gave him power over the wind *jinns* and *efreets.* He also taught him how to speak the language of animals. The Qur'an mentions he even talked to ants. Asef ben Barchia — Solomon's nephew had great knowledge of Mysterious Sciences bringing the throne of Belqeis, Queen of Saba in Yemen to Solomon in a second. Later he stole the stick from King Solomon and escaped to Moroco. That explains why Moroccans are so strong at sorcery.

The woman was more than impressed. She said that her problem was a bit different from Moza's. Her husband knew about her affair and was planning a divorce. In Oman, as it is everywhere in the gulf, divorce is simply sending the woman back to her family's house. Fatma feared the anger of her brothers and the scandal. But what she feared most was the poverty, after living in a highly comfortable condition provided by her wealthy husband.

"What would you have me do for you?" I asked her.

"I would like you to change my husband's mind about the divorce."

"Did he find you in bed with him?"

"No, but he saw me in my boyfriend's car."

"Is that all?" I asked, not thinking about the ramifications.

"Don't you realize that, in Oman, when a woman gets into a stranger's car, it is as good as saying, 'Let's go to bed?'"

"You could have given thousands of excuses," I replied.

"In Oman, everyone knows everybody. If a man meets a woman in a car, everyone knows what it means — you understand what I am saying to you?"

I thought to myself, even King Solomon, with all his wisdom, would back off at this point. I promised, nevertheless, that I would make him as the Arab proverb says, "like a ring on her finger." It would only take seven days or seven nights, I explained.

Then Moza left us and the woman became my wife for a whole week. We met secretly, of course, sometimes in my house very late at night, sometimes in her house, usually in the small bare room of the Filipino servant.

Useless to say that this time I was not successful, but at least I had my full pay. Then she and Moza disappeared from my life and I forgot about the thing. Actually, the dreary dullness took hold of me again. During this period of time, I stopped giving private lessons, so as the money stopped flowing, I sat at home more frequently.

CHAPTER 25

One evening, Hazem and I sat over a bottle of Indian whiskey. It was one of those rare moments when I drank cheap liquor.

"Tell me, Hazem, how did you become a Christian?" I asked. My question took him off guard.

"How did you know?" he asked.

"Are you afraid I might denounce you?"

"Yes — but I do not fear death — I fear the torture, the humiliation ..."

"I will never do it, Hazem — I simply don't care," I reassured him.

"How did you know?" He finally asked.

"A simple hunch," I said. I was about to say that I had actually seen his Jesus in a dream earlier, but I was too late — the moment had passed.

"It's a long story ..." His voice trailed off.

"We have all the night — don't we?" I asked rhetorically.

"Shall I tell you the truth, all the truth? Oh God! I'm ashamed of myself."

"We all have our little secrets," I encouraged him.

"It all started with a woman, five years ago. She was sipping a cappuccino in Lulo, Sohar. Her eyes were the eyes of a gypsy ... her lips were so inviting, and the color of her skin was like snow, and so soft and mysterious. Something about her made poetry meaningful and docile. There was something about the blue ocean of her eyes, or were they green?"

"But you said you have been here ten years," I cut in.

"That was the first time I came here." His voice trailed off again, this time because of me, I suspect.

"Was she a European?"I asked.

"Not exactly. Actually, she was from South Africa ... I wanted her at first sight and something in the far corner of my mind told me she had no man in her life. I do not remember how I introduced myself to her, but we spoke to each other. After half an hour it seemed to each of us that we had known each other a long time.

We spoke about Oman and then about the weather, and finally our talk took us to art, to the secret beauties behind the harshness of an Omani dune. Then we spoke about religion and she asked me if I was a Muslim. Curiously, a jolt of sexual awareness shot through me when she asked this question." Hazem smiled and I laughed.

"I lied and said that I was an atheist. I wanted her so badly — I wanted to make love to her right then and there and explore that mysterious aura that surrounded her. She said she was a devout Christian and she would pray to her Lord that I see the light. She believed every word of her sacred book. At the end of our conversation she gave me her Bible, and because of my desire for her more than an interest in the book, I took the gift and threw it in a drawer when I went home.

I don't know why, but one day I decided to see the nonsense written inside. Actually, I did not like the Old Testament. To me it was full of laws, blood and revenge like the Qur'an. But when I opened the New Testament, I immediately was caught by the greatness of this man they call Jesus. When I first read about Him, I was — how shall I put it — mesmerized by the beauty, the love and the compassion of this man.

In Islam, we only hear about the sword, blood, faith or invasion and concubines. But in her religion, I found peace and love — eternal and boundless. Still, I believed the Muslim Sadducees and Pharisees. I swallowed without reserve the lies they aired on television. After all ... a man of the caliber of Karadaoui said openly on Aljazeera, the Christian religion was a bunch of lies and Islam was the only true religion. Who was I to question such a well-known authority?

Yet, from that time on, I became, if I may say, Bible-addicted, and could not sleep without reading something Jesus said or did. I was not a believer. I just read it like one reads a nice, well-written novel. Sometimes when I was drunk and my mind was empty from all worries, I thought all religions were lies and if we human beings couldn't live without them, then what would be our recourse? If that aching thirst for the divine had to be assuaged, then perhaps that part about Jesus is the best lie, and consequently, the best remedy for this metaphysical pain that seems, to me, innate in every individual."

"Nice story," I said.

"As I was saying," he continued. "I started to read, but my transformation took too much time. I was born a Muslim and branded with the mark of Cain on my forehead from birth." Hazem said bluntly. I rolled my eyes and thought he was going too far. Hazem's eyes met mine, then a grin curved around his lips. "I see you don't like the bit about Cain," he said.

"I do not care about religion, but I hate prejudices. I think the world would be a better place if all of us simply respect each other," I said, then muffled my snort. I could see the irritation on Hazem's forehead. He rubbed the corner of his mouth with his thumb, and then went on.

"You are right. I remember I sympathized with her at that time. I liked her naivety, her raw faith, but I thought at that time she was a *kaffira* (an infidel) and there was no harm if I played with her heart for a short time of pleasure. After all, Prophet Mohammed had done it with Maria and then Safia. The next time we met, she gave me a cross — a silver pendant that I still wear around my neck. She said that she had another one at home. When I wanted to kiss her, she simply did not let me, though I knew she desired me as much as I did her. She said once that I was dangerous — handsome and sexy and that she had to be strong."

"Bad luck," I sneered.

"We continued to see each other for a month or so, and then one day she asked me to attend a fellowship in her own apartment. I said yes because I thought I would be able to make love to her as soon the people were gone. Oh God! I'm so ashamed of myself."

"I see no shame in what you did — you liked a woman and, of course, you wanted her. It happens every day," I tried to encourage him, but he was not impressed.

"In Islam, when you go to a Friday sermon, the people around you are usually stern, serious-looking. They show off their piety and their fear of an inflexible god — you know what I mean?" Hazem said.

I nodded and stifled a sigh.

"The people at the fellowship meeting were very happy, very spontaneous. They prayed with their hearts and souls, not like us in regular, boring ranks. There were no *ablutions*, no *adahn,* no *imam* ordering us each time we stood facing the *kaaba* for *salat,* prayer, to form close lines and forbid the *shaitan,* satan, from sifting through our ranks.

Someone had a guitar and began singing gospel music. Then each one of them opened his Bible and chose a chapter to read. Each one talked about what he understood from that particular chapter. Then, finally, they prayed in unison for all the people around the world — not like with Islam prayers. We always pray that God destroys Israel, the whole *kaffir* kingdom in the west. No, my friend, it seemed to me at that time, they were people from another planet," Hazem explained.

For a moment I too dreamt of a peaceful world based on love and nothing but love. For a moment I was impressed, but my *shaitan,* satan, was very powerful at that time.

"What happened when they left?" I asked.

"I tried to kiss her but she said she wouldn't allow me to. She told me that she did like me, but it wasn't right. I really respected her resolve. Were she a Muslim woman, she would have succumbed and then after two or three prostrations towards Mecca, Allah would have forgiven her or else He would have scandalized her. I tell you, man, with these people there is no two-facedness. What you see in the light of day, you see in the darkness of night."

"Not all of them — believe me," I countered.

"I'm not a sociologist, but they are definitely better than us once they are devoted," Hazem replied.

"We also have true, devoted Muslims."

"What do you think of a man like Karadahaoui?" Hazem asked me.

"He is one of the greatest *Olama,* Muslim theologians; in this *Omma* (Muslim world)," I said without wasting a breath.

"Well, he was caught red-handed with a young Algerian woman. He said she gave herself to him like in the famous story of Mohammed with that Fazari woman. Do you remember that story?" Hazem replied.

"Those are lies, but please stick to your story," I said. My tone rang with anger.

"As you prefer," Hazem said and continued with his story. "I said I was more than impressed. I felt a mixture of shame and anger, but I respected her and all the people I met that time. Yet of course, like every Muslim, I returned to my old habits and decided that those people were an exception. After all, they were *moshrikin* (polytheists) and Allah forgave everything but *shirk* or polytheism.

"I decided to read the Bible to see its various mistakes as voiced by the Prophet Mohammed. I browsed the Web and found so many arguments — the strongest from Ahmadiyya led by mirza Gulam."

He declared that he was the 'Promised One' of all religions, fulfilling the eschatological prophecies found in world religions. He stated that his claims to being several prophets (religious personages) converging into one person were the symbolic, rather than literal, fulfillment of the messianic and eschatological prophecies found in the literature of the major religions. The motto of the Ahmadiyya Community is 'Love for All, Hatred for None.' Later on, I became one of his fervent followers.

"I've heard of them," I said. "They say they are pro-British and the Jesus we are waiting for was nothing but Mirza Golam of Quadian."

I was about to admit that I, too, had been one of his followers when Hazem broke his thought and said to me, "I'm impressed — I 'm sure you will find your path one day. By the way, they are not pro-British, nor are they puppets in their hands."

"Actually, they are the biggest threat to Christianity these days," I answered. "I will give you an example. They say that since Elijah came in the form of John the Baptist, then it is logical to deduce that the spirit of Isa — Jesus — would come in the form of Mirza Gholam. What do you think about that?"

"It's nonsense," Hazem said. "Everybody will see Him when He comes. *'Then they will see the Son of Man coming in the clouds with great power and glory.'* (Luke 21.27)"

"You must admit, they have some truth in what they say," I countered.

"Like what?" Hazem asked. His voice rang with sarcasm.

"They have their evidence from the Qur'an. In Jomoa Surat, Allah spoke about some other people who did not come yet. The companions asked the prophet about their identity for three times ... only then he said they were people from *Faris,* Persia."

"Are you an Ahmadi?" Hazem asked.

"Actually, I'm a sympathizer. But, to be frank with you, I'm not decided yet," I lied.

"Watch your pocket if one day you decide to make *bayaa* (pay allegiance)," Hazem warned.

"I'm not that stupid," I replied.

"Good … as I said, Ahmadia seemed to answer, at that time, all the questions related to Islam and, of course, Christianity. I decided to fight those happy Christians in their own arena. I attended the second fellowship and threw what I thought was a bomb. When it was my turn, I said, 'I really like what is said so far and I think so far that Islam and Christianity are not very different. But I have a question to ask. If Jesus was God in the flesh, why does he say, 'Eili Eili lama Sabaktani?'

"The Australian priest smiled at me and said, 'Read Psalms 22 and you will understand. At that time the Jews called Psalms by their first sentences. God wanted them to read the prophecy about Him written hundreds and hundreds of years before Jesus was born.'

"I said to him, 'I never read the Bible, but it seems to me illogical that God comes in the form of a human being. Why should he do that?

"And the priest answered me. He said, 'It is very simple, because He loves us. Let me tell you something. In order to understand Jesus, you have to forget about Allah. The Allah we know from the Qur'an is totally different. He has no mercy. One of his divine names is 'al Motakabbir or the arrogant — don't forget this.'

"But I told him, 'He is God — he is the all-powerful, the all-knowing entity. Do you want him to beg the creation he made with his own hands?'

"He responded to me by saying, 'The difference between us and them is this: the notion of God. In Christianity, God is like a good father. In Islam, Allah is the other way around.'

At that moment, the *adhan* cried "Alklah Akbar." From out the window we could see the first streaks of dawn. A strange idea also dawned on me at that time. Only the *shaitan* could concoct such a religion in which the believer had to wake up in such an early time and splash his face with cold water. Hazem abruptly suggested that since we were not going to finish this talk till morning, he would make two nice cups of coffee.

CHAPTER 26

We sat over our coffee and lit cigarettes. "I should stop smoking," Hazem said.

"You don't need to. Better to be an active than a passive smoker," I replied.

"I have to quit from a religious point of view, as a Christian. I should preserve this Holy Temple," Hazem said, drumming his fingers on his chest. I could not see how a man spent his life preserving something doomed to be devoured by worms. I smiled at the thought.

"It is a question of faith," he pointed out.

"You sound like the *salafists*. They say the same things — *haram*, forbidden by Sharia law, and all that stuff. But when they are cornered, they have nothing to say," I snapped. Hazem smiled and shook his head.

"I will tell you something. I don't believe in anything. I'm like the Europeans ... I can live without God," I spat.

"I see you are on the verge of atheism — that's rather good news. It means you have a brain and you are searching. You remind me of myself ten years ago. By the way, I'm older than you by at least a decade. Am I right?"

I shrugged my shoulders. "Maybe."

"That means my first impression was right. Just keep searching."

I kept silent and Hazem lit another cigarette. Something in him, some fountain or spring that flew from inside his heart, had the power to fill the whole world with love and compassion. I really respected that man.

"You have not answered my question yet," I teased.

"Well, if you think that we Christians resemble *salafists* (people who have a literalist and srict approach to islam), you are completely mistaken. But, for your information, I can say that the *salafists* you spoke about are like the ancient Pharisees in the Bible. They follow the law and most of the time burden people with weights they aren't able to carry. Christians do it with free will. We are not slaves; Jesus paid with his blood for our sins. We are sons of the Most High God."

At that time Hazem seemed to me, an extremist in his own way. Therefore, he was not that different from all the other fanatics around the world who thought they held the truth that was final and complete. Of course, arguments and counter-arguments were different, but the result in my mind was the same. I was intrigued with his personal experience, however. I was avid — like King Shahrayar — the famous character in *One Thousand and One Nights* (Arabian Nights) to know what happened to him with that beautiful South African woman.

"Did you finally sleep with her?" I asked bluntly.

"Not yet. She said she would only sleep with a man after marriage. She had vowed chastity years ago."

"I thought Christianity is more open than Islam. When I watch films, I see they live their freedom completely," I countered.

"I am speaking about very committed Christians," Hazem said. "A very few in any western society live a totally Christian experience according to the Bible — especially in this day and age. In Europe, many of the people are actually atheists. But this is another story." He waited for his words to settle, then went on.

"I returned home very angry because I thought I was going to win and make my point. But the Australian priest was so humble; he just answered casually my questions, encouraged me to read Psalms 22 and then went to something else.

After I returned home I decided to read Psalms 22. Clearly, Jesus wanted them to read the prophecy. I immersed myself again in Ahmadia books, looking avidly for a stronger argument. After weeks of hard toil — for their books were banned all over the Muslim world ..." Hazem stopped when I cut in abruptly.

"Of course you know that last year the government in Algeria sent Internet experts to South Africa to help the officials get control over their Web and other webs they deemed harmful to islam?" I asked.

"I do not doubt it ... our governments are experts in these fields. They outshine the best — even the Chinese or the North Koreans."

"Did you find any argument that helped you in your battle?" I asked.

"Actually, I thought I did. In the New Testament, when Jesus asked his disciples, 'Who do people say that the Son of Man is?' And they said, "Some say John the Baptist; and others, Elijah; but still others, Jeremiah, or one of the prophets.' So I said why do they thought he were a prophet if they were not expecting another prophet to come?"

"Yes, even the Qur'an mentions the fact that our prophet was talked about by Jesus, but of course they changed everything." I said.

"Yes I know, but wait a second," Hazem nervously cut in. "When I threw this question out in my third meeting, Sharon herself answered me. She asked me to finish the verse, 'But who do you say that I am?' Simon Peter answered, 'You are the Christ, the Son of the living God.' And Jesus said to him, 'Blessed are you, Simon Barjona, because flesh and blood did not reveal this to you, but My Father who is in heaven. Matt 16: 13-17 (NASB95) and then explained that Jesus was the one meant by Moses. Her words still reverberate into my ears 'Read Isaiah 53, which was written more than 800 years before the coming of the Lord. Do not tell me it was written by Christians. Go onto the Internet and search for the Qumran scrolls ... you will see that they were written at least 200 years before the Messiah was born.'

"That night they prayed fervently for me. They asked the Lord to open the doors for me and to make me free. Late that night, as I slept, I saw Jesus in my dreams. I remember that His eyes were the greenest green I have ever seen. 'Lazarus, come forth,' He ordered as He held out His hand to me. And at that very moment, I was saved." Tears welled in Hazem's eyes. I felt uncomfortable and went to the bathroom. I thought about his story and it seemed to me, at that time, that it was not different from other experiences I heard about from various religions. Even Osama bin Laden saw visions, and I heard that the 9/11 plane attackers had experiences similar to that.

The alarm clock rang. It was already 6:30 in the morning. "Time to go," I heard Hazem call out.

"Tomorrow night, *Insha'Allah* (if God wishes), I will tell you how I stopped being an Ahmadi and embraced Christianity," Hazem promised. I was no longer interested, but I nodded agreement.

CHAPTER 27

The following night I did not stay home. I took a fast shower and headed towards Sohar. I felt a real need for fresh air, even if it was the stale air of that grimy, dingy and cheap Indian pub. When I entered the place, I found the Indian girls; sweat glistening on their pale foreheads. They were already dancing their cobra dance, hands moving so gracefully in every direction. Their necks and shoulders curled and twisted, and of course their feet followed the rhythm. Only their waists needed more action, I thought to myself.

I ordered two bottles of cold Heineken and rushed to drown my cares. That night I drank more than usual. As I drove my car and was about to turn the roundabout, heading for Shinas, I saw a beautiful woman. She looked English. She appeared to be in her early 40s, slightly overweight, but tall and graceful. She was climbing out of her vehicle and heading towards central Safir. Her arms were bare, and the v-shape of her tight shirt exposed her well-shaped breasts.

By Omani standards she was more than naked, but she did not seem to care and glided unaware of thirsty eyes, as if she were in Beverly Hills. I loved those pale-faced Caucasians. They lived like kings anywhere in the world because they had the innate and stubborn ability to preserve what is sacred to them: happiness. All eyes looked in her direction, even the eyes of the meek Bengali cleaners, I thought. I soon realized that I was the cause of a traffic jam. The Omanis, as usual, were too polite — only the one behind me flashed his lights. I changed my direction and pulled alongside her big Toyota four by four.

She was pushing her shopping cart, oblivious to the avid stares of long-bearded Omanis or the silent whispers and gawks of Omani women who were shrouded from head to feet in black. Their faces were hidden behind transparent black veils, while others, older in age, wore *burqas,* oriental eye masks, around the eyes. The blond-haired woman headed towards the ground floor, in the direction of the food department. The woman was special — she smiled innocently to everyone. Was it naivety or self-confidence? I wondered.

I decided to go upstairs and look for any gift that I might offer her as a token of my interest. We Arabs do not approach a woman without something in hand. I could not find anything that I thought might impress her, so I went to the perfume department. I stood there wondering what to buy. I looked for a special, but also accessible, perfume. She was accustomed to all the brand names, I thought, so after some hesitation I settled upon a small but cute Omani bottle of perfume. As I was about to take the elevator, I found two Omani women waiting. They looked at each other and then moved towards the stairs.

"Never mind," I said, "I will take the stairs." The women did not speak and went back to the elevator. Even the voice of a woman is *awrah* (a moral blemish) in Islam. When I reached the ground floor, I found the woman standing in front of a female cashier who was a *khala* (a black woman.) Only black Omani women worked as cashiers in the Gulf. Sometimes you might come across a white, black-eyed cashier but do not rush to conclude that she is fully Arab . She probably has some Persian origins, because no purely Arab woman would do this type of job, I thought to myself. A slight pang of jealousy cut through my chest, for, clearly, the glances of the cashier were not at all innocent. They had that special glow any woman had when she liked a man. I remember it took me several weeks to understand why the female cashier looked at a woman in that way. I safely concluded that in the Gulf there is no clear boundary between lesbianism and heterosexuality.

I waited at the back of a long line, but it was very long and there were too many dazed-looking Bengalis waiting to pay for a bottle of soda or half a kilo of onions. Also, there were many Omani men pushing what seemed, to me, shopping carts filled to capacity. That amount of food could feed a neighborhood, I thought.

I pursed my lips and shook my head. I made up my mind that I was not ready to lose her. As she was about to leave, I tucked the perfume inside my back pocket and followed her. No sooner had I stepped away from the cashier than the alarm started wailing. All eyes were staring at me — even that beautiful angel turned toward me to see my embarrassment.

A fat, dark-faced Omani security guard grabbed my arm and a young man in a yellow uniform ordered me to follow him. I was so ashamed, and I discovered that night that there are worse things in life than death. I was stripped naked and then spat upon and beaten for a bottle of perfume that cost two *rials*. I quickly realized it was my mistake and I paid double the price — four *rials*.

As I went out of the city center, there was no Toyota in the parking lot and no trace of self-esteem left inside me. I drove back to the hotel and, this time, I went to the Arab pub where sexy Moroccan girls danced under the severe protection of their Omani pimps. If you only said one wrong word to them, blood would be shed.

I drank two beers, but the burning inside my chest did not stop. It dawned upon me that if I burned my skin, I would know for sure which hurt most: the literal or the metaphoric. With every beer I had, I stabbed a cigarette upon the soft skin of my left hand. I remember that I drank four more, after the first two. I also remember hearing a vague voice at the far corner of my head. "This will make you know." The pain on my skin lasted a second or two, but the pain in my chest did not go away.

I reached Shinas at about three in the morning. I found the lights in my room were on, and I remembered that I had shut off the lights before going out. I pushed the door open and the first thing that caught my attention was a leather book — a Bible lying on the small table near my bed. Hazem must have left it for me to read. The cross on the book was golden while the leather was black. The cross reminded me of something familiar, something I had just been contemplating.

"Oh my God," I exclaimed. I looked at the raw wound on my left hand. The same cross was there, etched with amber and blood.

CHAPTER 28

That night I opened the *Koffar* (unbelievers) book. My hands were shaking and my eyes constantly looked around the room for fear of Allah's *ikab* (punishment.) My plan was very simple. I would read a few lines just to confirm to myself that it was just nonsense. I read about the woman who was caught in adultery. She was brought to the temple and Jesus happened to be there. "Let anyone who has no sin cast the first stone," (John 8:7 NAS95) He said. Then when they were left alone, he told the woman, "Go and sin no more."

This guy is different, I thought. For a Muslim is brought up on the assumption that a woman — as a case in point, like a dog, is a source of impurity. It was too much. Had Mohammed been there, I'm sure he would have stoned her without mercy and, of course, have tried his best to spare the life of the man involved.

This book was filled with love and compassion, whereas ours, the Qur'an, was filled with blood, hatred and terror. Even when we had sex with our wives, we had to pray Allah to protect us against Shaitan. If all religions were a myth, at least this one believed in a merciful God, I contemplated. I remember I went to sleep holding the book to my chest. From that night on, I became a Christian Bible addict, just like Hazem.

However, I did not realize my addiction until the night when Hazem took his book back. That night I tossed and turned in my bed and wished I had that therapeutic book to read, some nice fables that had the magic of putting me to sleep. I was like a kid who never got tired of his favorite book of fiction. I was not a believer and was absolutely not ready to give any hint to Hazem that I was interested in his myths, or experiencing his conversion to Christianity, but I remember that, after about an hour, I swallowed my pride and knocked at his door.

"I wonder if you would lend me your book for a while," I asked, a bit embarrassed.

"What book?" he teased

"Your Bible, I said, clearing my throat.

Hazem arched an eyebrow. "Don't you think it's a little late?" He was clearly enjoying the game, which was playing on my nerves.

"Actually, I could not sleep and I have nothing to read. I mean I've read everything except your book."

"I see. So you are telling me you need my Bible to be able to sleep?"

"Not exactly," I lied. "But yes, in a way, that's what I mean."

"Yes or no? It's not that hard a question to answer," he said.

"Then, yes" I said, swallowing my pride.

"Okay, just a second," Hazem stared at me for what seemed a long time before he returned inside his room for his precious book. "Here it is," he said, handing it to me.

"Thank you very much," I said taking the book from his hands. But, as I was about to retrace my way back to my room, I heard him ask, "Are you still an atheist?"

"Why do you ask?" I questioned instead of answering.

"It seems to me you are a believer now," Hazem replied nonchalantly.

"Well," I replied, "the fact that I want to read your Bible does not mean anything." I lied, because it meant many things. Hazem kept silent, but continued to look directly into my eyes. I looked down at the floor. "I read it just the same as I read *La Fontaine* or *One Thousand and a Night*. Understand?"

"No." He said abruptly.

His short answer stopped me. For a long moment I thought

about a retort. Then the words poured out of my mouth. "I'm what you might call a modern *ronin,* if you saw the film."

"The famous French actor Jean Reno and what was the name of that great American actor?"

"Robert De Niro," I responded, surprised at his knowledge.

"Yes, I like him. He is one of the few actors who can convince you, whether he plays the funny guy or the ruthless bandit."

"Yes, I agree, but I think that Jean Reno is unforgettable."

"So you are without a master — roaming the streets of this life for the highest bidder?" Hazem questioned.

"Yes, in a way ... except for one important thing ... I'm very well at ease without a higher authority," I said, confident in my answer.

"I don't know why I don't believe you," he said. His straight forward remark took me unprepared and anger swelled inside my chest. I remember I was about to throw the book in his face, but my fingers kept clutching at it as if it were the only rock in turbulent waters.

"Sorry, I'm sometimes unbearable," Hazem said. "I think I'm getting old." He gave a dry smile, and I thanked him again and rushed away with my booty.

I opened the Bible to John 8: 31-32, to where Jesus said to those Jews who believed Him: "If you abide in my word, you are my disciples indeed. And you shall know the truth, and the truth shall make you free." The guy was definitely different. Big names came to my mind — Alexander the Great, Plato, Confucius, Mohammed. Whoever you named, no one was his equal. I finally had to admit it.

Days went by very smoothly since that night .I was a false atheist in the heart of my hearts and a devoted Muslim In daylight. At night hazem's fables would breach the gap between reality and fiction.

CHAPTER 29

Two months had elapsed since I had last seen Moza. When I opened the door and saw her that Thursday morning, standing in the doorway and beaming with happiness, my old infatuation was revived once again. However, Moza stiffened when I first touched her hand.

"I tried to phone you, but you changed your number I suppose. I just came to thank you for all that you did ... by the way, this is Safia and she has a problem." A shy, tall and very thin woman stood behind her,

I could have said no at that moment and stopped her story right from the start, but something inside me urged me to allow Moza to continue. The woman who wanted my help that day was not a normal case. The woman had cancer and, according to her doctors, she was in the final stages. Nobody should play with a dying person, I thought. She came to me as a last resort and I saw it in her eyes. She was so pale and thin and what? The thought came to my mind that she was dying. Her mother, whom I did not see at first, was helping her walk and the child behind them — a girl about seven years old, implored me silently with her eyes. I wanted to say I was just an imposter, a charlatan — a mean, insignificant *khal* who wanted to live like anybody else. But, because of various things that really hurt, I chose to take everything I could get out of life, using Machiavellian strategies. I was about to tell the truth when words poured out of my mouth.

"I'm sorry, but I can't promise anything "Don't say that, I know you can help if you want. Please do not let her down," Moza begged. The woman had decided to believe in me — I could see it in her eyes. It was too late for a humiliating confession besides I found it difficult and unfeeling to simply turn my back and let the woman suffer alone.

"I've been to all the doctors — to India, Thailand and even Iran, my case is hopeless. I went to pilgrimage and prayed until I could not stand on my feet. I'm not afraid of death. I'm a believer and life and death is part of *khadar* (fate), but I have a family — two boys and a girl. They still need me. I ask pardon from Allah — who am I to question Allah's will?"

I listened silently and felt a growing lump in my throat. Moza reassured her that she would be healed. "This man has done miracles before, I assure you. You will see. Just do what he tells you to do. He is neither a magician nor a charlatan. This man has a real gift. He knows and uses Hebrew sacred words that were written on Moses' rod. He was taught the words from a Moroccan Jew who believed in his talent."

Moza went on, and then she stopped to let her words settle. She looked at me for help but I shook my head and gritted my teeth. She nonetheless continued in her mythical explanations of my powers, and of course the frail, dying woman was all ears.

"King Solomon, the Qur'an says, governed the wind and all the *jinn* or demons and *efreets* of the world. Allah taught him all the sacred words that were inscribed on Moses' rod. The Qur'an says, as you know, that Solomon was dead for a long time, but Allah did not allow his death to be revealed. Each time the *jinn* did their slave work, until the day the ants finished eating away at his rod and he succumbed in front of them. That was a lesson from Allah — to teach them that they were too weak and unable to see *ghayb* (the unseen)."

Moza stopped to clear her throat and then continued. "But meanwhile, Solomon's nephew, well before the *jinn,* knew about the death of Solomon. He stole the secret, I mean he copied the words etched on the rod and escaped to Morocco. From there he taught some of his Jewish disciples the secrets that transformed water into ice or moved a person from one place to another in the twinkling of an eye." Moza fervently recounted the entire story that I had fabricated.

"What is your name, again?" I asked the frail woman who was now busy straightening her *hijab*.

"Safia," she said.

"Safia, as Safiyya bint Huyayy?" I asked, but the woman did not seem to understand the insinuation. Neither did Moza or the old mother.

Safia bint Hoyayy was a Jewish woman whose mother, Barra bint Samawal, was from the Banu Quorayza tribe. Safiyya settled with her tribe in Khaybar(the name of an oasis about 90 miles to the north of Medina,Saudi Arabia) after being expelled by Muslims from Medina in 625 AD. Two years later Mohammed and his companions sieged the last stronghold In Khaybar and only spared children and women. Mohammad married the 17 year old Safia the day he ordered the killing of her husband, brothers and uncles. Curiously enough, she became a devout Muslim and recounted *hadiths* (sayings of Prophet Mohammed) to *sahaba* (companions.)

"I'm going to give a treatment, but I do not promise anything," I said.

"Of course," she said quickly. "But thank you from the bottom of my heart and may Allah reward you with His vast Heaven."

Suddenly, the *adhan* cried out, "*Allah akbar.*"

My frail woman started asking forgiveness from Allah and beseeching Him to give Mohammed the highest position in *firdaws* (Heaven). I lit a cigarette and sat on my sofa. "Are not you going to pray *dohr* (afternoon prayers)?"

Her question caught me unprepared. I shifted in my seat and thought about a suitable answer, but I knew in her mind she was beginning to question my offer. I could almost hear her thoughts — *What kind of a miracle am I supposed to receive from a beardless, cigarette-smoking man who does not even perform salat, prayer?*

"Do you still want me to do it," I asked.

"Yes," she said without conviction, "but can I ask you a question?"

"Go ahead," I replied.

"Are the *jinns* that serve you truly Muslims?" She caught me unprepared again. I smiled blankly and had nothing to say. "If you are not sure, I would rather you don't. What would be the purpose, if I gain a few years and then die and go to Hell?" She asked.

"The entity I'm going to ask help from will never forsake you now or in the hereafter," I replied.

"Astaghfirullah! I ask pardon from Allah" she exclaimed. A cold silence hung in the air. Safia shifted in her seat and scratched the back of her left hand. "I think I need to go to Sultan Quabous' mosque and pray. I feel that Allah will listen to my prayers and if He doesn't, then it is my fate and it is useless to fight." She then stood up and was ready to leave.

I felt like an Omani *khanjar* dagger was cutting through my heart. "Then I will respect your decision and I will pray for you."

"Just pray for yourself — the Qur'an warns against those who do not perform *salat* punctually," she answered cynically.

Inside my heart I had nothing but pity mixed with respect for this frail woman named Safia. "I will pray for you to the only one I believe is capable of miracles," I said. Safia smiled blankly, then left. I prayed earnestly for her in the name of Jesus, the Lord of miracles, the only one who brought people back from the dead. I prayed, while visualizing Benny Hin, dressed in white, as he performed miracles on the big stage of his church in the U.S.A.

Had I been a believer, I would have understood that a real miracle happened in front of my eyes; that The words of Hazem's Jesus won the battle against cancer.

In less than one week, Safia's health improved and the doctors were stunned. There was nothing, absolutely nothing. All the tumors — all the poisons were gone. The doctors, skeptical about everything that cannot be measured down-to-earth, as usual, decided that their first diagnosis was wrong and that all the chemotherapy she was taking was actually destroying her health. Of course it was nonsense and the woman knew it, but I did not care at that time. I actually believed the doctors' story and thought It was a happy coincidence.

I was told later, by a long-bearded *salafist,* that an eminent doctor was intrigued by her case and then offered his theory that it was the brain and all its remarkable healing power that was the cause of her healing.

"I wonder why they did not believe in Allah's might and the power of healing in the Qur'an and Sunna," the *motawwa* (a government recognized religious police) exclaimed. In fact, Safia's marvelous recovery became an Islamic triumph by which an irony of fate, or a miracle, became an instrument in the claws of the beast.

"It was a miracle. The woman read the Qur'an every night and God saved her — is it so hard to explain?" The long-bearded man went on. I recall that I wanted so badly to pull at the ferocious beard that covered most of his face. "They think in a box and they have to find another box, or else they will die. Besides, most of the doctors are pale-faced *Koffar,* infidels, they are not to blame. After all, we Muslims have not done our duty towards them. We should do all we can for *dawah* (preaching of Islam.) But instead of course, our money is spent in the casinos of Las Vegas or the brothels of France," he preached. I remember I just stood up and left him talking. Safia had completely misunderstood the true nature of what happened to her and the Muslim preacher, avid for a miracle like all preachers around the world, seemed to me at that time more stupid and misled.

CHAPTER 30

The big question that took me so long to answer was this. If Mohammed wrote the Qur'an and said it was from Allah, then how could I explain the marvelous, miraculous beauty of its *bayan* (eloquence). How did he create such a new genre that, according to *sirah* (prophetic biography), it astounded some great poets and made them believers in his declaration that he was called as a prophet of Allah? How did he do it, he the goat herder, the poor and illiterate orphan?

I soon found an answer to that prickly question. I knew a senior teacher from another school whose name was Talal. I was older than him and every now and then he sought my advice on some pedagogical matter. The law stipulated that all senior teachers should be Omanis; therefore, most of them lacked experience and needed the help of *wafideen,* or non-Omani Muslim immigrants.

I met my friend Talal one day and we went to Sohar. We had espressos in Lulu Center and I was stunned when he lit a cigarette.

"You are the first Omani that I know, who smokes!" I exclaimed.

"Oh, forget about these Omanis. They are just stupid," he replied.

We talked about the beauty of Lebanon; how easy the girls were in Thailand. He talked about his wife, who never missed *fajr* prayers (dawn prayers; it is the first of the five daily prayers offered by practicing Muslims) and never let him sleep in peace without performing them. We discussed the thousands of AIDS cases in the Gulf, which the governments continued to hide, and then we moved on to talk about religion.

"All religions are rubbish. Islam is a religion based on cruelty; invasions and blood … look at Somalia or Pakistan. Anywhere where the banner of Islam floats high, you will see only bloodshed," he said.

I nodded agreement and let out a deep, resonant sigh. "Those Afghani people make me laugh … they do not have enough to eat and I heard they refused some kind of food sent from the international relief on the grounds that the meat was not *halal* (slaughtered the Muslim way)." I laughed, but he only smiled a smile that did not reach his eyes.

"Have you seen those *jihadists* in Iraq? They slaughtered a man in the name of Islam. They cut his throat, like you cut the throat of a lamb during *Eid al-Adha,* the sacrificial Muslim Feast," Talal said with disdain. I realized that clearly his heart was heavy and he needed someone to listen to him.

"Who has not watched?" I sighed.

"I visited France last year — the *horma* (my wife) did not want to go back home. It was the first time in her life that she could dress the way she wanted without being afraid." He paused to let his words settle and then went on. "Nobody believes in God there — nobody speaks about religion except the North Africans, of course. Most of them were scumbags, no offense … yet the people respect you as a human being, help you when you need them. They do not mislead you or use you like our so-called Muslim brothers."

"I did not go there but I spent some months in Sweden. You are right, they are far better than us. Of course, they have scoundrels far worse than we have, but generally speaking, yes, unfortunately," I agreed. Immediately I felt a painful throb in my head.

"You know, I was a great believer until the day I read the

poetry of Omaya ibn Abi Salt. I asked a friend of mine who knew Arabic poetry better than me, who came first: the prophet or Omaya?" Talal went on with the same tone of disdain shrouding his voice. "Oh, I heard about this Omaya. The prophet, according to Sirat, biography of Ibn Hishem, liked him and always listened to his poetry. He was a Hanafi, a monotheist, a true follower of Abraham," my friend said.

Talal paused and looked out the window. He puffed at his cigarette with vigor and smiled, but there was a shadow of pain that went over his eyes. "Well, if I had found my wife in the arms of another man, it would have been much easier to bear. I was surprised when I discovered how similar his poetry was to the Qur'an that Muslims say was revealed from Allah!"

"Who is this Omaya and can I have a look at what he has written?" I asked.

"They say the man embraced Christianity, he wrote poetry about major biblical prophets way before mohammad became a prophet " he replied.

"By Allah — I think I have read about his spiritual journey somewhere," I cut in.

"The books recount that he came during the famous Badr battle when Mohammad first won his Koreishi tribe and killed seventy of them — saw the dead and all the bloodshed and decided to return to Damascus. He never came back. What is curious is that most of us heard something about this poet, but very few of us have read his work," Talal pointed out.

"It is not available. I always wanted to read his poetry and see what the prophet wrote, but unfortunately, I did not find anything," I said.

"Of course! now the Saudis, the Qataris and Emiratis are doing a good job in rewriting the Sunna — do you understand what I mean? he is rarely mentioned on TV or even the most specialised books. It's becoming a taboo. Sometimes I bemoan the little freedom we had 20 or 30 years ago."

"What is so special about his poetry? I mean, what makes it so threatening?" I asked.

"His poetry is like the Qur'an — almost the same style, the same metaphors and sometimes literally the same expressions," Talal said.

As he spoke, I had mixed feelings. On one hand I was happy, for finally I had what special agents would call a good leak. But on the other hand I was dismayed, for I knew the implications of that leak. For a moment, I could not even feel my legs.

What's the matter — are you okay?" Talal asked

"But I saw you in that mosque in Sohar," I said instead of answering.

"What do you expect me to do — bring all the shame to myself, my family and even my tribe? Do you want me to get killed if I speak my mind? Wake up, man, we really live in *jahiliya*, complete ignrance."

I smiled a dry smile, but I hurried to ask him, "You did not tell me where I can get his poetry."

"You won't find it anywhere, here I told you. But God bless the U.S.A. and the inventor of the Internet. Just write his name on Google and you will find all his poetry together with some other Christian poets before Islam. Make a mixture of all these and you will find our holy book."

"Are you a Christian?" I ventured to ask.

"No, I'm an atheist, or maybe the God who had created us lost his life long ago and consequently we have to live without him, if you know what I mean."

It has never ceased to amaze me how life, or something mysterious, has always helped me along my way, in my spiritual quest. Talal was a rare breed, I thought. He was poles apart from the Omanis I met there. I still remember the words he said before we parted.

"We have been fooled for 14 centuries, man. Cheer up, life is beautiful!"

CHAPTER 31

The desert preached ugliness and thirst. I could now understand why Jesus was tried there for 40 days. Why the brave Antony the Great (a monk who lived like a hermit in the desert of Egypt around the third century AD) fought Its harshness single-handed and wrote his famous desert sayings. This is the land where Moses and his people wandered for forty years .This is the land from which the cross was forbidden. This is the land where Mohammed did his notorious ethnic cleansing, I thought.

Bani' Najjar was a tribe of Arab Christians. When Mohammad sent his messenger to them telling them to follow his divine message or pay *jizya* (money tax) or fall by the sword; they sent him a delegation led by their most learned priests. They wanted to know if Mohammed was from God or Shaitan. They gave Mohammed some trick questions, and whispered into ears that Paul was the name of a pit fire in Hades and that Mary was the sister of Aaron and Moses.

The prophet swallowed the bait, repeated the misinformation and reported that it was from Allah. The Bani' Najjar were sure now that he was not from God. Would they fight the king of the desert? Would they stand fast against the dark legions of the false prophet about whom Saint John had spoken hundreds of years ago? In the end, they paid the *jizya* (money tax) and continued to pray. Muslims saw it as, finally, a great victory, because those stubborn *kaffirs*, infidels, gave up their property and chose to live in bondage.

On the other hand, the Jews of Banu Qurayza had welcomed

death with open arms. Mohammed dug a big pit and offered them two choices: Either live in slavery as second-rate Muslims or die by the sword. There was no third way out.

The last one who remained alive because of the prophet's companions interference on his behalf asked about the fate of his friends and relatives. He was told they had been killed by the sword. He beseeched Mohammed to cut his throat like them, for life meant nothing without his beloved.

More than 600 Jews died that day — only the women and the children were spared. The massacre happened five years after the *hijra* migration of Mohammed from Mecca to Medina. It is also mentioned rather vaguely in the Qur'an in Surah Al-Ahzab verses 26 and 27. But Ibn Ishaq, the famous Muslim historian recounts the whole story:

"Then they surrendered, and the apostle confined them in Medina in the quarter of d. al-Harith, a woman of Banu. al-Najjar. Then the apostle went out to the market of Medina (which is still its market today) and dug trenches in it. Then he sent for them and struck off their heads in those trenches as they were brought out to him in batches. Among them was the enemy of Allah Huyayy bin. Akhtab and Ka`b bin Asad their chief. There were 600 or 700 in all, though some put the figure as high as 800 or 900. As they were being taken out in batches to the apostle they asked Ka`b what he thought would be done with them. He replied, 'Will you never understand? Don't you see that the summoner never stops and those who are taken away do not return? By Allah it is death!' This went on until the apostle made an end of them. Huyayy was brought out wearing a flowered robe in which he had made holes about the size of the finger-tips in every part so that it should not be taken from him as spoil, with his hands bound to his neck by a rope. When he saw the apostle he said, 'By God, I do not blame myself for opposing you, but he who forsakes God will be forsaken.' Then he went to the men and said, 'God's command is right. A book and a decree, and massacre have been written against the

Sons of Israel.' Then he sat down and his head was struck off."
These last words of the chief of Banu Khoreida kept reverberating in my ears for a long time. I did not care whether Christianity was right or wrong, or whether or not Jesus really existed or was just a legend. All I was sure of was that this bizarre part of the world needed the beautiful story of the son of Nazareth — the unrestricted love of a divine symbol. Then it would not matter if they changed their minds afterwards, whether their offspring would become secular like everywhere in the world, whether religion would one day become a taboo word. It did not matter, really, for the seed of unrestricted love and mercy would be there, etched forever on their genes.

At *Maghreb* (sunset), the *adhan* cried, "Allah Akbar." Instinctively, I rushed towards the water tap. Then I remembered that I was no longer a believer. I washed only my face and then went out with Hafiz to the mosque. I had a reputation to preserve.

They stretched the *sajjad* (prayer mat) and lined up for prayer. The *imam* enjoined the believers to close ranks. Hafiz grabbed my arm and elbowed a space. The time was ripe for a choice, I thought. They beckoned to me to stand upright and respect the line. They wanted me to worship the beast, I thought. I chose to say no and left. Nobody cared.

I had never seen Hazem's face so thought-stricken. That night he entered into my room without even his usual three knocks on the door, or clearing his throat, if the door was open. I was reading the Bible, of course. I remember that Hazem's face was ashen that night; he truly looked concerned. My breath caught in my throat.

"What is it?" I asked.

He did not answer. He kept silent and clearly weighed his options.

The load on his mind is heavy, I thought.

"Something serious?" I asked.

"Yes," he answered. My heart lurched.

"What happened?" I asked.

Silently, he sat on a chair opposite my bed and then lit a cigarette. "I saw a vision," he said carefully.

"Is that all?" I snapped. "I was about to have a heart attack!"

"I told you, it's very serious, more serious than you can imagine."

"Do not tell me that I'm going to die tomorrow," I teased.

"I'm not joking, Jamal," he said.

"Okay, sorry — tell me about this dream of yours."

"It was not a dream, it was a divine revelation."

"Whatever," I replied.

"Do not talk like that — I'm serious."

"Are you a prophet?" I asked him.

"I'm not, but this does not hinder me from receiving a message from my Lord. Do you understand the difference between Islam and Christian beliefs? In Islam, prophet hood is sealed by Mohammed. After him God is dead, or at least vowed abstinence since Mohammed, as Allah claims in the Qur'an, is the last prophet, no other prophet should be expected to come after him," he said.

"Everything is explained in the Qur'an, any social, economic, legal or even scientific matter or so they say … so why do we need to hear from Allah now? Do you see what I mean?"

True, Christians, hear from God. He speaks to them through His Holy Spirit as they claim. In fact, Hazem had put his finger on a question that had always disturbed me. Only Sufis and some new sects such as Babism, Ahmadia, etc., believed that Allah is not dead and that He still talks to some of the saints. But those small groups were shunned and even ridiculed.

"I'd advise you not to stay here next year … I mean, do not renew your contract," Hazem said, which brought me back to reality.

"Why do you say that? Didn't you tell me that you are planning to spend five years here, just last week?"

"I was, but I'm going to return to Egypt this summer."

"Sometimes you surprise me," I said, suppressing a smile.

"This region is going to burn very soon," Hazem said.

"Okay, and how … Israel? Iran?"

"I'm not sure, but by the end of this year, a terrible thing is going to happen here in the Middle East," he replied.

"You are not the first. The Mayans — who were a bunch of human-sacrificing, jungle-dwelling primitives — claimed the world will end in 2012, but fortunately for us they ended before their chilling calendar. Do you really believe this?" I countered.

"I only believe what I see."

"Even Nostradamus spoke about this so-called imminent disaster. But I think he spoke about a great comet that would impact the Mediterranean, which is far away from here, I suppose."

"I don't care … all I know, and what I'm sure of, is that my Jesus never lies," Hazem responded.

"Even a man like Yisrayl Hawkins speaks about the 2012 catastrophe," I went on as though I was not listening.

"Do you think I'm stupid? I know all this, but this does not mean that what I saw is wrong," Hazem exclaimed, clearly frustrated.

"I did not say you are stupid..all I'm saying is that you might be influenced by these kind of cliché prophesies," I said.

"I wish I was … but the Lord showed me what is going to happen very soon. This world is going to see an appetizer of God's wrath," Hazem said.

"You know that I'm not going to stay more than two years with these people, but that is not the question … I mean, how can you be sure? Everybody sees visions, even the Chinese Shaolin monks. Apart from training in martial arts, they also follow the Buddhist code of conduct and customs and practices in their temples," I replied, unconvinced.

"I do not have the time or the energy to understand every creed or every doctrine. All I know is that the Lord I serve is real and He never tells me lies," Hazem kept repeating, more to himself than to me, I thought.

After all, I thought, the numerous predictions about the year 2000 turned out to be nonsense. I thought that Hazem, like any close-minded Muslim *salafist* (Muslims who emphasize the earliest Muslims as model examples of Islamic practice), listened to only one voice. The antenna of his brain could not detect any other frequencies. In a way, I thought that religion was not only an opiate, but also a boundary that separated human beings who shared the same problems and, therefore, the same destiny.

"We have a busy day tomorrow, we better get some rest my friend," I said. Hazem was slightly disconcerted though he smiled innocently and bid me good night.

CHAPTER 32

A day at school was a day in Hell. If it was up to me, I would have bombarded all the Shinas area with heavy artillery, I thought. Yet, that morning, I kept a smile on my face and was not ready to lose my job either in Oman or in Algeria. The only solution I knew was to finish this year peacefully and return back home. That way I could '*kill two birds with a single stone,*' as the proverb says. First, I will have gathered some extra money. Second, and most importantly, I will have preserved my job back home. But, as an Arabic proverb from the Middle Ages states, '*the winds rarely go according to our sails.*'

I really tried hard to endure this trial and swallowed almost everything, even my common sense. In the absence of girls, teenage boys sent love letters to each other, and from time to time had a secret meeting in the toilet or somewhere else. All this I accepted and told myself that it could be worse.

I saw teachers flirting with young teenagers and I turned a blind eye. Maybe I was wrong, I would comfort myself. I heard insults from some colleagues and turned a deaf ear. I worked twice as hard as any Omani teacher, received half his salary and said Allah would provide. I always said yes, to my superiors — the magic word in the Gulf. I went home each night totally washed out, mentally exhausted and physically drained.

Then, one day, something happened that really made my blood boil. I did not have class, so I was sitting in the teacher's room busy writing my lesson plan. An Egyptian colleague, Anwar, came in.

"Have you not heard the news?" He jerked his head left and right, and then said in a hushed tone, "Mr. Khalil was arrested last week."

"The history teacher, the one who speaks a lot?" I asked. "I just met him an hour ago."

"Yes, that's him ... but the investigation is still ongoing."

"What did he do?" I asked.

Anwar turned around to check and see if there was anyone else in the teachers' room.

"He was caught red-handed," Anwar said.

"What do you mean?"

"Do you teach the 11th grade?" Anwar asked instead of answering.

"Yes," I replied impatient to know what this teacher had done to get arrested.

"Do you know a student whose name is Antar?

I wracked my memory to recall his face. "Yes," I said. "He is a rather heavyset boy." *And very white in a country where the sun turns everything black, even the hearts,* I thought to myself.

"Antar was his *sbay* (sexual partner.) Actually, everyone knew about their relationship, but last night he was caught in *sih,* a desolate, uninhabited place. The father heard about his child's affair and called the police. They caught him on Friday night," Anwar related.

"Oh no!" I said. "You mean they were caught in the very act? I can't believe it! What a country! Don't they have women here? He could go to Dubai, for God's sake. It's a stone's throw from here ... there are more prostitutes there than anywhere in the world!" I exclaimed.

"Not exactly," Anwar said. "He has a tendency towards young boys. You didn't know this?"

"I can't believe it," I snapped again. "It's as though we live in another age."

"And they speak about piousness ... just yesterday he was

asking me about you, you know. Why you stopped going to mosque and everything, as though it was their business."

I knew though that it had been Anwar, who probably said to other teachers that I was absent during prayer. I was sure that he had ripped me apart behind my back. And Omanis in general adored gossip, especially if it was about *wafideen* (foreigners) because they thought we threatened their livelihood.

"He is so stupid," I said. "Now he has lost his career and will spend the rest of his life in jail. I can't believe that I just saw him earlier and he acted as if nothing had happened."

"Are you kidding?" Anwar asked. His voice rang with sarcasm.

"What do you mean?" I questioned.

"Listen to me. How long have you been here?"

"This is my first year."

"Well, I have been here for 20 years now. Do you think it is the first time something like this has happened? Let me tell you what will happen. The victim's father will get a generous compensation and the problem will be settled forever," Anwar said.

"I don't believe you. We live in the 21st century, for God's sake."

"You will see," Anwar replied. "I'll tell you something else. Do you think the father cares about his son? All of them have done sodomy sometime in their lives. I'm sure he is happy because the accused is a teacher. The reward will be generous."

"No, it can't be like this!" I said. "Where are human rights activists, the UN? I mean, we live in the 21st century," I kept repeating stupidly.

"The king himself chooses, from time to time, handsome boys and takes them to one of his numerous castles. Open your eyes, man," Anwar snickered.

"Do you mean those rumors about him are true?"

"I don't know — they say he just wants to be served by young handsome boys ... nobody knows why" he replied cautiously.

Then we laughed and Anwar, as usual, forgot himself and fell down to the floor. It was his way of showing how funny the joke was. I thought that after 20 years of teaching, most teachers became like kids — stimulus response stuff. I wondered when social scientists would study that field.

When an Omani colleague came in, Anwar stood up and resumed his air of stern piousness. He immediately changed the subject. He spoke about Islam and *taqwa* (piety) and each time he looked at me he spoke about the importance of *salat* or Muslim prayer. Later in the day — before the eighth period, I heard that Khalil gave the plaintiff the sum of 7,000 rials(around 25000 dollars). The student returned to the same class as if nothing had happened.

When I met Anwar on my way to my class, he smiled a smile of triumph. This pushed me to lose control, making a big mistake. I entered my classroom as usual and asked one of the kids to write the date. I told him to use two colors: white for words and yellow for numbers. Then I went out and lit a cigarette.

I was nervous, but I had to do it. I had to confront my fear and tell the truth. The class became noisy, and I knew Nawwaf, my only brilliant student, must have finished writing.

I waited for the class to settle down, and then I took a piece of chalk, drew a cross beside the current date and wrote in capital letters: (WESTWARD). "This is the real time in the West. Let's see now the real time in the East," I said to the surprised class.

I wrote: Tuesday, March, 1602. Then I drew a crescent and a star and wrote (EASTWARD). "Now, young men, this is the real time in the East. Which time would you like to live in?"

I looked at the blank faces around me for a long moment then thought about the witches of Salem Village, Massachusetts. It seemed to me that all people around the Gulf region; intellectually lived in the 17th century.

"The teacher has lost his wits," a mischievous student shouted and broke what seemed an eternal silence. The boys laughed and then screamed, yelled and quarreled with each other. The clamor was indescribable. One of the students told me he wanted to go to the toilet. Actually, he was a secret agent. In Oman, as everywhere in the Gulf region, every citizen was a secret agent. They did not report on each other unless it was a matter of state security or a revenge case. But if a *wafid* (foreigner) made a mistake, especially as big as mine, the world came to a full stop.

After the adrenaline rush, I felt tired. I fell onto the chair and started weighing my options. Would I be taken to the nearest madhouse? Would they put me in jail? If the truth be told, I was not sorry. I was proud of myself because I looked into Shaitan's eyes and told him, "I know your true face."

After a while the kids forgot about me and their fuss was mainly because of each other's ridiculous behavior. Some switched on their mobiles and showed their adventures to less reckless kids, others hugged and even kissed furtively.

There was a knock on the door after a while and I saw the headmaster accompanied by two burly, colleagues. I recognized the two men. The first was Fawaz Risi, the math teacher. The other was Ali Ftisi who taught Islamic education. The classroom was suddenly all discipline and respect. The devilish kids wore the mask of innocence and all eyes focused on me. The headmaster stretched his hand cordially and asked me politely to come to his office. He asked Ali to supervise the class for the remainder of the lesson.

I remember the principal kept smiling, but curiously, though the smile reached the eyes and shook even the long beard that hid most of his face, I felt it was artificial. Inside his office, the picture of the sultan loomed large on the wall. He was dressed in a red turban and the eyes, though icy and ruthless, were vulnerable and slightly concerned.

"Mr. Jamal," he began, "did you sleep well last night?"

I weighed my options and decided to use the outlet he offered. "No … I was awake until the first *fajr* (dawn) *adhan*,"

I said without conviction. The principal caressed his beard thoughtfully.

"You need a young *horma* (woman). I really believe that you need young blood in your life. I wonder how you manage to live with one single woman. What can man a do when she becomes too old and unable to satisfy his needs? It is against nature. You see animals walk on four feet, the seasons are four, and there are even four elements. How can you spend your whole life with the same woman, always having the same boring dinner?" He asked me and I knew he actually believed what he was saying.

The principal then smiled to cover the sting of his remark. I shifted in my seat and smiled blankly. "I think I'm going to give you one week off. You need some rest ... maybe you should go to Dubai, you know?" He offered it as a question, but I knew it was a suggestion to find a prostitute. He actually thought that would solve all my problems. How ridiculous he seemed to me. I guess it was a good thing that he couldn't see what was really churning within me

"I can't. I need permission and an Omani *kafil* (bailsman)," I explained, though he knew the system better than me. The principal shifted in his seat and faked sympathy and concern. But deep inside, very deep where there is the real Muslim legacy of two-facedness and greed, he was happy because only he and other Omanis had the right to taste the forbidden wine of the prostitutes that invade Dubai every day.

As he shook my hand, I knew he was going to write his *taqrir* (report) as soon as I left the office. But I was not ready to allow him to enjoy that opportunity of asking for my resignation. In Oman and the Gulf region in general, when one wants to resign he has to write his letter of resignation and submit it before April so that the educational authorities had enough time to recruit another teacher in his place for the next year. I still had time to think about it, but I was adamant in my desire to leave Oman and aware of all the consequences, so I decided to proceed with submitting my letter and I informed the principal of my decision.

"Are you sure you want to resign?" The principal asked, slightly edgy. Clearly, he wanted to be the one who suggested my resignation to the educational authorities In Sohar.

"I think I am no longer able to live away from my family; homesickness is very hard," I said. The principal was moved and he shunned Shaitan. But he still wanted to have the honor of shedding my blood as we say In arabic. I smiled at my skill of discernment.

"Well, you have enough time before the actual application is due. I want you to have some rest and think about it during this short holiday."

But it was already decided in my mind. I was no longer a Muslim and no longer able to live in the sacred kingdom of Shaitan.

CHAPTER 33

Before finishing with my experience in Oman, let me point out one last thing. While waiting for my plane back home, I stared at the self-inflicted wound on my left hand — the wound that I got from putting out cigarettes on my skin. It was then that I realized that the *koffar*, infidels', symbol — the cross — had never ceased to play a cardinal role in my life.

When I was a six-year-old frail boy, my father took me to a French Catholic doctor as a last resort. As we entered his examining room, I immediately looked at a big wooden cross on the wall. Then I stared at the man hanging on the cross — half-naked and smeared with blood and crowned with thorns. But the face beamed like a sunrise despite the horrible pain.

"Doesn't he feel pain?" I asked innocently. My remark won me some stern looks from my father, and the doctor followed my gaze and looked over his shoulder. The breath caught in my throat, but the smile on his face, when he turned, killed all the fear that rose inside my chest.

"Yes, you are right," the doctor said gently. "He doesn't feel pain because he chose it to save us."

It was on the tip of my tongue to say it did not make sense, but my father rushed to say, "They have the cross and we have the crescent and the star."

The doctor shifted in his seat. It seemed to me he wanted to say something, but on second thought he kept smiling warmly and never took his gaze off of me. "How old are you, young man?" He asked.

"Six — next month," I answered proudly.

"Do you know that you are the first one who noticed him?"

"I like him, I said. He does not deserve that."

The remark won me another frown from my father. "Sorry, sir," my father replied. "He is quite naughty sometimes."

The doctor shifted in his seat again. "No, he is a nice boy. I mean, he is intelligent ... I'm sure the Lord, or Allah as you say, has a great plan for him."

My father gave me a hug and tousled my hair. I was proud and felt the world was mine. The doctor examined me and told my father that had I come there one week later, I would have probably lost my liver and been dead. But I did not care at that time, I knew I was in good hands. My father loved me and had always said I was the apple of his eye. And from then on, the old French doctor treated me like one of his grandsons.

When I was 12, I had a big problem with mathematics. We were very poor and my father could not afford to pay for private lessons, so I thought it was my fate that I would not be able to continue my education. I anticipated that in two or three years I would learn a skill and quit my schooling. Again, a Christian came to my rescue. That year we had a new teacher. He was a tall, wide-shouldered Frenchman who wore the weirdest moustache I had ever seen. It was so long that a bird could have easily rested upon it. He always wore a silver cross around his neck. With him, all numbers became like chocolate, as he'd promised. The obscure Xs and Ys were now little kids like us or cute dogs or rabbits. We loved the teacher and we loved algebra. Again, I was saved by a man who had a cross.

I remember that I advanced from poor to fair, then excellent. During the 12th grade I was considered one of the best pupils in the school. After the baccalaureate (secondary school), I was faced with a major issue. What should I choose for my focus when I went to university? I was good at almost every subject except English. I had always managed to get fair marks in

English though, and even had a decent grade in it by the end of my secondary school years.

When Ronald Reagan sent his troops and bombarded Libya, I made up my mind to study the language of that man who dressed like a cowboy and seemed to me, at that time, prepared to destroy the entire Muslim world. I remember that I swore I would write a book in English, which would make the people in the United States discover the beauty of Islam, and therefore leave the cross and follow the crescent moon of Mohammed!

The irony was two-fold. Twenty years after that vow, I am indeed writing a book. But this book is to expose the true face of the *wolf in the lamb's clothing*. The second irony is to my mind even more revealing. The cross I swore to fight to my last breath is now etched forever on my left hand.

CHAPTER 34

As we flew over Al Huwari Bu Midyan airport, Aljazair, capital of Algeria, appeared in the distance like a bride waiting for a husband who would never come. I had never realized that my country was so beautiful, but now I knew it was too late for me. Unfortunately, because I had left my job in Oman I automatically lost my post in Algeria, because I was tied up by a written agreement I had signed before travelling to work there. I had 2,000 Omani rials(around 7000 dollars) in my pocket and a big desire to hug my old mum and sleep. *Oh God, I missed real oxygen,* I thought.

The passenger who sat beside me and remained silent for more than seven hours shouted out. He took a deep, long breath and miraculously the face that used to be almost inhuman, became full of life and excitement.

"I worked with those bastards for three years, three long years, in the desert of Saudi Arabia. I bore the lash of their tongues, the heat of their desert and the narrowness of their brains. My back was to the wall. I was forced to work in the middle of nowhere and obey the orders of a bunch of moneybags." Then, suddenly, he turned to me and asked, "And you, where have you been?"

"The Sultanate of Oman," I replied.

"Not bad! With Sultan Qabous? They say he killed his father — is it true?"

"Is there any Arab leader who does not have blood upon his hands?" I asked instead of answering.

"They call themselves Muslims! That is just nonsense! They

are just like Jews or even worse — Islam to them is a kind of habit, no more, no less. Praise be to Allah, we are not like them," he exclaimed.

I eyed the man for a moment. He appeared to be in his mid-50s, grey-haired and overweight. It was then that I realized that the Jews we hated — like we hated death — were more human than those people who hid themselves under the shield of Muslim piety.

I thought about Mahmoud Darwish, the famous Palestinian poet, who was born in Israel and had an Israeli passport. Darwish was originally a member of the Rekla, the Israeli Communist Party, before joining the PLO. According to a website dedicated to his memory, in 1988, one of his poems, *Passers Between the Passing Words,* was cited in the Knesset by Yitzhak Shamir. Darwish was accused of demanding that the Jews leave Israel, although he claimed he meant the West Bank and Gaza. Yet, when he died after heart surgery, in 2008, he was buried on a hill overlooking Jerusalem, as a respected poet of the Palestinian people. Three members of the Israeli Knesset attended an official ceremony honoring his death. Had he been in Saudi Arabia or anywhere in the Arab world, he would have been lucky to receive a clean death.

"We are the true Muslims — we are not *monafiki'in* (hypocrites)." The man broke into my thoughts. "When we are devoted, we are truly devoted … you see what I mean?" he asked rhetorically. I nodded in agreement, though I did not agree with him. The man ploughed on though:

"We abide by Allah's precepts — no adultery or wine consumption or exploitation of the poor. We are the true Muslims. We should be proud of ourselves, don't you think so?" he asked.

I could have simply smiled and said nothing, but suddenly, without any forethought, the words poured out of my mouth. "I'm no longer a Muslim."

I received a stern, contemptuous look from his beady eyes.

I don't know how Mohammed did it, but it seemed to me that everyone who sipped from his wine became saddled and forever enslaved to a philosophy that destroys all reason. The beast — the deceiving rock of the false prophet — blinds the eyes like a master illusionist, and only the most avid seekers are able to sniff out the real truth, I thought.

The man tipped his chin and weighed his options. "*Astagfirullah* (I ask pardon from Allah.) Shame Shaitan man … have you lost your mind? I know what you feel, but this does not mean you should lose your faith."

I was sure he knew what I felt, because he had also experienced the same backward thinking and repulsion of Muslims that he thought were his equals in the faith. But what I had come to understand was a mystery to him. I was aware that a sensitive chord had been touched. I wanted to say that the Muslim faith is a big lie — a fallacy in which a power-thirsty intelligent man fooled the whole Arab world — but the plane was about to land. The picture of my mum waiting for me in the "arrivals" section of the airport, made my heart leap with joy and forget about him.

As we moved inside the airport, the long-restrained silent anger inside my chest left me and I felt I was alive again. My gaze travelled around to other excited passengers, lining up for their turn to pass through customs. The short grey-haired man with beady eyes moved through the crowd and placed himself third in the line. It did not surprise me.

The airport was full of tired faces rushing to go through the last ordeal of the luggage check. Their legs were tense and restless with anticipation. Most of the Algerian women, who had hidden themselves under dark *abeyas* in Oman and elsewhere in the Gulf, were now dressed in tight jeans that exposed their *mafaten* (secret beauty), as an Omani might say. Curiously, I no longer imagined what was hidden behind the tight jeans; I simply caught a glimpse and went by. I discovered, at that very moment, another enlightening truth: the more the woman hides her beauty the more the man becomes ensnared within a purgatory of obscene thoughts.

True, Prophet Mohammad ordered the *hijab*, following Omar's suggestion, to hide his 12 wives, but he left the stern law of conduct loose as to the concubines and the ones who offered themselves to him freely.

I think he made a big mistake, for the hidden is always enticing, I suppose. More to the point, the bitter truth was this: *hijab* was for free women. *Tabarroj* (nakedness) was for second-class citizens of that time: *jawari*, or concubines, Malikat Yamin or female slaves, and of course black slaves. It was exactly like the yellow star pinned to the clothes of any Jew under Nazism.

A tender hand tapped me on my back. "It's your turn, unless you want to return back to where you have come from." It was a woman's voice. I turned around and saw a tall brunette. We both smiled. "Do not tell me you have been in Oman," she asked.

"I was — but threw my resignation in their faces."

She smiled. "A teacher, I suppose?" It was a statement rather than a question.

"And you?" I replied.

"A massage expert," she said timidly. I smiled a smile of recognition and she blushed.

The icy glare of the customs officer caught my eye and he motioned me to pass through the security machine.

Mum was there as I had expected. Her eyes were brimming with tears. As she threw her arms round me she wept. I felt her heart beat against mine and I welcomed the peace I was deprived of for a long year. Then her wrinkled hands shakily moved to my shoulders and face. All at once, the world was filled with beautiful orchids and a compassionate sun.

"I made you your favorite meal — couscous with grilled lamb. By Allah! You have become thin and your skin is scorched. This Oman has distorted your face out of recognition. I won't let you go back again. Do not tell me you are planning to return there."

Mum couldn't keep the concern out of her eyes or the tone in her voice.

"Mum, I'm almost 40. In Oman, people of my age have grandchildren."

Mum cast on me her usual look of reproach and hastened to counter. "What are you trying to prove? You are a kid in my eyes and as long as I live you will remain like this — do you hear me?" She was a bit vexed, but when I hugged her and kissed her hand she just became my good old mum again. Her voice became soft and her face flinched.

"I thought I was going to die before seeing you again. Thanks to Allah; I prayed to Him every *fajr* (dawn prayer). Thank Allah, thank ..." Her voice trailed off and she broke down again. I and some female passengers spent some time consoling her.

I had two bags of luggage — one for me and one for Mum. I bought her all the *abeyas* I could find — black as she insisted, but with different embroideries on the elbows and the neck. There were slippers, rosaries from Saudi Arabia or imported from Kom, Iran; Laban and incense from the famous Dofar region, prayer mats and of course the Holy Qur'an.

As for myself, I bought the finest and most expensive clothes I could find in Lou Lou and Carrefour centers. The clothes were mostly imported from Italy and France, but I bought some Indian t-shirts and some Pakistani jackets — made of silk, with special embroidery. If God did not exist, and Islam was a fallacy, then it was my right, I thought, to build my own paradise on Earth, even for a while. I decided that the lost concubines promised by the Qur'an for the believers would become real in my lifetime. I was not ready to forsake those nice rewards for which rivers of blood had been shed.

CHAPTER 34

I found the country on the fringe of turning back to the dark days of the early '90s. The number of women dressed in *hijabs* became phenomenal and the young who frequented mosques and wore beards became alarmingly greater. It was no doubt heading towards a dangerous zone — that dark zone from which Algeria has not yet returned. Two-hundred thousand lives became dust and the beast wanted more.

Only a few months ago, the worshippers of the beast had prayed daily and kept their faith to themselves. From their forced loss in the elections they learned *takiya* (to be double-faced) and feigned belief in democracy and the freedom of worship exactly like their brethren in neighboring Egypt, Tunisia or Libya. No doubt they became experts in masquerading into the crowd with their trimmed beards and their deluding façade of open-mindedness. But they will always secretly dream of a Muslim caliphate governed by Sharia law and so strong that it extends from the Euphrates to the Nile and from Spain to Madagascar. Only then would they show their true face and begin their sacred *jihad* against the infidel Christians or the cursed Jews, the everlasting enemies of Allah.

Now, as their number grew phenomenally, they would look you in the eye and lecture you about Islam, as if you were a small child. Some of them, for no reason, would ostracize you; others would look at you and shake their heads. Some bold ones would decide you were a potential target. It would not be long, I thought, before some of them would stab you because you were a *kaffir* (infidel) since you did not perform *salat,* Muslim prayer — exactly like in the early '90s.

But why should I care after all? I thought. I was going to die very soon — as soon as the *rials* ran out. That was my macabre decision at that time. So why on earth should I care? I kept repeating to myself.

The café, as usual, was full of people. The smoke filled the air, stung the eyes and hid visions, I reflected. My friend Ziad, who is short, stout and craggy-faced, came and I was snatched back to reality. After the hugging and the customary kissing of welcome that we Arabs tend to perform after absence, Ziad sat and ordered a coffee.

"Welcome home again — we missed you man," he said once more, but the tone in his voice rang with concern.

"What is it? Something is bothering you?" I asked

"My young brother, Hraq, sneaked through the borders yesterday … I never thought he would do it."

"That young kid? I saw him last night. Are you serious?"

"I am sure that no one suspected anything. He told his mother that he was going to *hammam* (the Turkish bath) and asked for five *dinars.* My mum gave him only three, but she was amazed that he kissed her and hugged her for a long time. I knew he wanted to go to Italy, but I never thought he would do it."

"How are you so sure he actually did it?" I asked.

"His friend came and told my mum. He said he was going to go with them but when he saw the condition of the boat, he changed his mind. He told Sami to postpone it for clearly it was too dangerous, but Sami refused to listen." There was another period of silence, but this time Ziad's face became dim and sad.

"Any news?" I finally asked, though I felt it was useless. The usual scenario was known to everyone, especially when the boat was too small and too old. Thousands had died trying to cross the Mediterranean and thousands more would drown in the future. It was only a matter of days when the half-devoured corpses would be recovered somewhere either north or south.

"We went to the police in the hope they were caught by the authorities, but the kids held in custody there were arrested one week ago on Algerian soil. Something wrong must have happened ... I know it ... I have a heavy heart and a bad feeling. *Astagfirullah,* I ask pardon from Allah. Anything that happens is already written in our books."

I recalled the young Sami, who once upon a time used to sleep in my lap. He was a very nice kid — handsome and intelligent. What a waste!

"What are you going to do? I mean, can't you contact the Italian embassy or something?"

"Are you kidding?" he asked incredulously.

"What do you mean?"

"Do you think they will be bothered? His own country doesn't even care."

"They have human rights and their hearts are filled with compassion, at least compared to us," I said.

"Do not start one of your lectures about human rights and democracy. You know very well they have learned everything from us — we Muslims are the best people brought out to the world."

His answer made my blood boil. "For how long should we continue to live in such nonsense? You said they have learnt everything from us; can you tell me a single thing?"

"I told you ... everything," he doggedly repeated.

"Out of this everything, can you mention just one thing?" I persisted.

"Science, your so-called human rights ... everything," he countered.

"The people of Mecca lived in darkness, unaware of the world around them. Only through *fath* (invasion) were they able to see the light of civilization. Those people, who had been conquered, translated knowledge into Arabic and then later — from the

4th century onward — came some learned men, mostly from Persia, with new ideas. Then, as *fath,* invasion, stopped for so many reasons, the Arabs returned to their most favorite pastime: *jawari,* concubines, and *ghilman,* homosexual slave-soldiers." I said. According to the Qur'an, the *ghilman* were creatures who work alongside their female counterparts called the *houris* in Paradise, in the service of the righteous Muslims. The promise of this reward is repeated four different times in the Qur'an,I thought.

"Nonsense," he snapped. "Omar Farouk could not sleep for fear that a single person of the people living under his rule could not afford his or her dinner."

"I doubt his motives were truly pious. Most of the stories related to this are with women who are either widows or whose husbands were in *futuhat* or Muslim conquests. Besides, can you answer this? Why did he conspire to usurp power from Ali, the fourth rioghteously guided caliph? Read books about him before you talk."

"*A'udhu Billah,* (I seek refuge in god) how can you speak such nonsense?" Ziad said with consternation.

"I'm just telling you what I read … I spent some of my time and energy — and often long hours after work, scrutinizing the personalities of these *sahaba* (prophet's companions) scattered here and there. It was a difficult task, for Arabs tend to misinform, but I think nothing is impossible for a genuine truth seeker."

"I can't believe it — this *shaitan* you have inside is an *efreet,* a very powerful demon." Ziad smiled to cover the sting of his remark and I laughed. "Shame, Satan man, you speak evil of Omar like the Shi'ites in Iran."

"Not only in Iran, my friend," I teased. "Don't forget the Shi'ites of Bahrain, Iraq, and even Saudi Arabia … they are everywhere, open your eyes."

"Are you a Shi'ite now?" He asked.

"Why do you ask this? Have you ever seen me whipping

myself and lamenting over a murder that had happened 14 centuries ago?"

"By Allah, you are right. They are fools. All of them will go to Hell as Prophet Mohammed, peace be upon him, had once promised," he said.

"They have some grounds for what they say," I replied. "I mean, you need to know why they said those things before you judge them. They are not like those *"imbeciles heureux"* (happy but stupid) in Saudi Arabia, who want to kill all the Shi'ites of the world in defense of *sahaba,* prohet's companions."

"You know what? If you continue to think in this way, I swear by Allah, the one who cuts your throat will go directly to *jannah* (Heaven)," Ziad said. I laughed at his cruelty, but Ziad only offered a smile that did not reach his eyes.

"The best example is that the prophet, when he was close to death, asked the *sahaba* to bring a *roka'a* (a piece of leather) on which he would appoint his successor. Omar, the second future caliphate and one of Mohammad's closest companions immediately refused, saying they had the book of Allah, and besides, the prophet was very delirious. They should give him some rest. Why on Earth did he behave like that if not from fear of being deprived from his part in the cake?" I went on.

"His reaction was normal. He truly loved the prophet. In fact, I would be surprised if his reaction was different," Ziad said. I heard his chair squeak as he shifted his weight.

"That old excuse no longer holds up. The people are no longer stupid, Ziad. There is what is called discourse analysis. People are starting to ask — secretly, of course. But, one day, the questions will be in public and every one of the Muslim world will become a Zachariah Boutros, for example," I said.

"Zachariah, who? Oh God, that devil who attacks Islam every day on the Al Hayat channel? Do not worry. Your mentor is going to die in the most obscene way," he replied.

Silent anger coursed in my veins. "That's not the question. I mean if, *la samaha Allah* (God forbid), he was murdered by some narrow-minded *salafist*, the real question is, can your sheikhs give answers to his innumerable questions about Islam? If so, why don't they do it? They have hundreds of Islamic channels," I said.

Ziad moved uncomfortably in his seat and twitched his left ear. "They do not think it is necessary to answer a mad priest like him who does not even speak good Arabic."

"That's not an excuse and you know it. But suppose you are right, though the man has a B.A. in Arabic, do you think some grammar mistakes would hinder the thousands of ideas he brings forth every week? Come on, give me something solid."

"He does not do anything, he just reads from old untrustworthy books of some people who died hundreds of years ago," Ziad argued.

"The books you speak of in a disapproving way are the very books mentioned by *imams* during Friday sermons," I said.

"*Imams* know what is right or wrong."

I looked him in the eye and decided to throw the bomb. "And if I tell you that, even in the Qur'an, there are many mistakes, what would you say to that?"

"What? How dare you say such nonsense! The Qur'an is full of so many scientific truths. Scientists in the U.S.A. are embracing Islam every day."

"I know that in the heart of your hearts you don't believe this nonsense. Believe me, there are all types of errors: scientific, linguistic, historical, etc."

"You must be hallucinating. The Qur'an is a living miracle. All prophets got their immediate miracles, but the Prophet Mohammed asked for an everlasting one and he got it — the holy Qur'an. Shame, Shaitan man, and have fear from an Allah who is *shadidu al ikab* (very severe in his punishment)."

I laughed again, but this time I received an angry fist on my nose. For a long second, the world went momentarily black. As

I overcame the sudden pain and opened my eyes, I saw Ziad holding a chair and about to hit me on the head. I ducked away and gave him a left hook, which made him fall to the ground, half dazed and writhing in pain. The desire to unleash my anger ebbed. It was useless to continue the farce. Perhaps, I was wrong after all.

CHAPTER 35

To my mind, "Cuba la Vieja" is the most beautiful café in the world. Obviously, it is not an impartial judgment, but *'beauty is in the eyes of the beholder,'* as they say. Its owner was a grocery store owner, but he got the brilliant idea of transforming his shop into a café. In a few years his place became one of the most prestigious cafés in Hydra ,Algeria, and of course he became a millionaire. Yet he still spoke in broken French, and dressed in the most unfashionable way. As my old mum says, "If money does not open every door, it surely transforms the monkey into a lion."

After the quarrel with Ziad and the usual nagging of my mum when she heard the news, I thought an hour or so at "cuba la vieja" make me feel better. My eyes were thirsty for beauty, craving a world that seemed to me full of life compared to the dreary atmosphere of the Gulf. That evening I knew I was going to meet someone special, I felt it in the air, brewing like the Arbi coffee (Turkish coffee) of my mum.

Part of me wanted to play the role of the gigolo — the handsome, strong man — but another part cried out for love and a family. I dressed in my best clothes and went to that beautiful place where the cheapest house in its vicinity cost $1 million.

As poor as I was, I needed to dress well, so I was forced to spend more time than usual in front of the mirror. If I did not present a proper image, I would be exposed and shunned with disgrace. The people who sat there were polite, extremely well bred and with good manners, but the moment they discovered you did not belong to their world, their eyes would mirror an unbearable disdain, and even hatred. Only the rich sat there. But luckily, at least theoretically, everyone had the right to sit side by side with those lucky few who owned more than 80 percent of the wealth in Algeria.

I took a seat at the far corner and started my favorite hobby: observing and meditating. Luckily, nobody noticed I was poor and the people watched me with respect and awe. I was filled with vanity seeing how favorably strangers looked at me. They assumed I lived in Europe, had a nice car and a beautiful house by the sea. My appearance as a rich and handsome man always contradicted the fact that I lived in one of the poorest neighborhoods of the Raïs Hamidou district, named after Raïs Hamidou and also called Hammida or Amidon (in American literature.) Hamidou was a famous Algerian corsair who captured many ships during his career. He was known for his gallantry and chivalry, but was killed by an American fleet commanded by Stephen Decatur in 1815. The commune of Raïs Hamidou in Algiers is named after him.

I had been sitting there for a while when I saw her walking like a goddess, and without even beckoning to any one of them, the waiters huddled around her like servants. In a second, the table was ready, cleaned and tidied up. The rare chairs were now available — one for her and the other for her Chihuahua dog. But the beautiful queen was not impressed. It was obvious that she felt they were only doing what they were supposed to do.

She was beautiful, like a light shower, following a spring sunrise; so delicate, like an Arab deer. Oh yes! She was that beautiful. In every gesture she showed a touch of grace and gentility. For a long moment the world stopped turning and my heart skipped a beat. Of course you know that feeling, but in my case multiply it by ten. At that very moment I knew I had fallen in love and my third eye told me what a great pain I was going to endure.

Then came the first blow to this lovely scene. One of the servants, whose teeth resembled those of a bulldog, brought her a hookah and a large cup of mint tea. She spoke with him about the *walaa* (hot coal) and he darted for a new one. I had always detested hookah. I thought it was coarse and vulgar. A hand like hers should not hold a *jabbad* (a hookah hose). A mouth like hers should not inhale the stale tobacco and make water gurgle by her feet, I thought.

On second thought, the hose of the hookah, in her hand, looked like a scepter in the hand of the Queen of England. That was the first lovely blow, I say, and the second best thing I liked about her.

She sat alone, unaware of the world around her and I, like a thirsty nomad, watched the beautiful fountain of fresh water and bit at my lip. From time to time she would flip open her expensive cell phone and I could hear her lovely voice and the excellent French she used in her conversations. It was curious how every word she pronounced seemed to touch some secret cord inside my heart.

The third time she answered the phone she spoke in Arabic, and clearly she was speaking to a man. "Where are you, *ya sakhta* (bastard)?" Her black eyes suddenly became almost wet and were full of that special glint when a woman addresses a special man. "Still in the U.S.A.?"

My rival lived in the U.S.A. I was relieved but for a short while. Then came the second hard blow. "I told you I'm ready to come and stay with you a whole year. The kids are old enough now, and to tell you the truth, I'm really bored here." A sword pierced my heart. I lit a cigarette and bit at my lip.

"Okay. When you arrive, call me. Do not forget, *ya khayeb* (mischievous man)" my princess said. She tossed her phone into her designer bag, her eyes happy and full of dreams. I finished my cigarette and unconsciously made a fist with my hand. Despite myself, I became like a teenager and secretly cast glances at her. I smiled at myself and my embarrassment when she turned round and caught me spying on her. She shifted in her seat, then passed a hand through her hair and smoothed a wayward lock.

Half an hour later, my princess gave the servant a note of twenty *dinars*. Not even waiting for the change, she lifted up the dog from her lap and stood to leave. She opened a new car from a button of her remote control and got in. I envied the dog, which continued to kiss her cheeks and her lovely neck.

The sky was gray now; though a short time earlier it had been azure blue. The servant gave me a smile, which meant he'd expected a generous tip. The beautiful "Cuba la Vieja" became empty without her. I lit another cigarette, then left.

CHAPTER 36

The neighborhood where I lived was not at all an ideal place in which one could live peacefully. The streets were narrow and dark. The houses were old as well as small. And the narrow turns had their own secrets — the perfect place for thieves to divide their loot, prostitutes to pay their pimps and customers to get their recreational drugs. Being born here, I had developed the necessary toughness and street smartness, without which no one could live safely.

When I reached Hamidou district, I found a fight going on not far away from my house. A drunk was threatening one of the youngsters with a knife while an old prostitute with blood oozing from her mouth was cursing and throwing large stones at the son whose left eye was swollen shut. He seemed indifferent to the danger. Actually, the young man, who was peddling every type of prescription pill, refused to give the old man anything without money.

As I took the second turn to the right, I found Noureddine, my neighbor, pounding on the door of his house with his feet and fists and sometimes his head. He greeted me, then resumed the pounding. His wife, Najia, a woman not to meddle with, refused to open the thick, rusted iron door. She simply reprimanded him for being drunk. Of course, she was right. As my mum always said, 'His children are starving and he spends the money he earns to buy muharramat (forbidden things.)' Najia, his wife, had stopped being prostitute years ago, but Noureddine could not forget the bitter truth ... even though he had been the pimp.

Mum smelled of garlic and tomato sauce. She's cooking either spaghetti or couscous, I thought. As I stretched my hand towards the pot, I received the usual slap on my hand. "Can't you wait? Go and sit … it will be ready in a few minutes," she said.

I turned on the TV and watched the Al Jazeera channel. Dhawahiri was giving one of his speeches promising *jihad,* blood and death to America. Then the nice-looking female newscaster spoke about the tolls of death in different countries: Iraq, Pakistan, Yemen, Somali and Afghanistan. People were dying by the hundreds, most of them by suicide bombers. I cursed under my breath, then switched it off, went to my room and opened Hazem's book.

The noise and clamor of the battle outside would not let me concentrate, so I too went out and, despite myself, enjoyed the action film that was still taking place. The old prostitute was now screaming in a raucous voice and beating her breast and tearing at her hair. Her loud voice could be heard above all the other voices.

"They are going to kill each other. Blood will be shed tonight," she lamented.

Her son was now armed with a bigger knife than the drunk. The two men were now threatening each other, all the while keeping a distance. When the wailing of a police car became audible, the crowd dispersed and calm was restored. The dust from the excited stomping feet rose from the ground in little swirls and dissipated into a starry sky. Whether it was summer or winter, down through the years, no day was spent without a fuss.

I thought about my encounter with the princess at "Cuba la Vieja." *How can a woman like her think of a man like me?* I smiled at the thought and went inside. I found a delicious dinner awaiting me.

If anyone in the world deserved my love and respect, it was no doubt my old mum. A few mouthfuls of couscous, the traditional Algerian dish, and a large glass of Laban were all that were necessary to restore the serenity of my mind and heart. As I lay down on my bed, the picture of my princess sifted through my mind again. The darkness of her eyes brought me serenity and comfort, but I kept tossing and turning.

Only Hazem's book could lull me to sleep. I cursed under my breath, and then I opened the Bible. I read about how Jesus blessed the little children and said, "Let the little children come to me, and do not forbid them; for of such is the kingdom of heaven." (Matt 19:14) It was hard to believe that such a highly humane message was written more than 2,000 years ago.

The next morning a demon oppressed my spirit once again. Love to a person like me was a kind of joke. The story of Jesus was a nice story, but gone were the days when one could love his enemy or turn the other cheek. At least the world in which I lived was full of wolves, and there was no place for lambs.

I remember that I decided, once again, not to read it anymore — I was getting too weak, too sensitive, I thought. I was becoming an addict and each time I read the book, something inside me was gone forever. My conscience pricked at me even when I looked at a woman. I was being transformed into a saint and saints had no place in the 21st century. In the absence of Allah and his nice reward, it was futile to live like a hermit, I thought. Besides I had only a few days to live — as soon as my pockets became empty, I had decided to kill myself.

I welcomed the day with a renewed desire to pursue my best hobby and therapy: chasing women. The rich neighborhoods abounded with them and all I had to do was to dress up like a prince and live, even falsely, the illusion of being rich. If Allah did not exist and his *jannah* (paradise) was a fallacy, then only that addiction brought real bliss and distraction to my storm-tossed mind.

Those women of high birth — born in silk and fed with a spoon of gold were the perfect prey for my revenge, the revenge of the poor, if you know what I mean. My *foutuhat* (invasions) had no limits. I did not really understand by what miracle, these women, whom every man was after, became like puppets in the hands of someone like me. I felt I was like Ibn Arbi, the great Sufi who wrote a book called *Futuhat Makkiyah* (Meccan Invasions), but in my own way, of course. I had a Sufi twisted heart and a Mohammadean metaphorical sword — all that in the body and soul of a *ronin*.

CHAPTER 37

I had never gone out with a woman who wore a *hijab* and was serious about religion. And the spectacle of a woman black-gowned and doing very intimate things was no doubt a great experience that I did not want to miss before I died.

The woman that caught my attention drove a luxury SUV. She was the only daughter of a man who owned half the businesses of a middle class district not far away from where I lived. It was said that he had started poor and climbed the ladder slowly and very painfully. That explained the lack of etiquette as she climbed out of her car and slammed the door shut. That clumsiness I recognized — it went with the genes and never disappeared, I thought.

Our eyes met in a Hydra shopping center. She smiled and I smiled back. Then we pushed our shopping carts in opposite directions. I forgot about her and she must have forgotten about me. After about half an hour, as I was about to turn the corner towards the cashier, our carts collided.

"We are destined to meet again," she said with a smile. The tiny bluish bruise on her forehead meant she never missed a *sajdah* (prostration.) She was sad-eyed and dry like an old palm tree branch, but her faith in Allah's destiny was almost insane.

"Have you got a name?" I asked. She laughed and the bad smell of her mouth filled my nostrils. She must be fasting, I deduced.

"Is there anyone who does not have a name?" She asked instead of answering.

"There are people who have no names — prisoners, for example. And people who have more than two names — artists, as a case in point." It was on the tip of my tongue to mention terrorists, but I opted for silence.

"If I were a prisoner, then how could I be strolling along with my cart in a prestigious Hydra neighborhood?" she asked. Again, it was on the tip of my tongue to say that, in fact, she was a prisoner. "Nobody knows — anything is possible," I said and she laughed and I tried to imagine what she was thinking. *He's handsome, smart and funny. Oh Allah! Thanks for such a generous reward.*

"My name is Fatima, and you — do you have a name?"

"Actually, I do have one. My name is Jamal. But I'm planning to get another one someday." If the truth be told, I always dreamed about changing my name to John. I did not know why until I read the Bible of Hazem.

"Are you an actor?" Fatima asked.

"Why do you ask that?"

"Because you look like you could be one, she said. "May Allah grant peace and honor to our prophet and his family," she added. To shun the evil eye, people in Algeria tend to ask God to pray for Mohammed each time they admire or gloat about something.

There is no *hishmah* (shyness) in religion," she continued.

"Do you work?" I asked.

"I prepare dinners for ambassadors and diplomats. Actually I'm rich and do not need to work, but I love cooking. This evening I'm going to the Japanese Embassy.

"You cook Japanese food?" I asked, rather amazed.

"I can cook anything."

"You must have studied somewhere."

"I never studied at any cooking school. I only watched some cooking programs on the national channel or read about their food in some cookbooks. But most of the time I watched international cooking programs, and then copied what I learned. I learned everything by watching. It is not difficult, you know. You just need the gift and a desire to learn. And you?" she asked.

For a moment her eyes brightened with big dreams. I assumed that she was in a hurry to know the reward for her long hours of prostrations in front of an all-knowing Allah. "I'm a teacher ... I teach English."

"My sister is a teacher. She lives with her husband in Saudi Arabia!" she exclaimed. Her tone conveyed a sense of boasting, as though that hellish kingdom was a kind of paradise or something. I grimaced at the thought.

"I was in the Gulf this past year," I said.

"You don't seem to like it. Where were you?"

"Sultanate of Oman."

"There is not any money there. I've heard it is called the India of the Gulf."

Actually, she was right, I thought. Oman was poor and I believe that the Omani people are some of the stingiest people in the world, but compared to Saudi Arabia, Oman was a real paradise.

" the salary is the same everywhere," I said instead.

"Yes, but in Saudi Arabia, Kuwait or UAE, you can give private lessons."

"You know the situation very well. I'm impressed."

"My sister told me everything — what a coincidence, *sobhana Allah* (praise to Allah)," she replied.

I did not see the coincidence she saw, but I nodded in agreement. "Do you do *salat* (prayer)?" she asked. Her question caught me unaware, but I was decided to tell her the truth. As I said before, the Bible of Hazem had contaminated my mind.

"No, I don't even fast Ramadan."

Fatima laughed and seemed to enjoy my frankness. "Shame on you! But do not worry; Allah has put me in your way to make you return to Him."

I smiled mechanically. She had a divine mission now. She had appointed herself my savior and I was the lucky man astray who needed her sacred help.

"Where do you live?" she asked. That question had always been a thorn in my side. Where I lived people still fought using knives and swords; where I lived people drank petrol mixed with alcohol to get intoxicated. "Sidi Yahya," I lied and prayed she did not ask for the address.

"I thought you were from Dreira. I think I saw you there once. I live In Hydra, but my father's house and business is in the old Kouba — not far away from where you live."

Though she was dressed in a moderate way and the cheap scarf around her pale face covered most of her bosom, I knew by instinct that she lived in a rich neighborhood. She gave me her number and we agreed to meet the following day in Casbah Park, a beautiful place by the sea where one could have a nice walk, drink a good cup of coffee or perhaps kiss a woman away from prying eyes. As I left the bustling mall, my conscience bothered me, but that time I decided not to listen. I just smiled and said to myself, *'Pourquoi pas?'* Why not?

CHAPTER 38

We met outside Casbah Park the next evening; I found Fatima waiting for me in her car. I was late, but she was calmly playing with her cell phone and did not raise her head until I tapped on the window.

"Didn't you see me?" I asked.

"I was listening to some Qur'anic verses … did you expect me to stare at every passerby?"

No doubt Fatima was pious, but I felt she was showing off a little. I noticed the green beads around her wrist — the beads of a Meccan rosary, most probably a gift from her sister in Saudi Arabia.

"What is this in your hand?" I asked.

"A rosary. You have never seen one?"

"Do not tell me you have been praising the Lord on our first date?"

Fatima laughed and climbed out of her car. "I was asking God to protect you and your mother, the *hajja*, (old mother). I was also asking God to help my sick dad." Though there were tears in her eyes, I do not remember feeling the least amount of sympathy. "I'm sorry," I said without conviction.

As we strolled around the park we saw a couple hugging each other and stealing a kiss from time to time. Fatima swallowed a sigh and then whispered almost to herself, "Astaghfirullah, I ask pardon from Allah."

I laughed and she smiled. Her face was red with embarrassment. "Nowadays, most girls do not care about Allah. They commit *haram* (forbidden things by islamic law) and do not care about their family or even the *ha'kem* (police.) Did you see what she was doing? She was —"*Astaghfirullah.*" I ask pardon from Allah."

"They were simply hugging and kissing," I said, and laughed. She did not smile. "Do you think it is okay for that woman to be kissing a man that is not her husband, or even her fiancée?"

"*Les moeurs ont changer* (habits have changed)," I said in French.

"To some, maybe." She gave me a strange glance out of the corner of her eye. "I believe that *haram* is *haram*. We cannot change what Allah has decreed."

"You are right, but after all, who told you she was not his wife?"

"His wife? Are you serious? Why meet in the street? They would have a house for that!"

"Maybe they are bored — anyway, they were just kissing," I said.

"I will tell you something … *rijal* (men) no longer desire to marry because they have these sluts in every corner of the street. Why marry if they can get everything they want anytime they would like it?"

"Marriage is not just a sexual relationship," I countered with a smile to cover the sting of my remark.

"Allah almighty refers to marriage in the context of sex, or *nikah*. You know better than Allah?" She asked.

I wanted to ask, what if Allah was not the real God we should follow. What if Mohammed had, for some reason or another, decided to become an important person and chose prophet hood to reach his goals? What if all you had ever heard since you were young was not true at all? What if you discovered that you had been praying to the real Shaitan? Instead, I said, "I think sex is very important in a relationship."

"If it is *halal* (permissible by Islamic law), it is the best and most important thing," she said.

"Will you believe me if I tell you something?"

"Why shouldn't I?" I replied. Truth be told, I didn't know why, but I had decided not to believe anything she was about to tell me.

"I saw you last night in a dream — the same hair, the same shoulders, the same eyes." Her revelation caught me unaware again and aroused my curiosity, but I kept silent. "You were dressed in green and you told me not to think too much, for you were there to stand by my side."

She stopped for a second, sized me up, and then continued almost to herself. "I did not want to go shopping yesterday — normally, my sister's husband goes instead. But he was sick and his car had a problem — the battery, I think. Anyway, I didn't want to go but my mum kept whimpering and complaining so I got my keys and stormed out. *Sobhana Allah* (praise to Allah), I never anticipated I was going to see you there. It was definitely *maktoub* (fate.) It is something written."

I was only half-listening. My eyes locked on her red lips and her hazel eyes, which looked to me so thirsty for rain. "Life is full of wonders," I said.

"It is not life — it is Allah and *al-Qadar* (destiny)," she replied.

I wanted to tell her that what the Muslim world calls al-Qadar was mostly a human choice, or more probably a reaction to an action. If the God of the Bible was really true, then we should believe that we are created in God's image and therefore we are free to choose and to create al-Qadar. But again, on reflection, I decided to remain silent. I looked at my watch and was amazed at how slow time was passing.

"Are you bored (déjà) already?" she asked.

I wracked my brain for a suitable answer. "No … there is a football match: Algeria versus France. A friendly game, but you know, France is France," I offered as an excuse.

"Don't worry; they will air it at 10. My sister's husband spent the whole day speaking about it. It always gets on my nerves when he speaks about football, but I try my best to keep my feelings to myself. Tell me about yourself; do you have any brothers or sisters?"

I lied and told her I had only one sister. Again, I was ashamed of myself and fell silent. I secretly cursed Hazem's book.

"Don't you want to have a family … beautiful kids and a warm home? Don't you want to return to Allah? Life is so short and nobody knows when death comes." She looked me in the eye and went on. "My only dream is to visit the holy Mecca, but I need a *mohram* (a husband or a very close relative)) for you know I can't do pilgrimage alone."

I looked past her. Did not she know that during Jahilia, period before Islam, women used to hover around Mecca naked and that the Hajj (pilgrimage) probably came from *hakk* (rubbing), a form of pagan ritual in which women used to rub their period cloths against the black stone for fertility?

"I think you can go through an agency," I said instead. Dismay clouded her face. "Yes, but most *olamaʾa* (theologians) do not like it. They say it's *makrouh* (detestable)."

"In Oman they offered me a free ticket to the Hajj," I said.

"And of course you went. How lucky you are!" she exclaimed.

"No, I thought they were going to give me an extra bonus for the trouble. I mean — the hard journey and the long days in a densely-crowded spot, almost naked but for a white cloth around one's waist and shoulders."

She laughed and shook her head. "Is there anyone in this world who gets a chance to visit the holy Mecca and does not go?"

"Yes — me," I said as my blood pressure began to rise.

"*Allah yahdik,* (may Allah lead you to his righteous path,)" she whispered.

I smiled wryly and fell silent. As we walked I took her hand and found it hot and sweaty. I pushed her against a tree and gave her a long kiss. She responded like a tigress at first and then she pushed me back.

"Have you lost your mind? Do you think I'm one of those sluts?" she asked.

"Don't you like it?" I teased.

"No, it is *haram;* I have to do my ablutions again."

"What for?"

"You are going to lead me to Hell," she cried out.

"Kisses are nothing; you may kiss and then do *salat.* Prophet Mohammed used to kiss his wife Aisha in the middle of the holy month of Ramadan."

"He is a prophet, I am not," she replied.

"You said half the truth. Normally, he should have set the example."

"What do you mean?"

"If he were a prophet, he should have behaved in a more pious way, and his wife should not have told these intimate things to other people."

"You sound as if you are not a Muslim," she said.

I weighed my options and then decided to spell everything out. Again, I inwardly cursed Hazem and his book. "Yes, I have my own doubts. A man at the age of 53 who marries a nine-year-old girl makes me think not only twice, but a thousand times, about his true character.

"A nine-year-old of that time is like 17 these days," Fatima said.

"Why, do you think 1,400 years is such a long time in what scientists sometimes call genetic evolution? But let's pretend you are right. Do you think it is fair to see an old man with a girl as old as his daughter? What would you think if I married a 16-year-old girl?"

"The people would laugh at you and she would most probably cheat on you," she spat out.

"Exactly. And how do you accept such a scandal by a *qudwa* (a model) like him?"

"Before, people did not think in the way we think nowadays," she said.

"If so, then let's do away with some verses from the Qur'an because they are no longer appropriate for our time."

"*Astagfirullah,* are you nuts?"

"You said it yourself."

"I did not mean that …" She stopped, looking for the right words. "I wanted to say that every age has its customs and traditions. Nowadays, we live in a different world. The people are no longer ignorant — you see what I mean? But the Qur'an fits every age and every country."

"Okay, would you accept the fact that I have sex with a young, handsome boy?" My question took her unprepared.

"*Astagfirullah,* if you do it, you don't even deserve to breathe the fresh air of *jannah,* heaven." she said, obviously appalled at the idea.

"Do you agree with me that it is absolutely wrong?"

"Yes, of course. Are you kidding?"

"Then, since times have changed and there is an international law that condemns pedophilia, we should delete all the verses in the Qur'an that speak about the *wildan* (young children)."

"What do you mean?" she asked.

"The *wildan* are the reward of the pious in the hereafter, together with al hour al ayn (beautiful virgin concubines)."

"I never heard about this. Are you drunk or something?" Fatima asked, visibly shaken.

"I'm in my complete intellectual capacities. I can even tell you why you don't hear about these things. Because the *olamaʾa* (Muslim theologians) know it is wrong. So, as it's their custom, they tend to hide and misinform. But you can trace it in a more blatant way in the Gulf region, especially with the old generations, the ones whom anthropologists would consider not contaminated by the civilized world."

"I wonder why you use your time following trivial things. It is very easy — just do *salat,* and fast Ramadan (the holy Muslim month), then live your life like everybody else."

"I wish I could — actually, I tried but there was always that emptiness inside my heart. You see, I have lost ten years of my life studying the Qur'an. I remember that, at the beginning of my spiritual quest, I was looking forward to dying as *shahid* (a martyr.) I wanted, no I dreamed that I would blow myself up like the hundreds I saw on the Internet. I wanted to be a soldier in the sacred army of bin Laden. I even saw him in a vision about one year before the September 11 attack on the U.S. He wanted me and I had thought I let him down. But I began to wonder about ... too many difficult questions. When I was in Oman, I immersed myself in books and now ... I'm a free man." I was about to say that the Jesus of Hazem had a special place in my heart now, but in reality, I was a *ronin*.

"I wonder why you don't try to live like everybody else. I mean, you are handsome; you have a good job, why on Earth do you bother yourself with things that are so complicated? I mean, everyone knows that if we do *salat* and fast Ramadan and go to Hajj — if we have the means, of course, then everything will be okay. Even if we are tortured by the fire of Hell, it won't be for a long time. That's enough for me and any ordinary Muslim," Fatima concluded.

"You seem so sure of what you say," I cut in.

"What I say is written in the Holy Qur'an. No Muslim — whether Shiite or Sunni — would question it."

"And if I tell you that the Qur'an is not from Allah, what would you say?" I had finally thrown a bomb and her face darkened with gloom and concern.

"I thought you were kidding ... are you sure that's how you think? I mean, because even a child knows that the Qur'an is above every suspicion," she said while she pressed the rosary in her hand till her knuckles were white.

"Who told you so?" I questioned.

"Every person ... even the prophet himself."

"Who told you he was a real prophet from God?"

"What do you mean?"

"I mean, he was a genius, no doubt, for he was able to con everyone, or at least most. I personally like the Wafd of Najran (Najran commission). They came and asked him trick questions. His most blatant mistake was in Surat Mariam. He pretended that the mother of Jesus was the sister of Aaron and Moses. The commission knew they were in front of a false prophet about whom Saint John spoke more than 500 years ago. They paid him *jizya* (Muslim tax), provided he let them live in peace and free to practice their faith. He let them depart in peace, but shortly after, most of them were killed or exiled. I also like Abu Jahl. He fought to the end and then died like a hero. When Ibn Masoud put his feet on his neck, Abu Jahl smiled and told him that he would remain a shepherd and a slave nonetheless. Ibn Masoud cut Abu Jahl's throat and brought the head to the prophet, who became very glad and prayed to his Allah a prayer of thanks," I explained.

"It is not you who speaks right now. I believe it is the Shaitan (Satan) inside you," Fatima countered.

"At least my *shaitan* fights for freedom and for human rights. At least he knows what is right and what is wrong. Without my *shaitan,* this country would have been another Taliban."

"We do not need your *shaitan*. Boutafliqua has already imposed it on our heads and you see, now, the consequences." Her voice rang with sarcasm.

"Do you know that even Boumedian, the former Algerian president, is better than Mohammad? At least he did not concoct a doctrine by which ordinary men and women are suddenly transformed into murderers in the name of Allah."

Fatima weighed her options, then decided to opt for diplomacy. She was over 40 and she needed a husband. "I think it's your opinion after all, and I'm sure you will change one day. As for me, I believe in God and I respect the prophet, may he rest in peace."

I smiled and took her hand. When we kissed again, it was me who pushed her away. As we drove towards the Japanese Embassy, where she worked that night, I thought how stupid I was for precipitating things. I could have postponed my debate for a week or so, but, again, it was all because of Hazem's book. I should not have read it. I should not have opened the door to that Son of Man called Emmanuel.

As we walked up to the entrance of Japanese Embassy, she turned to face me and as our eyes met she knew and I knew we would never meet again. I smiled then I left her as she was greeted at the doorway with the traditional konbanwa (good evening.).

Pervasively, in my heart of hearts, I was proud of myself. I was forever free from the bondage of Islam, though, for the first time in my life, I had allowed my prey to escape unharmed. Late at night I tossed and turned in my bed and my firm decision about the Bible began to melt little by little. Only when I read the prayer that Jesus taught to his disciples was I able to sleep.

"Our father in Heaven,
Hallowed be your name.
Your Kingdom come.
Your will be done
On Earth as it is in Heaven.
Give us day by day our daily bread
And forgive us our sins,
For we also forgive everyone who is
Indebted to us.
And do not lead us into temptation,
But deliver us from the evil one." (Matthew 6:9)
(For thine is the kingdom and the power and glory forever.)

CHAPTER 39

The next morning was a Sunday, which meant flea market day. The flea market was the place where I used to buy my second-hand clothes, but at that time, my suitcase was crammed with Italian and French clothes. Still, the desire to be the false, happy, wealthy, young man ebbed. Deep in my heart there was a growing desire to be who I am.

My mum was, as usual, busy praying to a heedless Allah. It seemed to me that the more she prayed, the more her dream of seeing me happy and well off went away. Or probably, she was in fact worshipping the beast without noticing it, as Hazem had once told me. I remember his words very clearly: "I believe in this book because 600 years before the arrival of Mohammed, John saw in his revelations the false prophet, the beast and the Shaitan. Your skeptical mind is searching for a solid truth — here it is, my friend, as bitter as an Omani coffee."

As usual, mum and I spoke only about the necessary things, but our bonds were so deep that a simple "*Sabah el Khir*" (good morning) meant countless things to both of us.

"Your coffee is in the kitchen and your eggs also," she said while she held to her rosary, her rock in turbulent waters. Without even thanking her, I went to the kitchen and ate my breakfast. "Our neighbor is going to circumcise his son; the celebration is for tonight." By that she meant I needed to come early and prepare a 20-*dinar* note to give the father of the child.

"Wasn't he circumcised some years ago," I asked, annoyed.

"That was his grandson. You forgot he married again after

the death of his wife, may she rest in peace." I cursed under my breath and went to the bathroom.

"You do not seem to care. Last year he gave a 50-*dinar* note for your sister's wedding, and his late wife gave 20," she called through the bathroom door.

I washed my hands nervously and cursed under my breath again. The 20 *dinars* I was ready to sacrifice were not enough.

"You do not seem to care about anything," Mum continued. People younger than you are married and have their own houses and their own kids, but you continue to behave as if you were 20. Do you think I don't know about prostitutes you chase every day and over whom you squander your money?"

It really hurt to hear her say that to me. My hands turned into fists and I could see my knuckles turning white, but my old mum had diabetes and I had to keep my mouth shut.

"You do not even listen when I talk to you." She had a captive audience now and she would not quit. "When are you going to have a brain and be like everyone else? Look at Ahmed, your friend. He works like you and started working after you were appointed to your teaching position. Yesterday I saw him driving a brand new car, his wife by his side. He has even built his house on the third floor. All your friends have done something with their lives and you continue to live like a vagrant."

Actually, my mum was right but she was uneducated and could not understand why I was like that. Ahmed, whom she thought was the perfect model, was a very frugal man who worked like a slave and deprived himself from everything. He didn't even go to a café. I never saw him wearing new clothes or having fun. That kind of life I had lived for so long a time when I was young. My reasoning was very simple: if I was destined to finish the rest of my days in that way, I would rather not live at all. As I had lost my job forever and had decided to spend all my money and continue to live my false decent life until the time when my money ran out and I was no longer able to live with a modicum of comfort. When that happened, I had already decided to kill myself. I just hadn't decided the method by which I would leave this world for the next, and hopefully better, life.

A friend of mine did it; he had been happy that day. He was so happy that I had been amazed, for he had been always depressed and gloomy. We had gone to the Turkish bath that day and I remember he had asked me to rub his back. In the dressing room he had prayed two *rakaʿat* (prostrations). I had never seen him performing *salat* (prayer.) I watched him, unable to figure out the secret behind the sudden transformation. "Life is so beautiful," he said, "especially when you find a way to leave it to go to a better place."

"Have they granted you a visa to Holland?" I asked, because he had always dreamt to visit Amsterdam.

"No, but where I'm going, no visa is needed," he said matter-of-factly.

"You are going to sneak through the borders?" I asked, questioning his wisdom. "You know the risks, man. Thousands die in the sea."

He smiled, but it was a false smile. I remember, he gave me a strange look and invited me for a coffee. That day, I remember that he kissed everyone and behaved nicely to them. Then a strange cloud came over his face. "It is high time for me to go, my friends. Would you mind taking my bag with you, Jamal? I have to meet someone in Dreira."

Like a naïve bystander, I believed his nonsense and let him go alone. I took his bag to his house. I remember that his mum had been very anxious.

"Where is Hasan?" I heard the trepidation in her voice.

"In Dreira," I said.

"I don't know why, I have a bad feeling," his poor mother said.

Later, when I heard he had thrown himself in front of a train, I felt pain and guilt. I wish I had been perceptive enough to understand the situation. I could have stopped him when there had still been time.

What kind of hopelessness pushes a young, educated man to kill himself in the most atrocious way? Was it the hopelessness of poverty or the fear of its ruthless strike? Or was it simply his inability to cope with the pressures of life? I guess I will never know the answer to that question because, unlike me, Hasan never had a Hazem to tell him that, in an instant, his life could change because of a man that died in his place.

I went to my room and closed my door, took off my clothes and lay down on my bed. I recalled the princess I had seen in "Cuba la Vieja" and everything around me became perfect again, like a palm tree. For a brief moment I felt the whole world needed a woman like her. The whole world — I meant that our Middle Eastern world did not need the United Nations or a security council; it only needed the mesmerizing smile of her eyes. But, little by little, the old worries started to emerge from my subconscious: the poor neighborhood where I lived; my compatriots ready to sell themselves for the beast; Allah as an entity or superstition; Oman, that little hell where I had lost two years of my life; my lost job; the Jesus of Hazem — did he really exist or was he a legend? I opened the Bible and started to read. Like magic, I felt peace and hope.

This man was either a big lie or the real son of God, I thought.

I shunned Shaitan automatically. How could God have a son like we humans? If God loved humans as the Bible said He did, then he may have the same desire to beget a human child. Moreover, if he had appeared to Moses in a bush of fire, then it was more acceptable to my mind that he could have had appeared in human flesh. Slowly, precious sleep came to my eyes and soon I was lost in a beautiful, peaceful slumber.

CHAPTER 40

As I awoke, the *Maghreb* sunset started spilling its blood around the horizon and the *adahn* as though sad for its departure cried, "*Allaho Akbar.*" Mum was sitting on her prayer rug, holding to her rosary — her sword and shield. She looked at me and I knew she was about to start her customary nagging, so I hastily got dressed and went out.

All the men of my neighborhood have become conscience *salafists*, I thought. Most of them grew beards that reached, in some cases, to their navels and some of them dressed like the Taliban. As to the girls in my neighberhood, in general, most of them were prostitutes and their clients were usually from Italy or expatriates who lived in Europe, and visited Algeria during their yearly holiday. Sometimes some rich, local man might appear in his expensive vehicle, but it was very rare because the rich knew more high-end prostitutes, or at least women who were acquainted with etiquette and had good manners.

The Italians loved the dark Mediterranean silhouettes of our girls, so most of the time they took them to their country as their mistresses. From time to time you would hear a nice story. An Italian got married to one of the girls of our neighborhood and had a family. Of course, he was required to proclaim *shahada* (there is no god but Allah, and Mohammed is his messenger), but it was only a formality.

My friends stood in tight knots and watched with a mixture of hatred and lust as any woman not wearing a *hijab* passed by. One year ago, the nicest one among them would have been drunk or engaged in a quarrel with fists or even knives, but now they became devout Muslims and spoke about Islam most of the time. Lots of blood was going to be shed, I thought.

I used to know my friends, and they used to know me, but now they became like strangers — they were not the people I grew up with. The *shilla* (group) watched me, apparently expecting me to join them as they made their way to the mosque. After all, I was in the Holy Land — how could I miss *salat,* prayer? They were deceived, for I was wearing short pants that barely hid my knees.

"That's *awrah,* nakedness, man. Aren't you ashamed of yourself?" said Lotfi, a tall and skinny man in his early 30's. Then he smiled to cover the sting of his remark. I wanted to say that the girls went out almost naked and nobody said a single word. But a man, according to their twisted minds, had to cover his knees and stomach when he went out.

"May Allah cleanse me and show me His righteous path," I said instead.

"Aren't you going to *Maghreb* (sunset prayer)?" He asked.

"No — I do not pray," I said very quickly. My short answer took Lotfi unprepared. Now it was the turn of the man dressed like a Taliban. His name was Faysal. He was short, stout and had spent six years in prison for a rape, I think.

"You know, brother, you can play with anything but *salat.* When you face *kaaba,* you are actually facing Allah, and if you do not face him now you will have to face him in another day." His words stung, but I did not flinch.

"But then you will have to pray on brazen stones and you will have to kneel down before his majesty and our prophet ,peace upon him, could not intercede on your behalf," added another.

I had luckily developed a thick skin — that hard shell of courage that was needed to counter the everlasting intimidating message of Islam. I was no longer afraid of the terrorizing messages I read in books about Islam, or heard on TV, let alone from a bunch of blind sheep like them.

"Anyway, I believe you will have his *shafa'a* (intercession) since you are so sure you are going to Heaven," I said, trying to keep the anger out of my tone.

"Nobody is sure, man," exclaimed Lotfi. "Do you know that Abou bakr Siddik — the first companion of the prophet and the first caliphate, was not sure, and said once he did not trust the cunning of Allah?"

The Allah they prayed for was malicious, intransigent and spiteful. No wonder they had the same nature, I thought. Their Allah was no longer my god. At least not the one I wanted to pray to. And if I was destined to go to Hell, then I probably would say, "*Que la fete commence.*" (Let the party begin.)

"So why does one pray, if he thinks that Allah, at any time, may provoke him to sin and therefore condemn him to Hell?" I asked and smiled to hide the sarcasm that rang in my tone.

There was a brief silence and most of them stared at me in disbelief. Then Lotfi again took the lead, but this time he was visibly irritated and it showed on his face. "God is ruthless, but also merciful. We perform *salat* five times a day to beseech him not to lead us astray, and of course he would not because he is merciful towards His *abid* (slaves.) May the Lord open your eyes, friend." He tapped my shoulders and said "*Salomo Alaykom,*" with mischief in his eyes.

There was also venom in some eyes. Was it a warning or a threat? I wondered. They left me and went to the mosque. It took quite a while to pull myself together. Off in the distance, I could hear them gossiping about me, devouring my flesh with their pious tongues, but I did not care. I had a princess to see and a real goddess to adore.

CHAPTER 41

Cuba la Vieja, the café I often frequented, looked like a flower garden. The rich had their own way of looking at life — and things, and the aura of their comfort caressed my nostrils like a kiss. I sat at the far end with my back to the wall — a perfect spot for meditation and observation. I simply waited for that princess who ruled without a crown. Actually I waited for that sweet skin prickle from head to toe that I experienced the first time I saw her. The world around me was almost absent, I just sat and watched.

"Hello sir," the waiter said. "The usual or would you like something else?" He was ready to lick my shoes for my tips were generous — one of my tricks to hide my true social background.

"No, I want a change this evening. Would you bring me a Shisha, hookah, please?"

"Ok sir, what flavor would you like — or shall I bring the menu?" I never expected that rotten tobacco had a menu of its own.

"I saw a woman a few days ago; she was the only woman after all who smoked Shisha. I liked the smell of her tobacco."

"Madame Dorra, are you ok with mint flavor?"

A slight pang of jealousy pierced my heart. Everyone knew about her, except me the one who burnt for her like a candle. "But I must warn you she brings her special M'assil, tobacco, with her, so do not blame me if it is not that good."

"I won't. Thanks," I said. The man's face became alive again — I mean without that nervous twitch of someone who wanted to please. I shifted in my seat, drummed my fingers on the table.

No doubt I was nervous. I was about to witness the coming of the most beautiful woman in the world.

Falling in love is a strange chemical reaction. In an instant one's heart becomes a rebel and the mind, miraculously, loses control and becomes like a slave if you know what I mean. When Dorra was present everything became pregnant with orchids and jasmine but when she was absent the place was barren and taut. She was that good.

All of a sudden the world stopped turning and my heart lost a beat. I saw her step out of her car, dressed in a blue dress, spotted with white. Her hair was long and loose, thick and generous like the night. Her eyes were dark and wide and fixed in the distance. Our eyes met and for a brief moment of time I felt I could fly.

The way she looked at me was neither casual nor special. It was a cross between the two. But there was a slight glint in them each time our eyes met for a brief second. That connection was very familiar to me. It meant that at that moment I was not any man to her, but someone dangerous enough to turn her upside down.

She sat in front of me but I could only see her back and savor her smell, a mixture of sea breeze and the caress of a smile. Her skin was the color of bronze. She must have spent long hours under the sun wearing perhaps a bikini somewhere — Jerba maybe, for only the sun of that wonderful island created such a magnificent effect.

When she turned to call for the waiter she gave me a quick glance. Her eyes were not as black as I had thought. They were dark hazel; the color of an Arab coffee brewing slowly on brazen coal. There were some slight wrinkles at the corners of those captivating eyes. She must be in her late thirties, I thought.

Then it came — the big blow. I saw her angry for the first time. Strange how those angelic eyes could spark with mischief. Even her voice could be heard like any common woman, saying "No Sir, I was sitting for more than fifteen minutes and you did not come. I'm not sitting in a cheap, popular café in Beb el Wed or Hamidou that would make me wait all this time. Besides I'm not any woman so, *khouya,* (brother) do not do it again. Everyone knows how good I am, but the one who disturbs me pays dearly. I noticed that there are people who are worth nothing and were served before me," she blurted out. The anger that was lurking in those two beautiful eyes had the power to set fire blazing anywhere, I thought. The poor waiter did not know what to say. His face became pale like unripe dates. I never saw a man so afraid of a woman. Of course, I have seen worse — a man beaten up by his wife or kicked out of his own bed, but that man's fear I had not seen in my life.

The nicely manicured fingers were now transformed into brutal iron claws, the claws of a lioness who felt humiliated. I knew her astrological sign at once, a Lion no doubt.

"I swear by Allah I haven't heard you and I did not see you. Do you think I'm stupid to let you waiting?" The waiter explained with a slight tremble in his voice. Dorra's face flinched and she immediately softened her tone, but her shoulders straightened with pride. "*C'est pas grave,*" it is not a big deal," she said in French and then gave one of her smiles that made the whole universe shake while it danced the sexiest oriental ballet.

"As usual, but add a good *walaa,* not like the one yesterday," she ordered.

"*Min inaya*" (with my eyes, I will serve you,) He said. Like a dog, happy when offered a bone for completing a task, the tall, large-shouldered waiter rushed to satisfy his mistress. And they say slavery was abolished.

The crown of my princess was actually a rod, I thought. Her angelic smile was angelic as long she was treated like a queen. I smiled at the thought and the woman sitting in the next table by my side thought it was for her and smiled back. If God existed, I would thank him for only one thing: those good looks he gave me that made me a temptation to every single woman, at least once. Oh yes! I would say, you treated me like a dog, never gave me what I wanted, made me a psych case; but for those lovely moments of self-esteem, I forgive everything, especially all your tenacious tendency not to hear or listen to my prayers even once.

Those things were brewing in my mind when my princess stood up and went to her car. She looked over her shoulders and her gaze locked on me for a long moment. The way she looked at me indicated she was slightly intrigued. She knew all the rich people of Hydra and most of the prestigious neighborhoods of Algiers. I did not belong to her collection. Was she wondering if I was false or genuine? Had her intelligent eyes taken in the fervency of my admiration for her? She was holding her Chihuahua dog and caressing its ears. She looked me in the eye, started the engine of her car and left.

CHAPTER 42

After "Cuba la Vieja" I went for a walk around the rich neighborhood of Hydra. In those lovely houses my mum had worked as a servant. She used to wake up at five a.m. prepare our breakfast and then go on foot to those rich lucky few. She washed their clothes, cleaned their floors and even changed the diapers on their babies. When she returned in the evening, exhausted and most of the time in a very bad mood she never shirked her duties at home. She would clean up our mess, prepare our dinner and wash the feet of my late father.

Father also, after losing the ill-paid job of an *imam* in a mosque not far away from where we lived had worked as a park keeper there. Like a dog, protecting his family, he would faithfully keep his eyes sharp like an eagle on their fancy cars. At times, he would boast that one morning, the nephew of the President bid him good morning. Then there were the times when the hopeless, unemployed would line up in front of our houses, clutching their *curriculum vitas* (copies of their identity cards and resumes, either typed or neatly handwritten.) They would beseech my father to talk to one of the President's family or those who are close to them. My father never said no to anyone who asked for help, but as far as I know, I never heard he was able to find a job for any of them. But people kept coming, and father kept collecting their CVs. He knew they had no chance but kept, nonetheless, listening to their pleas.

He knew some secrets about the most influential families In Algeria. At times, he would swear by Allah to my mum that they were a bunch of drug addicts and losers, but my Mum would not believe him and neither did I, nor did my older sister.

My parents worked hard to protect us from poverty and provided us with a good education. But the germ of hatred and the feeling of injustice were deep in my flesh and soul until I reached that farcical point — jobless with only a few *dinars* to spend before I died.

My late father used to say, "If you look up too much you will get tired, always look at those who are inferior to you." I had never believed in his wisdom and if truth be told I started to regret when it was too late or so I thought. I could have lived like everybody else, took care of my only daughter Zeineb and re-married the woman who loved me more than her life. I could have stopped the critical thinking of my rogue brain or at least could have tried harder.

Mahdi came and saved me from gnawing thoughts. "enjoying yourself as usual, I really envy your peace of mind … I thought we were going to play a game of cards, last night," he said.

"I forgot," I replied.

He chuckled. "I know why. You were in the company of those birds (beautiful women). Lucky you! You are the only one who breathes real oxygen," he said. I looked at him and then a long way past him. He had never ceased to envy me. I wondered if the friendship we had was nothing but enmity in disguise.

"You think too much these days," Mahdi prodded. I wanted to say that I was going to die very soon. Would he believe me? Would he feel sorry for me? Would he try to dissuade me? Or, most probably, would he gloat over my misery?

"What is it? You look tired man, I know that look," he went on. "These are the looks of someone who thinks about tawba (repentance.) I went through that."

I laughed and lit up a cigarette. He looked at me then swore," By Allah, you will never change."

"*IL n' ya que les imbeciles qui ne changent pas*" (only imbeciles do not change.) I said in French.

"Yes, well said. I think you are right," he confirmed.

"It is not me who said it, but do you know who last said it in front of the United Nations?"

"Most probably our president," he whispered.

"No, it was Colonel Ghaddafi," I said.

Mahdi laughed and I laughed too.

"That man is truly mad," he said.

"Do you know he is a writer?" I asked.

"Yes, his famous, Kitab al-Akhdar (The Green Book) a third theory they say, neither capitalism nor socialism, but something very complicated to my simple mind," Mahdi added cynically.

"I did not mean that, He writes short stories and he is quite gifted," I explained.

"I admit he is a highly educated man, but each time he brings a new thing that destroys what has been planned before, do you know that Libya could have been richer than United Arab Emirates or even Quatar," Mahdi said.

"I know, but the guy is special that's the least thing we can say about him," I countered

"I think he is round the bend," Mahdi replied.

"There is no doubt about what you say but do you know any other president of the Arab world who could improvise so well in front of a camera?" I questioned.

"Yes, Bourguiba," Mahdi said. Actually he was right but he was talking about a man who was already dead, I thought. "Nasser, too," He added.

"Give me a living one," I said, taking a slow drag from my cigarette.

"Maybe Colonel Beshir," Mahdi responded.

"Are you kidding? The man is not even a politician," I retorted.

"May be our President, then," he said as he looked at me very cynically.

"Come on, he can't even read correctly from his papers, let alone his iron fisted generals." Mahdi laughed but I only smiled.

"Anyway, in our Arab world everything is planned by USA, so no president can speak freely," Mahdi continued.

"Let me tell you something — if an Arab has an unfaithful wife he would blame USA"

"I wonder why you love those bastards." Mahdi asked

"I do not ... Nor do I hate them ... I simply try to be truthful."

"Nonsense!"

"Typical"

"What do you mean?" Mahdi asked with a scowl.

"We Arabs love the conspiracy theory, the two-facedness, etc. I think our opinions reflect our true nature — don't you think so?" I asked.

"I think I better go," Mahdi said suddenly. "I'm in no mood to hear these absurdities," Mahdi spat then sprung to his feet.

"Ok, stick your head in the sand — very typical," I challenged.

"You have lost your mind," Mahdi said and left.

Maybe I was losing my mind I thought. But at least I was sure of only one thing. I was free ... so free, like nobody else around me.

CHAPTER 43

Late in the evening, I sat over dinner with my mum. She stared at me for a long time. Then she let out a big sigh. "I wonder when are you going to return back to your job? All your friends are working now. Are you sure you need to wait until you receive a letter from the ministry of education?'

"Absolutely," I said and then resumed eating. She fixed her worried gaze on me and I could hear the wheels of her mind turning. "But you said last week, that you were going today, is something wrong?"

"Nothing mum, you know the system … it's just administrative stuff, don't you worry. It's okay. Do you think I'm stupid to lose my job?"

"So you are telling me there is nothing wrong?" She said as she looked me straight in the eyes.

"Of course," I said and did not flinch.

"Don't tell me you are going back to that place?" She responded with some trepidation in her voice.

"Never!"

"Good … you know that woman I told you about?" My mum said.

"Who?" I asked relieved that she was changing the subject away from of my situation.

"Last year, just one week before leaving for Oman, remember?"

"Mum, if you ask me what I ate yesterday, I probably wouldn't be able to answer."

"She saw you last year and she fell in love with you — she

never stopped talking about you. She is very beautiful and now she has become a teacher like you."

"Are you bored with me?" I cut in.

"How can you say such thing? Is there any woman in the world who gets bored with her own child?"

"I thought that maybe you wanted me to leave," I teased.

"You are the apple of my eye. How can you say such a thing?"

"I was joking, Mum," I said.

"You know I don't like those kinds of jokes."

"Sorry," I said.

Then as I was about to clear my plate, she said "Leave that to me or to your future wife *Insha'Allah* (if Allah wishes.) That woman who left you and opted for the money of Quatar will one day regret her decision. I just feel pain whenever I remember your daughter Zeineb who is the true victim here," my mum said with a sigh.

I felt a sword thrust inside my heart. At that time I had lied to her again. Knowing she was utterly convinced that divorce is a sin. I told her that my wife did not want to return with me because she found a better job in Quatar.

"I just wanted to help," I said.

"Don't worry, I'm still able to take care of my child," my mum said. "But not forever and that's the crux of the matter, son. You need a wife. You need to start your life again while you are still young. I want to see your children and hold them in my arms. I did not even have the time to play with Zeineb. Astagirollah, I ask forgiveness from Allah."

An Omani *khanjar* (knife) cut through my heart again but I was not ready to back down. Maybe it was because I knew that my back was against the wall.

"I don't want to re-marry now. I still haven't found the right woman. Besides I'm still legally tied to her," I said, hoping that this conversation would end .

"That's exactly what she wants. She just wants to keep you

waiting while only Allah knows what she is doing there. Your hair is almost white and you are telling me you are still waiting. Men that are your age have kids on the edge of adolescence, wake up!" She exclaimed.

"Mum we have spoken about this subject thousands of times."

"I will keep on talking until you do something with your life," she cut in.

"Can I go now?"

"Right, run to you room and close the door behind you." Her words trailed off as I slammed the door of my room behind me. Inside I hit the wall with my fist and instantly blood gushed out. My mum was right and once again I was wrong. But it was too late and even the Jesus of Hazem could not find a way out for me now, I thought.

CHAPTER 44

I woke up late in the morning. After a delicious cup of coffee, brewed by my mum, my mind cleared and the entire burden that had lain heavy on my shoulders the night before was as light as a feather. That morning, my mum unexpectedly opted to keep silent. She just cast one of her looks that meant, our second round would be tonight. I thanked the Lord of heaven and blessed every sacred name. Outside, I found my friends sitting in the middle of the street. Some of them were squatting, others were literally lying down. It was very rare that a car passed by, because the street was so narrow. Even if it did, the driver, no doubt, was a visitor. In that case he had to beg to make them give him some space. Otherwise, he would be beaten like hell and his car would become unrecognizable. The police could not be of any help — our eyes were accustomed to tear gas and our skins too thick for their rods. Unless someone was killed, they would prefer to stay in their quarters or enforce law and order in much calmer neighborhoods.

Zied gave me a cynical look, "Still chasing those girls of high birth?" He teased. There was a burst of laughter. I weighed my options then opted for a sharp answer. "Better than staying here and counting how many flies I have waved off." Ziad smiled, but I knew I had made my point.

Mahdi interjected. "Last night I went to Hydra beach. As soon I got out of the taxi with my fiancée, I saw three Hummers driven by three women. I told the *horma*, my wife; let's go back, this place is not for people like us." There were bursts of laughter but, somehow a cloud of pain went over most of their eyes. They were able to laugh but it was evident that, given the chance, they would relish being one of the privileged in that same situation.

"Sit down man, or have you become one of them?" Zied chuckled.

I looked Zied in the eye. "Do you think I was born with a silver spoon in my mouth?" I said, then I squatted down beside him.

Mahdi, who was the youngest, and had a barber shop around the corner, said "You know what? We really do not live. Actually our lives revolve around providing services to the wealthy."

"You forgot an important thing," I said. "We are here to do the jobs they don't want to do."

"*Alhamdolillah*" (thanks to God') said Ali who was not only a *salafist* but wished he could find a way to the sacred army of al Qaida.

"Why do you say thank God?" Mahdi asked.

"When God hates someone, he gives him everything during this life, but we will go to heaven and the day will come when they shall weep and grind their teeth."

"At least the rich people here are living their lives to the fullest, but in our case, no one knows what will happen to us, "Mahdi said.

"They also have the means to gain paradise — they tithe and we do not. They build mosques and help orphans, if they wish to. They can gather lots of *hasanat* (good deeds.) And of course, the poor, it seems to me, are unable to purchase these *hasanats* for themselves," I said. My statement just thrust another sword into almost every heart.

Ali weighed his options and chose diplomacy. "At least the poor have nothing to answer for during *hisa'b* (judgement.) God forgives those who repent — just keep faith and start going to mosque. Life is nothing Jamal. It is a peace of dirt. May Allah bless you and enable you to visit his *kaaba,* (the holy house of

Allah) in Mecca, where you may cleanse yourself and be born again," he concluded.

"Do you know how much it costs to go there?" I teased.

"Don't you worry, Allah will open doors, just keep faith and you will see," Ali said. But there was no conviction in his voice.

"My grand mum went last year; she had been waiting for five years. She paid five thousand dollars for just two weeks. She told me that everything was expensive in Mecca. I understand that all the money goes to Al Saoud, the governing Saudi family, in the end," Mahdi said and Ali cleared his throat.

For a while a cold silence hung over us, then suddenly Lotfi, who had a pleasant voice, started to sing a Mezouad song, *Ikhsir w'Farigh* (Lose and then leave everything behind.) It was a beautiful song sung by a famous folk singer from nearby Tunisia. And they say that only the educated can create good art. I believe pain and real experience make a good artist, but this is another story.

The *dohr adhan* broke in suddenly and Lotfi said "*Astagh-firollah.*" In Islam singing is *haram*, music is *haram,* and painting is *haram* — even having a dog at home is *haram*.

But people, even the most serious about religion, had developed a certain margin of freedom for themselves, and even some recent *mofties,* specialists who give *fatwas* where the Islamic jurisprudence is not clear, like Kalbani had declared music was not totally forbidden, provided it reminded someone of Allah. Maybe I should mention that his *fatwa* (legal opinion) provoked a storm. Some enlightened Sunnies in Saudi Arabia allow music during certain celebrations, but only drums are allowed. At times, it seemed to me, Islam is like that famous Auschwitz concentration camp where only a lucky few were able to gain their freedom back. Anyway, some of us went to the café and others went to mosque. Mahdi and I began to stroll up the tortuous lane that led to the highway. Mahdi was silent and I did not want to ask why he did not go to *salat*.

Years ago, I had that fear that if did not pray I was a *kaffir* (an infidel) and an infidel had no chance to enter heaven. But by now I had developed a thicker skin, and of course a more skeptical mind. Who would believe that King Solomon talked to a *namla* (ant) and a *hodhod* (bird)? Who could believe he had an army of *jinns* (spirts) and could travel by wind? But the sacred always puts a veil upon a person's eyes, which makes the mind unable to question the veracity of a legend. The Bible of Hazem was at least realistic and the legend of Jesus, if it was not true, at least it was beautiful; at least it built and never destroyed anything, I thought.

"They say the heat is going to reach its peak tomorrow," Mahdi said.

"Today is already stifling," I replied.

"It's the end of the world," Mahdi said, quoting Zied.

I looked at him for a while and then a long way past him. I saw Dorra in my mind. She was my princess without a crown, smiling to herself and the people; happy like a lilac and so different. She was indescribable.

"Actually I do not think Zied is right," Mahdi corrected himself. "Before the end of the world, the *al-dabbah*, the beast, should appear and then Yagog and Magog. Then the *dajjal* (Antichrist) will descend and make most of the people worship him. But luckily 'Isa, Jesus , peace be upon him, together with Almahdi, would fight him and prevail. Then they would break the cross and kill the pig and govern all the people of the world with Sharia law, as our prophet had once told." I listened and did not know why I recalled, once again, John's vision about the false prophet and the beast.

CHAPTER 45

"The girls have become mad these days, they walk almost naked, smoke cigarettes in the middle of the streets and do everything. Last night I was about to break the virginity of my fiancée. I could not help it Jamal. Nakedness is everywhere. Do you know what I mean?" Mahdi said.

I chose not to comment. I thought about marriage in Islam, Why on earth does Allah call it *nikah* (having sex) and not something else? Why, according to the Qur'an, does Allah not see marriage as more than just a physical act?

I had begun to receive many kinds of strange thoughts as soon as I started reading the *kaffir's* book. In fact, each time that I decided not to contaminate my mind with its lies anymore, I felt a strange hunger to devour some more of its pages. Maybe the Lord of the Christians was close to us. Or maybe His story and His words were just enchanting, even if they weren't true. I didn't know the exact reason but, I knew that I was no longer able to sleep if I didn't read something He said.

Our clothes were almost wet with sweat when Mahdi and I reached the café. As usual it was already full of people — mostly the young. In a country where unemployment is always high, a café is the best financial project, I thought. People started playing cards at ten in the morning then played chess at twelve and *Shkobba* at two.

"Two Cappuccinos, as usual," Mahdi told the sad-eyed waiter, and headed towards the toilet.

I sat at a table at the far corner almost near the hookah

counter and lit a cigarette. Mahdi returned to our table and, as usual, greeted everybody and appeared to know everyone there. I watched him, jealous of only one thing: His ability to remain happy all the time. In fact, the idea of a clean suicide had come to my mind several times in the past, but now I knew I was going to do it very soon.

"Why are you so silent? I'm tired of always being the one to speak," Mahdi asked.

"Words have lost meanings — don't you think so?" I said almost to myself.

"Yes you are right, of course. What we do at night, we do also in the morning, *Astagfirullah*. I can tell the future. After one month, even five years from now, you will find me in the same café, sitting in the same place, doing the same things." Mahdi spoke as if he had resolved himself to this eternal boredom.

"Isn't it sad?" I groaned.

Mahdi rolled his eyes. "Listen if you are going to be sad and start nagging, let me go to another place. There is "Cuba la Vieja" on the corner, thanks to Allah. Listen, we all are going to die and the most beautiful thing about death is that we do not take with us anything. We are all suddenly equal at that moment."

I smiled and scratched my head. Actually, we take with us our memories, the beautiful moments we have spent, the lovely kids we have left behind — and we are so sure they will live in comfort and ease."

"Say *Astagfirullah* man. When we die we will meet Munkir and Nakir, the two questioning angels, in our tombs. We will start to pay from the very moment we are thrown into the grave," Mahdi continued.

"Do you know Umberto Eco?" I asked.

"How should I know about him? Have I been to university like you?" Mahdi said with some disdain.

"Umberto Eco is a writer," I replied.

"Oh please! They are mad, these people," Mahdi cut in.

"Just let me finish the story man," I spat out.

"Ok, sorry Mr. Jamal, I beg your pardon, go ahead," Mahdi said with a malicious grin on his face.

"This man was a novelist. In most of his books, writes about atheism and encourages his readers not to believe in what they don't see," I said.

"Ha! What a son of a bitch!" Mahdi interjected.

"If you don't be quiet, I'm not going to finish my story," I snapped out.

"Sorry man. It's the last time — go on," he promised.

"He was asked by a French intellectual, I think the presenter of *Le Cercle de Minuit*. 'Mr. Echo what will you say to God, if he really exists, and you are wrong?' The man thought for a while then said *'Je lui dirais que la fete commence'* (Let the party begin.)"

"So?" Mahdi interjected.

"Good heavens! You are so stupid. Doesn't he make you laugh?" I asked.

"At your stupidity or Eco's — which one?" Mahdi questioned.

"What if God does not exist?" I asked suddenly.

"Shut up!" He exclaimed.

"What if Islam is a false religion and we have been living in a big lie for more than Fourteen Centuries?'

"What if you are going crazy and deserve a strong punch?" Mahdi said.

"I mean, only the stupid do not question." I said.

"So according to you Mr. Genius, more than two hundred million Arabs are stupid?" He countered.

"Exactly!" I responded. "In fact, what if all of us are wrong?"

"Listen man — you are treading on very dangerous ground. I would advise you to stop asking these stupid questions or else God will make you pay — never underestimate Allah's wrath."

"What if the Allah we fear, is In fact, full of love and mercy? I mean, what if he is a father and not some strange entity that should be treated with fear and awe?" I asked.

"*Astagfirullah,* how do you want to behave in front of the One who has created us? Are you nuts?"

It is useless to argue, I thought. Hundreds of questions were brewing in my mind. Suddenly there were hundreds of thorns that never stopped gnawing at me. Besides, I was not sure of myself. It was funny to think that more than twenty centuries ago, in that very place In Algeria, philosophers were strolling along the streets, asking, arguing and fighting intellectually. It is curious how history in this cursed part of the world is always moving backward, or maybe I was wrong, or just exaggerating.

"Do you still think Barcelona will win her next match against the Real?" I asked, switching subjects. Mahdi's face became alive again. Finally he found a subject he liked and something he excelled at.

"Do you doubt the gift of the Maestro, his majesty Lionel Messi?' He said.

"Last time, against Dortmund he did not do anything. He was dead, man! I taunted.

Mahdi's lips curved in a cynical smile, "I know you wish your team had someone like him, but please do not tell me he did not do anything. He was like a German Diesel engine, and the two goals were because of him. By Allah, real Madrid fans are jealous. Don't worry, the maestro will teach you a lesson."

"You are hallucinating; the king will impose his style," I responded.

"Who are you talking about? That stupid Ronaldo … He is a good sprinter no doubt, but only when the field is empty. I swear By Allah if he was in Barcelona he would be *bannnack* (back bencher)."

"Ronaldo, sitting on the bank?" I asked, incredulous at his statement. " He is he most expensive football player in the world. Are you kidding?"

"You know that I say the truth, he has nothing in his legs man!" Mahdi replied.

I admit, I am not an expert in European football, like Mahdi, but his words hurt my pride. "When you win on Sunday, then come and say this, but not now. Real is about to hold the trophy once again."

"Yes, as long as you rely on Ronaldo," Mahdi countered.

"If your Messi is good, I wonder why he doesn't do anything when he plays on his national team?" I asked.

"A prophet is without honor in his country," Madhi said.

"Do you know who said these words?" I asked.

"It's a proverb for God's sake," Mahdi said.

I weighed my options and then decided not to say that it was Jesus — that beautiful entity I read about every night. There was a long pause of total silence. Mahdi had always been an expert in football and I wondered why people like him were not on TV instead of those announcers, who know nothing about football.

"I heard yesterday that Ronaldo was caught red handed cheating on his girlfriend," Mahdi said, then glanced at me.

"How do you expect a rich man like him, to remain faithful to a single woman?" I asked instead of commenting.

"Hah! Just rich!" Mahdi snorted. "He has millions and millions man. God has given him everything: money, fame, talent and good looks."

"Do you know that one Omani teacher said he is a *khal?*" I said.

"What do you mean by *khal?* (the Omani slang for a slave) A homosexual?" Mahdi asked and his interest brightened.

"No, the son of a slave. And you know what? In the kingdom of Oman and the Gulf in general, no respectful man will give his daughter to a former son of a slave."

"But he is white and slaves used to be blacks," Mahdi said.

"They don't care about the color; they follow the shape of the nose. If it is big and the nostrils are large then he is a *khal*. I tell you something. I knew a teacher in Oman. His tribe is from Blushistan. He was green-eyed, white etc … nobody wanted to give him his daughter because he was a *khal*. Evidently his grandmother was black and everybody knew it. He married a *khala*, (an Omani slang for a female slave); in the end, one of his family members. Do you see the kind of world where I have been?" I asked.

"Good God! Didn't Islam abolish slavery?" Mahdi asked.

"No, there is a law of *kasas* (punishment) in Islam that says a freeman should be killed for a freeman and a slave for a slave."

"Ok, was not Bilal the private Muezzin of Rasoul?" I did not want to enter into another futile debate with him." I told you what I have seen with my eyes, and experienced every day for two years," I said as a matter of fact.

"You are exaggerating, as usual; I know you won't be happy even on Mars. But of course your USA is always perfect ... the land of racism."

"You mentioned the USA. Okay, I will tell you another thing. Iman Haramayn was a *khal* so the people in Mecca did not want to be led by a black iman and soon he was kicked out. In the very Mecca we face five times a day. But in USA, the one you think is racist ... President Obama, whose father is Hussein from Kenya, became president of the most powerful nation in the world. Now you tell me — who will go to heaven, them or us? As I said that, I gave Mahdi a slap on the shoulder.

Mahdi scratched his head and then knitted his eye brows. "Still they are *Koffar*, unbelievers, and God forgives everything, except not believing in Him or his messenger."

"Who said so?" I challenged.

"Allah, I mean it's in the Qur'an." Mahdi said.

"Who said the Qur'an is from God? Have you asked yourself this very simple question?" I asked.

Mahdi took a long breath, and replied, "I think I better go."

"See you later then," I said and fought hard to keep my voice even. He did not answer, but I knew I had lost a friend ... forever.

CHAPTER 46

As I was crossing the street, I saw Dorra's car parked near the green grocer. I never thought I would see her in real daylight. And there she was, right here in my own poor neighborhood, wearing a lovely flowered dress. Her dark hair resembled a crown, pushed back on her head. There was no makeup on her face except for a very faint amount of eyeliner. I never thought she was that beautiful; but today she looked exceptional. Her skin was so soft and glistening. It was as though the sun had never dared to cause her skin to become rough and dry, as is common in this region. I heard her say to the grocer, "I might come tomorrow if I find time — anyway, call me when it is ready to be picked up."

I realized at that moment that the grocer had her phone number and he talked to her as if she were his mistress. I was jealous. He smiled when she in got her car and revealed a set of decayed teeth. My princess smiled back and then slammed her car shut. He stood watching as her car slowly moved into the traffic. The fifty-*dinar* note was still in his hand and he kept caressing it as though he were embracing her hand. If the truth be told, I never felt that jealous! But my envy was mixed with a strong curiosity.

I never thought that one day I would ever buy anything from that crocodile faced man. There were so many rumors that circulated about him: Dishonest, too expensive, never sought to do business with the poor etc. But as they say in Algeria, "if you depend on a dog, then say to the dog that you are in need, and the dog will be at your beck and call."

I walked over to the grocer and said, "Give me one kilo of bananas, please." Unexpectedly he gave me the freedom to choose what I wanted. In Algeria, most of the sellers do not let you touch anything, "What a hot day today," the man said while still caressing the fifty-*dinar* note. I was ashamed of myself that I had gotten the wrong impression about the man. Actually he was not only sympathetic, but had a genuinely good heart. Suddenly his ugly face became compassionate in my eyes, and I ventured to ask an indirect question, "Nice car," I said glancing at Dorra's car as it moved away from us and down the street.

"That woman owns half of Hydra and ben Aknoun. That car is nothing. Every two or three days she comes in a new one, Mercedes, BMW, Hummer, you name it."

"I wonder why she comes to such a poor neighborhood." I asked.

"These people do not look for the cheapest price like us. They are different. She buys from me because she was once looking for dates and could not find them anywhere. She came to my small shop and found some. She wanted half a kilo so I gave it to her free. She insisted that I should get my money and I insisted too. She looked at me and said, "from now on I will be "*Une cliente fidele* (a faithful customer.)" And she kept her word. That woman is something. She speaks as if she were a poor helpless woman, '*Il n'ya que les bidons vides qui font le bruit*' (only drums make noise because they are empty inside) she once said to me, and it is true."

I wanted to ask if she was married. 'Did she have children? 'But the question remained on the tip of my tongue. Instead I opted for diplomacy and gave him a compliment, "You speak good French."

"Well, all my customers are surprised at first. Actually, I have a Master's degree in Physics. But for many reasons I ended up here. Alhamdulillah (praise to God), I earned more money than a university professor. Actually I was young and got involved with Abbasi Madani party, The Algerian Islamic front. I went to prison and the years I had spent there were enough to teach me a good lesson. I started a new life and that's it — could I help you with anything else?"

"No thanks — I think I know her husband, isn't he the owner of that café in El Kobbah." I asked gingerly.

"No sir, you confuse her with someone else. Her husband is dead, a car accident, she said."

"But she is still young, she can marry again?"

"These people do not think like us — you know what I mean?" I nodded in agreement, even though I really did not understand what he meant.

"Maybe you will understand one day," the unsaid sizzled in his words.

"Tell me what you mean," I said.

The green grocer thought it over then said, "Yes, she can marry anyone she wants to, but I think she doesn't want to remarry. She once said she had a daughter and did not want her to have another father. You are right! Everyone will want her money, but you said she is young, do you know how old is she?" The man asked.

"Early forties, I think," I surmised to him.

"Hah!" He snorted, "She is fifty-two. These people do not grow old, do you know why?"

I was shocked, not just surprised. A woman like her, of whom the deer would be jealous of her beauty, was almost the age of my mum.

"Comfort," I said almost to myself.

"Not only that, those people do not think about tomorrow like us. All they have to care about is how they spend their money. My wife is thirty-two. If you look at her you would think she is sixty. She does not even wash up her teeth. My friend you have just brought up a big question," he said.

"Her name is Azza I think," I said to him hardly listening to his reply.

"No, it is Dorra. Do you know that a famous singer had written a song about her. I wish I could recall his name."

"Me too but I know the song you are speaking about. It's a beautiful song." I said.

"Well it was written about the time of her fifth birthday, I think. I will tell you something. These people belong to another world. They do not think like us or even speak like us. She speaks in a soft low-pitched tone and never gets angry. My wife is always in a bad mood. When she is really out of her mind the people who live in Hydra hear her shrill voice." The man lamented. I laughed despite myself, and the man laughed with me.

"You know what? By Allah, if I did not have kids I would not have stayed with her a single day. But, *Haslitni,* she trapped me, with three daughters and a son."

I wanted to say that a normal man could be fooled once or twice maximum, but I preferred to keep my thought to myself. Why add salt to the wound?

"Do you believe in *sihr* (magic). Well, my wife made me eat the meat of a donkey."

I laughed gain and thought he was kidding. The man did not even smile this time and went on.

"You know if you want to goad a man like a donkey, make him eat its meat. Of course she had to know about putting a spell on a man, but these women we have, they know everything."

I smiled and wondered how an educated man still believed in such nonsense. For a moment the picture of Oman and then Mosa flickered through my mind.

"You don't believe me, do you? Well do you believe in the Qur'an? To your knowledge it is stated inside a *sourat,* I forgot which one '

"*Sourat al Jinn,*" I said.

"Yes exactly! And you know the story of Harut and Marut. They were two angels in heaven and saw the degree of vice done by humans, so they started grumbling about it. God heard them and said to them would you behave any better in their situation? They said of course we would. So God transformed them into flesh and bones and sent them to earth. To Babel, or Iraq, in our modern world ... to make a story short they got drunk and slept with a beautiful woman then killed her. After that they started teaching people *sihr* (magic.) As a punishment God put them in chains and hung them between earth and sky. Actually He asked them whether they wanted to continue living until the Day of Judgment, or get their punishment in this life. They chose the second option of course and now they are dangling between sky and earth, till *kiama* (Day of Judgment.)"

I looked him in the eye and then a long way past him. If an educated man like him believed in such nonsense then what about the layman of the street? Would he believe me if I told him I had been a magician? 'And where?' he might ask me? 'In the holy land of revelation, of course,' I would answer.

"Every *kayd* (deceit) comes from women, as it is written in the holy Qur'an ... they cast a spell on Prophet Mohammed himself, peace be upon him, and do you know how?' He continued in earnest.

Of course I knew the story but he was going to tell it even if I said yes.

"They cut some of his hair, peace be upon him, while he was asleep and buried it in a forgotten tomb. The prophet could no longer see to the duties of his wives. For a whole month he remained in that state. Then the Archangel Gabriel came to his rescue. He told him where the spell was buried and he sent Umar to find it."

Actually it was not buried in an old forgotten tomb as he had said. Rather, it was hidden in a well, and the Shi'ites and some Sunnis believe that Ali was the one who retrieved the spell from inside the well, and saved the prophet.

"And do you know who did that — the Jews may be cursed till the end of days; they knew he was a prophet but were jealous because he was not a Jew, but because they are cowards they relied on a woman to cast a spell on Mohammed, may Allah confer his blessings on him." The man went on.

That story brought back a memory I had of the old days when I lived in Oman. There were so many Algerian Jews. They were kind and honest and everyone knew that. Ask any old man in Algeria and he will tell you they were hard workers and had an extraordinary gift for commerce. The old women would praise their excellent food. Till now, we played their card games, hung a *khomsa* (a carved hand) to shun the evil eye. Until now, our best dishes were in fact, Jewish dishes.

"You see my friend, if the prophet himself was not immune against their *kayd,* do you think I could be immune? May God protect us all and exterminate all the Jews from this world," he concluded sadly.

"Why?" I asked.

"Aren't you A Muslim?" he asked. I weighed my options and kept silent.

"Without Arabs they would have been exterminated. During the inquisition period they fled the persecution of western Christendom and came to North Africa. They lived among us like our brothers ... But again as it is their habit, they started plotting and conniving. They spread *sihr,* and all kinds of vices among us. See what they are doing to our brothers in Palestine now?"

The most dangerous nonsense is always filled with some truth. True; the Muslim world offered a better protection to Jews, though of course they were obliged to pay excessive *jizya* (tax) and dress in a special way. I think they had to wear a yellow belt round the waist. I may venture to say that Hitler got the idea of the yellow star from such a great heritage of soft persecution. Even today in the Gulf region a *wafid* did not have the right to wear a dashdasha (a white long robe) during work. Only the *muwaten* (the native) had that sacred right. I asked why once and they answered in unison: 'It's just the law,' they would reply. But I knew it was something else, something ugly like apartheid or the separate but equal philosophy of the nineteen sixties, which was practiced in the USA. I remember that when I had stopped praying they had kept nagging at me, 'come and pray, beware of Allah's wrath'.

My decision was firm. No sir, as long as I was treated like a second rate Muslim, I will never go to pray and if your Islam is the only way to Heaven, then I prefer to go to Hell with my dignity preserved.

"You think too much, rely on God and you will never be deceived," he said. I detected a pitying glow in his dark, small eyes.

"Well, it is very nice to meet you," I said attempting to conclude our conversation. "My name is Jamal and, of course, I would be pleased to be one of your regular customers."

His face softened, "I'm Mustafa." We shook hands and I left.

CHAPTER 47

My mind was brimming with thousands of thoughts. I was in love with a woman for whom one of the greatest artists in Algeria — El Hachemi Guerouabi — wrote one of his best songs. And the woman was 52, almost the age of my mother. No doubt I was going to experience real pain, but, after all, it was a new experience to add to the last chapter of my storm-tossed life. I could rest in peace, confident that I had seen almost everything. The time was ripe for a sweet death.

As I reached home and knocked on the door, I heard my sister weeping and knew she must have been beaten once again by her cowardly husband. As she opened the door, she threw herself in my arms. My heart was broken for her, and my eyes were blinded by a fit of anger.

"I'm going to kill him, that son of a bitch," I said angrily.

My mum held my arms and my sister closed the door. By and by, my anger subsided. I knew I had to calm down because my mother was diabetic and had *dhagt* (hypertension.) I didn't want to be the cause of any more problems with her health.

"I did not do anything!" my sister said. "The boy was crying and I didn't know why and I had to take care of him." I knew she was speaking about her son that suffered from Autism.

"Suddenly, Hamid, started yelling and breaking everything in front of him. When I asked him to stop because the boy was scared, Hamid started beating me. He thinks that it's my fault that his son is ill. He has forgotten that when I was five months pregnant, he kicked me in the stomach when he was in one of his fits of anger. He said I shouldn't have another baby. He even said to me, 'I'm working all the time and you sit at home like a princess and you want another baby? Who is going to feed him?" Her voice trailed off as her body began to shake and tears streamed down her cheeks.

The truth is that her second pregnancy had been my mum's idea. She wanted my sister to have a second child in order to make Yasin unable to even think of divorce in the future. A second child was a guarantee that his cell was firmly locked. Very few men would have enough courage, selfishness and of course the means to cater for the needs of two children and then start a new family.

"The boy is abnormal because of the kick, and the bitter days that I've spent with him since that moment," my sister continued while my mum nodded gravely.

Autistic children needed special centers, a thing we still did not have many of, in Algeria. Besides, the list was too long and the lucky ones had to have connections above all. "I have told you a thousand times to apply for a divorce and I will find you a job. By law, he will be forced to pay for the expenses of the child," I murmured, knowing she would never take my suggestion. I don't remember how many times I had said this to her, but the result was always the same. She would return to him and replay the same scene over and over again. It was her destiny, I guess, to live the life of an abused wife. But I knew in my heart that it was the culture and religion that relegated her to this life, not divine appointment.

"Do not listen to him, my dear," my mum said, then cast me one of her stern looks that I was so familiar with. "Think about the children. At least your husband does not cheat on you. He works very hard and I know you, *binti* (daughter), you do not take care of him the way you should when he comes home exhausted."

As a matter of fact, he had cheated on her many times. I saw him with one of those low prostitutes in his old car. And his work was the easiest in the world. He had to sit in a café or some other public place and listen to what the people who were sitting around him said. Then he would write a report. That was all. I told her not to marry him. But, of course, she was head over heels in love with him. If there was a reason to hate women for something, I would hate them for being so stupid with little forethought when falling in love. I recall now she had spent a whole month not speaking to me because I had said "no" to her marriage.

Now she was weeping and cursing the very day she did not listen to me. *Bon appetit,* I said to myself rather than to her, and went to my room. She would weep for some time and then wait for her husband to come in the evening and take her back home. In two weeks or so she would be here again and my heart would be saddened anew. With time and her inability to see the plight of her situation, however, my compassion towards her had become a bit cynical.

CHAPTER 48

After a quick nap and a shower, I snuck out of the house while my mum was still comforting my little sister. I never thought I would cross paths with Dorra twice in the same day, but the miracle happened when I saw her fancy car parked in a Hydra shopping center. I watched as she pulled up and got out of her car. She was like the sun when it is hidden by a cloud, then suddenly reappears to add bright light and color to everything it touches. Dorra deserved not only that beautiful song but all the beautiful songs of the world, I thought. If I'd had enough time, I would have written for her the most exquisite poetry ever produced in the Arab world. The famous poem titled *al matar, Rain,* by Al Sayab, would be nothing compared to my poem. Then I heard her speak to a lame man in the park.

"Your windshield needs some cleaning, mum," he observed.

"I forgot to take it to be washed," I heard her say.

"You do not need to, mum. I will do it for you."

Despite his lame right leg, he walked faster than an athlete. I thought it was probably due to the adrenaline rush or that famous *tai chi* talked about by Chinese martial arts experts. His bucket and a rag were carefully hidden behind a small tree. The man looked happy, happier than spending a good night with his wife, I thought.

For a brief moment, my Dorra watched the obedience and faithfulness of the old man. She was unemotional, as if his offer was expected and an entitlement of her status. I stared in amazement that this simple, unappreciated act of helping someone could produce such pleasure in the old man.

If she was that accessible, I thought, it shouldn't be that risky to talk to her. I never considered it a good idea to follow a woman while she was doing her shopping — very risky and most of the time pointless. Experience taught me that every woman hated being stalked.

Dorra loved fruit and each time she stood in front of a new box, she looked, smelled and then ordered a kilo or two. When she went to where they sold fish, I was quite amazed. Those silky hands selected a large fish and actually picked it up. What kind of woman — especially one of her status — would even touch a fish, let alone hold it in her hands?

"How much is the *karous*?" she asked the grocer.

"Thirty-five, mum," he replied.

"I don't think it's fresh," she countered.

"It is today's catch, mum," he responded.

"Are you kidding me? I'm *bint bhar* (a daughter of the sea), look at its eyes. This is from yesterday, at least," she said, correcting his remark.

The man smiled to cover the sting of her remark or probably the embarrassment. He turned his head sideways and his small eyes glanced at me for a second.

"Give me two kilos of Dorado; at least it looks fresher," she said.

The man started to pick up the fish, but with each one, he asked with his eyes if she approved of his choice. The innocence that I had seen in her hazel eyes was now full of light mischief. The rich are always skeptical, I thought.

"Do you want anything, sir?" the seafood grocer asked, which brought me back to reality.

"Do not buy *karous* today," she remarked. "That's only my advice, of course. *Après tout* (after all), we live in a free country, *bon je l'espere* (or at least I hope so)"

She was addressing me and suddenly the look in her eyes was what, full of probabilities? I smiled and she smiled back. The teeth she revealed were not teeth, they were real diamonds — so white and perfect that I wondered if the so-called side effects of smoking, especially the hookah, really equaled five packets of cigarettes, as doctors stated.

"I think I should follow the advice of a nice lady like you," I said, then gave one of those smiles that I made use of only in times of real need.

"Are you a visitor or have you just moved here?" my princess asked.

"How do you know I'm not from Hydra?" I asked instead of answering.

"You are kidding. I live here and I know everybody, especially a man like you."

"On a visit," I lied.

"Let me guess. You live in France … most probably in the south, judging from the tan."

"No, in the Gulf, unfortunately," I lied again. As if I was a part of the story of *Pinocchio*, I began to feel my nose grow longer.

"Why unfortunately? It is there where the real money is. Do you work in Qatar?"

"No, a worse place — Oman," I lied.

"I have a friend who works in Dawha in Qatar as an economic analyst. He also teaches in Sorbonne, France, and every two months or so goes to Qatar," she said. "You must have seen him. Sometimes he appears on Aljazeera channel."

"Probably, but I do not watch it so often."

"What do you do there?"

"I'm a teacher," I said.

She fixed her glance on me, and the interest and the sparkling warmth suddenly lost some of its heat. "At university?"

"No, in a secondary school, in a place called Shinas, about nine kilometers away from the UAE."

"So, most of your free time must have been spent in Dubai, Abu Dhabi — those wonderful places?"

Actually, I was not allowed to visit even Al Fujairah, which was less than ten kilometers away from where I lived. In the evening, when I was really bored, I would watch the lights off in the distance and imagine what it would be like to live in the city of sin — Dubai.

"You are not a great speaker, I like your type," she said, changing the subject.

"Thanks," I said, relieved that I did not have to convey that information to her. Again, I threw her one of my best smiles. Dorra did not smile back, but scrutinized me for what seemed a long time.

"Are you renting a place here?" she inquired.

"No, actually I stay with a cousin in Ben Aknoun." I said Ben Aknoun because it was another luxurious neighborhood, and I judged that she would not find out where I was supposed to be living.

"I have a house in Ben Aknoun. I'm there almost every day, and I have never seen you there." Then, with slight disdain she continued, "Unless you are staying in Medina El Arbi, the old Arab city."

"I'm not from here, so I can't tell which is which," I said, then swallowed. Finally her maid came and saved me. She was well dressed for a servant, but her manners were, of course, still uncouth.

"*I am glad you came, Lilla, mum!*" Dorra exclaimed, her voice ringing with sarcasm.

The lady did not speak, but only took the fish and put it in the shopping cart. She then stood away, waiting for other instructions. The hidden wall between a master and servant was made of concrete, I thought. I recalled my mum. Most probably she had toiled in the house of a woman, like that beautiful woman standing in front of me now.

"I still don't know your name," she finally said.

"Oh, it's Jamal."

"Nice to meet you; mine is Dorra. Will I see you in the evening at the café Cuba la Vieja, about 7:30?" She smiled like an angel, then through a glaring glance towards the servant who, eyes down, pushed the cart in front of her mistress. I do not know why, but the scene brought to my mind the sad-looking Bengalis of Oman.

"Oh, I almost forgot — give me your phone number, please, and take mine," she rushed to say before leaving. As we exchanged numbers, she whispered, "Do not look at me in that way — there are people around."

I had been found out. She had noticed the desire I felt for her, but I didn't care. My goal had been achieved. I would finally be with my princess tonight.

CHAPTER 49

When I saw Dorra get out of her car, I lamented the years eaten by the locusts. On reflection, I discovered that even my language repertoire became biblical. Once again I cursed Hazem and his book. I had lost my job, and for the first time after my return from Oman, I felt painful regret burning inside my chest. My phone buzzed. It was a message from Dorra. 'Please do not talk to me in the café. I will tell you how to meet later.'

When our eyes met, she smiled but the smile did not reach her eyes. The waiter hurried to find for her a suitable table and then rushed for the hookah. Then, as she was about to leave, I received another message. Wait for me at the corner on the opposite street near the big palm tree. I left the café and walked to the appointed meeting place. There I waited for her in the darkness.

"Sorry, I'm well-known in this neighborhood," my princess apologized as she stopped her car and rolled her window down. I got into her car and told her it was alright. My nostrils sucked in her mesmerizing smell; it was alluring. She pulled away from the curb and began driving down the street.

"You lied to me," she said suddenly, which took me by surprise.

"What do you mean?" My heart pounded inside my chest.

I did some research about you, you know — actually, I know many powerful people here." She stopped to let her words settle. Her voice rang with sarcasm. I swallowed and shifted in my seat, my shell of falsehood cracked.

"I do not care if you are poor," she continued. "I just do not want problems. I'm not ready to help anybody … I have helped so many and I'm tired of playing the role of the angel guardian." I could see that she was fighting to keep the frown off her face.

I was embarrassed and felt my heart being torn to pieces. "I don't know what to say." I replied.

But she cut into my forced confession. "You see, I love young, handsome men or maybe it's the other way around. The problem is that most of them are from deprived neighborhoods. Once, I was almost killed by a lunatic who did not understand the simple meaning of an adventure. He was in love with me and wanted to marry me. You see, it's impossible. We do not belong to the same world. I could never marry someone who is below my social status. For me, having sex is like having a nice dinner. Do you understand what I mean? This year I was planning to make pilgrimage and wear *hijab,* but I saw you and I decided to postpone everything. Like Shaitan, you caught me in your snare."

"Do you believe in God and in Islam?" I asked unexpectedly.

A shrewd light shone from her eyes. "Do not mention Khadija — may she rest in peace — please. I know she was richer and much older than Mohammed — may he rest in peace — but he was a prophet, after all. Anyway, times have changed," she answered.

"I did not mean that," I replied. "I simply meant you are wrong … Islam does not change the hearts. Consequently, it won't make you holy."

"What are you saying? Are you drunk or something?" Dorra asked as if she could not comprehend my question.

"You see, what I hate about Islam is this pilgrimage that is supposed to make you clean of every sin. Could you please stop the car?" My request took my Dorra unprepared.

"What? Right here in the middle of the highway?" she asked.

"Yes. Just pull over to the right side of the road and stop so we can talk."

"Okay, I get it. You are really mad," she said.

"I was. Anyway, thanks for the ride." I hopped out and closed the door behind me. She blew her horn and flashed her lights, but I kept walking, my eyes fixed in the distance. I'm not sure why I was walking away from this beautiful woman. Was it because, for the first time, I saw myself? Or was it because I was beginning to realize that what I wanted, no, needed, was something much deeper and more fulfilling than just a "one-night stand" that would go nowhere? I don't know for sure. I just know that this event signified what was to become the beginning of my life, not the end.

CHAPTER 50

The throbbing inside my head was unbearable and I almost swayed on my feet. But I kept walking despite my shaky knees and my dry throat. As I reached *Houma* (my neighborhood), I needed to do something, anything. So, as I passed by Mahdi's barbershop, I decided to go in.

As usual, the place was crammed with people — mostly our neighbors — who liked to idle their time away there. Mahdi, like any barber, I suppose, liked to gossip and hear the new stories. His favorite subject was international news. Most of his information was either superficial or biased because of the Al Jazeera channel but, if the truth be told, it was fun to hear him speak or comment on world events. When I entered, the topic of speech was about *Hezbollah* (literally 'party of Allah,' it is a Shi'a Islamic militant group based in Lebanon) and the murder of El Hariri, the former president of Lebanon.

"I told you, Hassan Nasr Allah didn't do it," Mahdi was saying. "Last night, they brought an important man on Al Jazeera. I think he is a leader inside the secret service movement."

"Yes, I watched it, in the *Milaf*, or file program," Fathi responded. He was a frail man in his 40's who had spent most of his life either sleeping or idling time away in Houma or in the café. Sometimes, when he was drunk, he would quote beautiful poems about bravery or love.

"He said it point blank," Mahdi went on. "The man talked about the case of a spy, a Lebanese, who sold information to the Jews. He said that many times the soldiers of Hezbollah had the opportunity to eliminate the target, but their plans were always aborted — usually because there were innocents at risk: the target's wife, his kids or even his friends." Mahdi stopped to scrutinize the effect of his revelations on his captive audience who had become "all ears."

"The man said that Hezbollah preferred to wait for long months before carrying out a very successful and clean operation," he continued. "I'm sure he is telling the truth because you could tell he was really pious. He had a long beard and a *zabiba* (prostration seal) on his forehead." Mahdi stopped this time to see if there was any potential threat to the credulity of his story. "The man said that even if the Hezbollah had wanted to eliminate Hariri, the former Lebanese president they wouldn't have carried it out in such a cowardly way. I mean, his wife and most of his family were all killed."

At that time, it seemed to me that what the high official claimed on Al Jazeera channel proved only one thing: Hezbollah eliminated targets from time to time.

"I will tell you, Mahdi that I'm sure he was killed by the Americans and the Israelis in a covert operation to spread discord in the region," Zied, another listener, pointed out. Despite myself, I burst into laughter. All eyes became fixed on me.

"What is it, Jamal? You do not like his analysis or as usual you think yourself smarter than everyone?" Mahdi said.

"I'm now pretty sure that if a man can't get along well with his wife, he would say that the Americans and the Jews are the cause. It's ironic that nobody would dare question his claim … nobody would doubt if the couple is simply incompatible," I said sarcastically.

Most of the people laughed, but Mahdi gave a crippled smile that barely reached his cheeks. "You think that Hariri was not killed by the followers of Shaitan?" he asked. His voice rang with contempt.

"Of course not," I replied.

"Think about it — who benefits the most from his murder?"

"This is a wrong question. You should ask who is armed and murders without being questioned," I countered.

"The Jews," Mahdi answered without losing a breath.

"Bullshit! You know the answer to my question. They have free press, and democracy — the only democracy in the Middle East … every two weeks or so their prime minister is escorted to court for a charge of corruption. Their free press reports everything about the government. Tell me about any Arab president or king who has been just criticized in an article. Transparency, my friend, that's the key word!" I exclaimed.

"Your problem is that you take in anything they say. Open your eyes, man — look at the racism there, against the Flasher Jews (the black Jews of Ethiopia, or even the Mizrahi Jews, Jewish communities of the East). It is useless to mention the Arabs of 1948. What about the freedom of press and the transparency you mentioned during the Gaza campaign? "

"I don't mean they are perfect, but they are definitely better than us. Actually, they are far better … unfortunately."

"In what way?" Mahdi asked, the scissors in his unsteady hands almost cutting the ears of his elderly client.

Thousands of examples came to my mind, but I do not know why the case of Mahmud Darwish — the famous Palestinian poet — came to my mind. "Have you heard of Mahmud Darwish?" I asked.

"Of course, who hasn't?

"You know that all his poetry is anti-Jew?" I asked.

"Sure, he is a great *mona'dhil* (freedom fighter)," Mahdi said, then rushed to ask "What do you mean? You think he was an *amil* (an agent?)" Mahdi's tone sizzled with poison and sarcasm.

"I just wanted to say he had an Israeli passport. But it simply means he lived in a real democracy, not a fake one like the one we have in Algeria. Had he been in any Arab country, he would have died mysteriously in one of our numerous Guantanamo — like prisons. Know what I mean?"

"You are right about the unfathomable number of Guantanamos in the Arab world. Actually, we have far worse. But to talk so well about the Jews is completely stupid. These people are very cunning and play on our naïve gullibility. Take my word about this," Mahdi said. I burst into laughter again and a dark cloud appeared across Mahdi's face.

"You think I'm wrong? Ask anyone around here or better, go and ask any Arab in the street — from the street cleaner to the doctor at university. The answer would be one and the same — you are wrong," Mahdi said, defending his honor.

"Why you are angry, then?" I responded. "If you think that I'm wrong, then I'm wrong. Just accept that I am wrong and go on."

"He is angry because you think you are smarter," Fathi said. "The years you spent at university have dimmed your wits, I'm afraid." While he spoke on Mahdi's behalf, I noticed that he shifted uneasily in his seat.

I thought about his comment for a long time. King Solomon once said, "He who corrects a scoffer gets shame for himself, and he who rebukes a wicked man only harms himself." Hazem's book was right once again.

There was silence, and the one who suffered most was the old man whose hair was being cut in an almost aggressive way. He kept looking at me through the large glass in front of him, as if he was beseeching me to stop, for Allah's sake. When the news finished on Al Jazeera, Mahdi hurriedly switched to the Algerian channel. Half-naked girls were dancing and an old man was singing a Rai song — a form of folk music dating back to the 1930s.

"See? This is what our girls excel at!" Zied exclaimed. He had remained most of the time silent.

"You're telling me — we have become exporters of prostitution?" Mahdi said and then lit a cigarette.

"Have you heard about the questionnaire on Facebook?" Fathi asked.

"No!" Again, Mahdi answered on behalf of all the people.

"They asked a large group of Algerian women about virginity and then found out that two-thirds of Algerian women admit to having had sex before marriage."

"I'm sure it's true," Mahdi said after a moment of silence.

"Don't worry. Before marriage they will go to the gynecologist and have an operation that will make them virgins again. The poor husband would be proud of the chastity of his wife ..." Fathi exclaimed, then let out a strong curse (cursed is the god of Mohammed).

"*Astagfirullah!* Do not curse inside my place again, I warn you," Mahdi threatened. "Listen, you moron, only the *hmar* (stupid) can be fooled."

"What do you mean?" I asked.

"A woman who is not virgin walks differently," Mahdi said.

"How?" I challenged.

"First, when she walks she tends to press heavier on her right foot. Second, when she sits, she relaxes her legs. She doesn't keep them tightly closed, you know what I mean?"

"If what you say is true, then my little daughter, who is four years old, is not virgin, *Lasamaha Allah* (God forbid)," Fathi snapped.

"You are right, but the blood is the only clue. The blood of a real virgin tends to be rosy-colored while that of a fake one is red. Besides, it's very easy ... use one of your fingers before you have intercourse," the old man said, speaking for the first time as he handed Mahdi a note of ten *dinars* and kept his wrinkled hand stretched out for the change. Despite the burst of laughter, the expression on the old man's face remained unflappable.

"So the problem is solved. One needs to use one of his fingers and then see the blood — thank Allah, who always guides those who truly believe in him," Mahdi concluded on behalf of everyone.

"Unfortunately, you are wrong, Mahdi," Fathi said.

"I think Fathi is right," I said. "I have a gynecologist friend. He told me that nobody can know for sure whether it's a true virginity or a fake … even he who did the operation." I stopped to let my words settle.

"He said that if he performed an operation on a certain woman and you brought the same woman to his office wearing a veil over her face and asked him if she was a virgin, he would tell you, 'Yes sir.'" An exclamation was then uttered in unison: "*La Hawla wa la Kowata Illa Billah* (There is no power or might except by Allah's side)

Then Mahdi cursed and stubbed his cigarette out. Fathi let a long hiss through his teeth and Zied kept drumming his fingers on his thighs. I was enamored by the twisted charm of 19th century sordidness.

"I guess they are right when they go out with the French or Italians. At least they are sure they won't be mistreated or used for not being virgins. But when the time is ripe for an Algerian or any Arab husband, they would simply go to a gynecologist, by Allah! We are the greatest fools!" Fathi groaned.

I remember that I had a gloating feeling about their pain — that burning of helplessness inside everyone's chest.

"Why are you silent, man?" Mahdi asked, snatching me back to reality. The sarcasm that rung in his voice meant, "Do you like being a deceived fool?" I shook my head in disbelief.

"They say that prostitutes in Italy made a demonstration asking the government to stop the flood of prostitutes coming from North Africa," Fathi finally said. "After two or three years they would buy a new house in our best neighborhoods, drive a brand new car. Who would not marry one of them?"

"I wouldn't," Mahdi said, looking me in the eye for a long second. "Even if she were as rich as *Balkis* (Queen of Sheba.)"

Actually, he was the only one in the group that I was sure loved money more than anything else, but that was not the question.

"The real question is how would you know? She could dupe any one of us with any story." Zied's voice trailed off.

"Finally, you raised the right question," I pointed out.

I heard almost a general sigh and Mahdi looked at me. "If true Islam was the rule, we wouldn't have had these kinds of problems," he said.

"You are confusing Islam and tradition," I said.

"What do you mean?" Mahdi asked.

"In an ideal Muslim society governed by Sharia law, the problem is worse: There are various cases in which a Muslim can commit adultery in a genuinely *halal* (permissible) way. First of all, Islam sanctions *saraya* (concubines); *motaa* marriages (pleasure marriages) bounded by time; and *misyar* marriages, in which, essentially, the couples continue to live separately from each other as before their contract. They only see each other to fulfill their needs in a permissible, *halal* manner when they please. Normal marriages allow Muslim men to marry up to four women. "I stopped to let my world settle and then continued.

"And if all these outlets are not enough, then a Muslim can commit adultery with a married woman and escape stoning very easily. By Sharia law, adultery is recognized as such only if there is a penetration and four witnesses testifying they have seen it. If they are caught naked in bed and doing anything besides penetration, then it would be only *moda'aba* (just kissing) and therefore completely sanctioned legally. In order for adultery to be proved, the deceived husband has to tell the couple to remain in the act while he goes out and looks for four reliable witnesses!" I spat.

"That's Islamic mercy, something you and your type do not understand, and the polygamy you seem to scandalize is a divine law — the right of every Muslim man. Besides, it is the only solution against spinsterhood," Mahdi countered.

"I don't think you are right, but let me suppose you are, Mahdi. If a Muslim man has hundreds of ways in which he enjoys himself, in a so-called *halal* manner, what about women? Do you think a woman who is unsatisfied either sexually or affectionately would resist the temptation of adultery? You make me recall now the famous prophetic saying enjoining the faithful not to enter their own houses at night after a long absence in *Jihad*," I said.

"That was for something much more important, something a person of your type can't see. Our prophet did not want to make men shun their wives. He wanted to give the women enough time to clean themselves and be in a good shape." Fathi shouted as he got shakily to his feet. On second thought, he resumed his seat.

I laughed to myself and realized how stupid I was to speak my mind in such a blatant way. But I remembered that I was going to leave them forever very soon so I said to myself, why not?

Mahdi's eyes were blazing now. He nervously swatted a fly with his right hand. I was not prepared to back down, though, and went on. "Imagine you have a sister, or a wife, and then in one way or another she got caught by a divine *Mujahed* — a Muslim warrior who wants to spread Islam through war — and takes her as a *sariyya* (a spoil of war). This woman would be his. That means he could sleep with her, sell her to the highest bidder or simply exchange her with a friend who, in his turn, got bored with his *sariyya*. Think about what I'm saying?"

"These are things of the past. Nowadays, there are neither concubines nor slaves."

"That occurred thanks to colonialism, unfortunately. Slavery was abolished by the French. In countries like Mauritania or Sudan, we still hear about cases of slavery. What I want to say is very simple. In an ideal Muslim society, the question will arise again. Do you know why? Because, we try to colonize other countries in the name of *Fath* (Muslim conquest). Ask yourself a simple question: 'What would happen to the women of a country that loses war against us?' " I said.

"You speak as if you were not a Muslim," Mahdi said cynically.

"I am no longer a Muslim — I'm a free man," I said, looking at Mahdi in the eye.

He glanced away and shouted. "*A'udhu billah,* I seek refuge with Allah … you have sold yourself to those pigs."

"We are the true pigs, Mahdi, and you know that." I said.

I do not remember what was said after that because I felt an angry fist hit my mouth and I reacted. The scene became like an old western film. Chairs flew through the air and there were screams, broken glass and blood. I left the scene I had created and hurried home to safety and solitude.

CHAPTER 51

At home I hurriedly took off my clothes and took a bath. The cold water washed away the pain I felt in my right ribs, my swollen lips and my bruised eyes. My face was messed up, but that was not something new to me. I remember that when I was a kid I would return home after a fierce boxing fight. My mum would scream and wail, but my father would look at me with pride and say to her, "Shut up, *horma* (woman), don't you see he is tired?"

On that night, my mum came to the bathroom door. "Shall I come and rub your back?" she asked.

"No, Mum, I'm not a kid anymore. Besides, I know you know. Stop your game."

"What game? You are my son; there is nothing wrong about it."

"I did not mean that."

"I'm going to enter," she said as she knocked on the door.

"Mum, I'm naked," I cried out terrified, then rushed and put a towel round my waist.

"Put something on," she said. Then I heard her cry, "Ya, Allah, there is blood on the door. What happened? Ya Allah, what happened to your face?"

"Nothing serious, Mum, a guy hit me by mistake … He thought I was his nephew or something. It happens."

"Do you think I'm stupid … I will bring some ice." I knew how much she loved details. For a long hour I would be caged in a witness box and she would cross-examine me until she was satisfied. I cursed under my breath.

"Do you think you are still 20? Look at yourself. Ask a simple question: Is there any teacher in the world who behaves like you?" She pressed the cold ice on my left eye.

"Ouch!" I cried out in pain.

"You remind me of those days when kids loved football and you, of course, you got infatuated with boxing ... your face was not unrecognizable. I thank Allah for that accident."

"Mum, I could have been a champion. I could have been someone ... you would have been very proud ..."

"Stop it. Do you think I would be proud ... seeing all that cruelty? And they call it a noble sport."

"It is the noblest sport in the world. You know why? Boxing teaches humbleness and love. The cruelty is only a means ..."

"Reserve your lecture for the women you are wasting your life with."

"I told you, I know you know," I said.

"Of course I heard about your fight. You made me ashamed of myself. I was proud of you. I thought you were a teacher, not a gangster. Mahdi's mother was here. She is threatening to sue you ... her son is in hospital. Do you want to go to prison? Do you want to lose your job and be a vagrant like your friends?"

"It's him who started it," I mumbled.

"He is a stupid, uneducated fool. Do you want to be like him?"

"I am like him, Mum, except that I read some English books and spent some years at university. If I was different, I would not be his neighbor, would I?"

"The place you are ashamed of is now becoming very expensive. Yesterday, someone gave Noureddine, your neighbor, 90,000 *dinars* for his dilapidated house. Wake up and see how lucky you are!"

"Mum ... would you mind? I want to put on my clothes."

"You are going to pay for all the expenses, do you hear me?" Mum ordered as she pointed a menacing finger towards me. I nodded agreement and then punched the wall when she went out. At that time I knew I had broken nearly every bond with my shallow world and my suicide was imminent. I just had to pick a suitable place and method to carry it out.

CHAPTER 52

That same night I could not sleep. The pain in my broken ribs seemed nothing compared to the pain in my broken heart. Deception and grief pulsated through every inch of my body. I tossed and turned and kept staring at the ceiling. Dorra, whom I thought was gone forever, was still hiding at the back of my mind, in that dangerous zone that felt like a thorn. I slipped a weary hand under my pillow fumbling for Hazem's book, my only rock in turbulent waters. I fumed with rage when I could not find it. I searched every corner in my little room. The book had simply vanished.

"Mum, have you taken my book?" I cried out.

"What book?" she asked, her tone filled with indignation. I fought hard not to scream at the top of my lungs.

"A leather-bound book ... black."

"The one on which there is the *kaffir's* cross?" she asked, knowing full well the book I meant.

"Yes!" I exclaimed in frustration.

"I threw it ..."

"What?" I screamed.

"I threw it away ... do you think I will let my house be desecrated by your filth?"

"Damn the day I was born," I lashed out, pounding my fists and my head against the wall. Suddenly, the door of my room opened. Mum, pale-faced and shaking, threw the Bible to the floor before slamming it shut. A sigh of relief hissed through my teeth, but a pang of self-recrimination cut through my heart. I should not have behaved like that. Besides, she was frail and had diabetes.

I knocked at her door and asked forgiveness. Though she did not respond, I knew she felt much better. As I opened the door of my room, I heard her call out, "Come here, Jamal, I want to tell you something."

She was sitting on her red sofa watching a Muslim program, a rosary in her right hand and the old, big remote control in her left. She lowered the volume and looked at me for a long while. "People have started to talk … they say you don't believe in Allah. Some of them claim you say bad things about, *Sidna,* our master, peace be upon him."

"They do not speak the truth," I lied, avoiding having to look at her in the eye.

"I just want to tell you something. If you leave Islam and become a *kaffir,* you would no longer be my son. I would kill you with my own hands before someone else does it." I knew she meant every word.

"I won't," I again lied, but this time for her sake.

"Why do you need that book in your room then? Do you want to follow their filthy faith … those uncircumcised pig eaters?"

"No, I'm just doing some research. I'm going to get my master's degree next year. Do you think I'm crazy?" I said, then felt shame and remembered what Jesus had said to Peter when he swore he would never deny Him. However, I managed to look her straight in the eye or else she would have died instantly and I would never forgive myself. Her face flinched and blood seemed to rush to her cheeks.

"May Allah help you, son. I know you read many books, but do not forget you are a Muslim. Better to be a murderer and a rapist than follow the path of those damned infidels."

I bid my old mum good night, then went to my room. The Bible was still flung open on the floor. I realized Mum had torn the cover where the cross was etched with the golden blood of Jesus.

278

Several questions brewed in my mind: Why on earth is the cross so abhorred around my world? Why was it so difficult to believe that God has a son? If God has his own house in Mecca, around which people must turn in flocks to pray, then with more reason: Why do we not accept that He has a son that has paid with His blood for our sins? Why did Mohammed — while agonizing — recommend to his companions to eliminate all the Christians and Jews from Arab Jazeera? Was he afraid the people would one day find out the true sources of what he claimed to be revealed from god? Or was it because he knew that the Christian faith in particular offered freedom and hope, not slavery and despair?

CHAPTER 53

Looking back at my first impression when I had arrived back in Algeria, I remember that I felt that the country had seen so many changes in the short span of only 11 months. Apart from the exorbitant rise in the price of goods, I saw that the people — especially the young — were turning by hundreds to fundamentalist Islam. Big brother oppression boosted *salafism*. Or maybe it was a general trend or a prophecy being fulfilled. The shackled beast had managed to get free at last, I thought.

Islamic Banks — owned by some pious long bearded financiers In the gulf region had paved the way for other Islamic initiatives in Algeria: Al Baraka bank, Abu Dhabi Islamic Bank and the Kuwait Finance House. Every institution promised divine salvation to the poor who saved their money in their *sharia*-ruled corporations. The sponsored Islamic channels mentioned almost every morning that their banks truly shunned rebate, but endorsed *mora'baha*, by which the bank does not lend money, but sponsors any customer's project — with interest, of course. On reflection, the system was worse but the people did not care — they just rushed by thousands to invest in the righteous path of Islam. The world around me was so small and tight that I welcomed the idea of an escape into the virtual world of the Internet.

I was amazed when they asked me for an identity card inside a cybercafé. "Are you serious?" I asked in disbelief.

"It's a new law, sir. I can't keep my business open if they find out I served you without an identity card," said the frail long haired woman from behind her desk

I refused at first and made a fuss, then gave her my driver's license. I had no other choice. They would ask for it everywhere else also. I remember that I was given an identification number of 666: the very mark of the beast.

The woman hastened to add, as she saw the frown on my face, "It's just a number."

Obviously, she did not read the Revelations of John — but how could she read about it? After all, she lives in a country where it is still illegal to own a Bible. I wondered, at that time, when the United Nations would finally do what was right and impose, by force, freedom of worship in the Middle East.

That day, I discovered that YouTube had been shut down and a customer said that Facebook would be banned very soon. Big brother was afraid, I thought. Yet the dictatorship of the army generals and sons was being weakened every day. The people hated them and though out of fear kept silent, the indignation inside their chests was so tight that it threatened to explode very soon.

I sat at my desk at post number 13; the old computer took its time to open. I typed my code and then again waited. After about four minutes, I was finally allowed to navigate the Web. But there was nothing left to log on to. The books I wanted to read were only downloadable if you paid $1 or $2. The problem was that we Algerians did not have the right to transfer foreign currency.

Chatting with a woman from the civilized world was like plowing a barren field. Once she knew you were an Arab North African, she would take to her heels. I virtually visited the cities I always had dreamt to visit: New York, Paris, London and Amsterdam. The woman who sat beside me did not stop chatting with an Italian in Palermo. Her high-pitched voice disturbed the ears of every customer, but she did not seem to care and kept talking in her broken Italian and smoking like a chimney. Somehow I pitied her eagerness, her almost impossible attempt to start a new life. After about an hour I left and went to the café.

CHAPTER 54

As usual, the place was full; the youth represented the overwhelming majority. That made sense in a country where more than 40 percent of the population was unemployed. Khamis, in his late 30s, was tall and skinny, with a face blurred with a long beard, beckoned me to join him.

"I haven't seen you for a long time … five years?" I said as we hugged.

"Seven … since the day when we shared that crazy old German woman, remember?" Khamis had mischief in his eyes.

I wracked my memory. "Yes, that old grey-haired Hindu who always spoke about the Yin and Yang stuff," I said.

Khamis burst into laughter, but I only smiled and wondered if the smile reached my eyes.

"By Allah, you have not changed … except for the grey hair."

"You too, except for the beard."

"We did so many bad things in those days," Khamis said, returning to his seat.

"You are right … We were hungry for sin."

"May Allah forgive us. Sit down, man."

"What happened to your once-handsome face?" I teased.

"Don't you think the beard fits me? Women love it, you know."

I recalled Aisha, the beloved wife of the Prophet Mohammed. She said that beards made men handsome and virile. The problem was that Mohammed was *ajrad* (hairless).

"I think you are far better without it," My remark did not

seem to please him. Khamis was an intelligent, ambitious man, I thought. He had an extraordinary gift for commerce. I remember how poor he had been, but by sheer will and hard work had become relatively well off. His specialty was secondhand clothes; he'd started as a small salesman and then became one of the biggest providers. But now he was clearly drawn by the *jihadists* and *salafists* line of thinking. The previous happiness and eagerness for life that had once formed an aura of charm around him was now blurred by the stern piety of a devout Muslim.

"I heard you bought a house in Dreira," I said after a long moment of silence.

"May Allah pray for Mohammed ... do you want to hit me with an evil eye?" Khamis asked and then smiled to soften the sharpness of his rebuke.

"I'm very happy for you. Don't you worry, I will never envy you ... especially now," I teased.

"What do you mean?"

"I heard you are on your second divorce."

"The third, in fact. What shall I do? Arab women do not want to live with a real man. They want to go out now and then, and spend money on clothes and make-up."

"Do not tell me you are planning to marry a fourth?" I asked incredulously.

"Actually, I am, but this time she is a real Muslim. She has worn a *hijab* since the age of seven — you see what I mean? Prophet Mohammed enjoined us to choose the pious over the rich or the beautiful, but we men always follow our eyes. What about you?" His question caught me unprepared.

"I have a daughter," I finally said.

"Okay ... I see ... have you planned to start anew?"

"I don't know. I might return to my wife; we are separated, not divorced. I'm losing my daughter. Yesterday I heard her call the husband of her sister 'dad.' A sword went through my heart."

"Is she a devoted Muslim?" Khamis cut in.

"No, but she does her prayers ... at least very regularly during the month of Ramadan."

"I don't want to advise you, but ... the sister of my fiancée is really beautiful and very rich. She wears *hijab* and she knows how to treat a man. You know Prophet Mohammed enjoined women to worship their husbands. These women we see in the street are not for *kisba* (possession). The real women are inside their houses. You don't see even their faces." Khamis stroked his beard thoughtfully.

I wanted to say that I did not need a slave woman anymore. I needed a woman who truly loved me and truly cared for me. I wanted a woman who was like a tigress at night and like a friend — or better, a mother — who cared after her clumsy, awkward child. I wanted someone divided evenly well between East and West — like me.

"What has happened to you?" I asked after what seemed an eternal moment of silence.

"What do you mean?" Khamis inquired.

"The beard ... the piousness. The sudden devotion ... everything," I explained.

"It's a long story," Khamis replied.

"We have time. In fact, it's the only available commodity in this country."

"Do you remember how I used to live?" he asked.

"Of course, like a vagrant," I teased.

Khamis smiled, but this time the smile did not reach his eyes. "Three years ago, I was drunk. I had two prostitutes in my bed when I saw Sheikh Bin laden say, 'Come and fight with your brothers in Afghanistan.' When I woke up at *fajr* (dawn), the *adahn* cried, '*Allaho Akbar*', I knew it was a message from Allah. I was deeply moved. I kicked the two sisters out, washed my face and went to the mosque. I found a long-bearded old man and I told him the story ... I said I was drunk and didn't know what to do. He said that I was very lucky and enjoined me to do *ghusl* (whole ablution)."

From that day on I never missed a prayer ...' Khamis' voice trailed off, but I could hear his mind questioning. Could he trust me? On reflection, he opted for trust. "Allah wanted me to fight for Islam. I did not lose much time. After two months or so I travelled to Pakistan. There I met some other Muslim brothers; but unfortunately, we were sold out by a rat, a *kabyle* from Algiers.

I was tortured by the *Salibiyin,* crusaders, and Muslims as well. Then I was extradited and here I spent more than one year in prison. They were, without a doubt, the darkest days in my life. I was released, but I have to sign in every morning at the nearest police station."

"Have you seen Bin laden in a dream again?" I asked.

"No, only the once ..."

"What happened to your business?"

"I lost almost everything, but I started from scratch again. I'm going to open a new store with my brother-in-law. Allah never forsakes the one who truly believes in him."

"Will you go to Pakistan again if you see the same vision?"

My question caught Khamis unprepared. He swallowed hard and lit a cigarette. Clearly, he had no answer. Two women passed by, one half-naked, the other black-gowned and veiled. Hand in hand they walked, unaware of the stares around them.

"One has a foot in *Jahannam* (Hell) and the other has a foot in *Jannah* (Heaven)," Khamis commented.

"Which one is which?" I asked.

"Are you kidding? Don't you know that prophet Mohammed said no woman would enter Heaven if she exposed some of her hair to outsiders? Look at her, man, she is almost naked."

"What about their hearts?" I asked almost philosophically.

"Would you let your daughter or your sister walk like that in public?" Khamis asked instead of answering.

"I would, very probably, if I knew she had nothing sordid in her heart to hide. Besides, would you be able to tell her what to wear in 15 years' time? Look, gone are the days when the man dictates everything to a woman. Even if we wanted to, we would not be able … times are changing."

"Bullshit!" Khamis exclaimed.

"Well, there is another alternative. You can live like a hermit somewhere away from the civilized world."

"You mean getting dressed like that makes you civilized? Wake up, man, this the new *jahilia* about which Sayd Kutb has written."

On reflection, I decided to change the subject. "Where were you imprisoned in Algeria?"

"In various prisons, but most of my time was in Serkadji."

"A high-security prison … full of dangerous men," I observed.

"You won't believe what you may find behind those cruel walls … I met with a *sheikh* who has a doctorate in nuclear physics. People could not speak to him because they could not understand his intricate explanations of some phenomena that you and I might consider simple or trite. He is a great man indeed. I, myself, when he started speaking about the scientific miracles in the Qur'an, I would tell him, 'Please stop, my mind is about to explode.' But the man would smile and say it was just the tip of the iceberg."

Khamis spoke fast, almost wrapped up his words. Clearly, he was excited. Clearly, he blindly believed the so-called *miracles* in the Qur'an. Dr. Zaghloul al Najjar made a fortune out of this and millions of credible minds believed his nonsense.

Luckily, a single man named Zacharias exposed his lies and bravely fought the hundreds of channels destined to spread Islam using falsehood and disinformation. He fought them singlehanded, armed with a cross that he held like an arm in his right hand. He prevailed, for he said the truth — without embellishment, without speciousness.

No doubt, the tension was growing in Algeria. The gap between rich and poor was growing at a fearful speed. The naïve, disconcerted poor were lured by the recent Muslim channels sponsored by the two eternal enemies: Saudi Arabia and Iran. One fought for a Wahhabi kingdom, the other wailed for the sacred Imami Shia leadership. The two poles accused each other with infidelity, but caught in the quagmire were the ensnared youth who turned by thousands to mosques and spoke about *sahwa* (renaissance of Islam).

The young kids, who one year ago used to steal during the market day to pay for illicit pills or cheap pharmaceutical alcohol, were now in flocks hurrying, lest they miss their *fajr* (prayers.) It's funny how they grew their immature beards. How they valiantly spoke about Allah's kingdom — how distrustfully they looked at me, the grey-haired adult who was supposed to be their ideal.

Clearly, Algeria was moving towards that no-return zone to which Somali had moved some years ago. The country was moving towards a disaster. I lamented, for a short while of course, about my lost country — my lost freedom. Most of the excited new soldiers of Islam did not know the true face of Islam, did not see the real ugly face of the beast. They would wake up one day and find themselves swimming in a pool of blood, but then it would be too late. Too many innocent lives would pay the price and of course only the poor would suffer at the end of every analysis. Bourguiba, the late Tunisian president, saw the beast and did all he could to postpone its rebirth in his own country. Without him, all of North Africa would have been an Afghani quagmire. He was a man — a real man of state.

Then I asked myself why I should worry. I was determined to die very soon, sooner than I had once imagined. Let them caress the iron teeth of the bridled monster. Let them believe the hypocrisy and the lies broadcast by channels like, Al Jazeera, Annas and Iqraa.

"Poetry is *haram*," Khamis said, pulling me from my musings.

"What did you say?"

"I said these Gulf moneybags squander their petrol fortune on a poetic channel that only praise kings and emirs. Don't they know poetry is *haram?* Unless, of course the poetry has a lofty motive such as praising Allah and his messenger. Hassan bin Thabit, the famous prophet's poet, was the sword of God, swerving the threat of divine revenge at anyone who criticized the prophet, Allah's blessings and peace be upon him," he corrected.

I remembered Hassan bin Thabit. The *sira* recounts that during *Ahzab* war, he sat with the women in *Al Medina* fort when all able men went to war with the prophet. Ibn Hisham recounts that one day a Jew soldier was inspecting the fort. Hafsa, the prophet's aunt, asked Hassan to go and kill the man. The poet was afraid. To save the women and the children, she put a belt round her waist and, armed with a big stick, descended towards the soldier and fought with him. She prevailed and killed the Jew. She went back to Hassan and asked him to take off his arms and clothes as loot, for he was a man and she was a woman. Again the poet said no. I wondered secretly if such a man truly meant all the praise he said about Mohammed.

"Painting, too, is *haram.* If someone paints a creature with a soul," Khamis said, snatching me back again to reality. On reflection, everything beautiful was *haram,* or not permitted, in Islam: Music, theater, cinema — anything that enriches the soul and refines sentiments. Pervasively, everything is *halal* (permitted) provided it honors Allah or his messenger. Consequently, innocent blood, revenge, deceit and even incest were sanctioned and sometimes rewarded. Nobody could concoct such a devilish scheme except the devil, I thought.

"You know, if we really practice Islam, we will live in Heaven on Earth," Khamis said. His eyes were confident and firm. My hands became fists, but I forced a smile. "You would never see any poor in the streets and all the society would be cleansed. They say in Mecca that nobody steals. Leave anything valuable and return to it after a long time. You will find it in its very place, do you know why? Because the people there fear Allah, and they are pious." Khamis cleared his throat then went on:

"God gave them petrol as a reward and a response to Ibrahim's (Abraham) supplications. If they decide one day not to sell, the entire world would tumble down. They are the true masters of the world." Khamis' eyes narrowed as if he was daring me to say the opposite. I saw that it was useless to argue.

Actually, the Saudis, Qataris, Emirates and Kuwaitis were extremely lucky because they dealt with honest people who paid for what they bought. Wait for China in another ten years or so, and you will see if they will speak so arrogantly about their petrol again. Like their forefathers, the Moguls who invaded Arabia and spilled blood until it had reached the knees, will turn them, once again, into tent-dwelling and goat-raising Bedouins. Let them cry out for Allah's mercy then, and let them tell me if their Allah truly hears prayers and supplications, I thought.

"*Sobhana Allah* (praise to Allah). You know, our father Ibrahim (Abraham) had prayed for Mecca, oh Allah, make it safe and rich forever. Curious how all the world is in turmoil except that tiny place in which Allah's house had been erected." Khamis said .He did not know about the massacres done in the very sanctuary he thought had always been safe.

"Did you know that Qara'mita invaded Mecca and killed many people there?"

"Before or after Islam?" Khamis asked.

"The question is irrelevant. Ibrahim was born thousands of years before them. But, to your knowledge, Qara'mita was a Shiite sect born long after the advent of Islam. They even looted the black stone and kept it in their custody for more than 23 years."

"I don't know from which source you bring these things. I wonder why an educated man like you believes in that Internet nonsense," Khamis challenged.

"Go to any library and you will find the information in any Muslim history book."

"Maybe," Khamis said with half conviction. "I think we better stop talking about religion when we are together, don't you think so?"

At that moment Mahdi came in and sat on the chair opposite me. Khamis stared at him. "What happened to your face? By Allah, I did not recognize you."

"Nothing!" Mahdi said, shifting in his seat.

Khamis understood everything at once. "I think I have to go now. Don't forget to call me," he said, offering a small, embarrassed smile.

There was a long moment of silence. "Does your eye still hurt?" I asked.

"Not too much," Mahdi said, producing a cigarette out of his left pocket. I watched calmly how he nervously struck the match across the box. Twice there was nothing. I finally took out a lighter and lit it for him.

"Thanks." He sucked feverishly at his Hoggar cigarette.

"My mum made a scene last night," I said.

"You did not see my mother," he said and shook his head.

"I can't sleep on my right side," I moaned.

"I still can't eat.. I think my jaw is broken," Mahdi almost smiled.

"Sorry …"

"It's me who should be sorry … I was overexcited … I think I deserved it." He stood up and kissed me on the forehead. I kissed him back. For a second, I felt warmth in my heart. I knew, then, I was wrong. My friendship with Mahdi was stronger than religion or Shaitan.

CHAPTER 56

Masoud was a young, ambitious youth. Like every young man of his type, he was thirsty for opportunities. He was a *huissier de justice* (court bailiff), but still without a good name or good contacts. He knew how lucky I was with those rich, well-dressed women, so he forced his friendship on me, and I, knowing that I was going to leave very soon, did not mind. At least I would have someone to talk to, someone with whom I could kill time, as they say in Algeria and very probably everywhere else in the world.

After three missed calls I agreed to meet him in a café not far away from where I lived. He came dangling the keys of his old car in one hand and holding a packet of Algerian cigarettes in the other. Decidedly, he had some potential, but the way he dressed, walked and showed off the rusted keys needed a lot of work and long hours of refinement. If only I'd had time, I would have made him a pro, a gentleman who looked like any genuine man of high birth. Hard luck to him, that I neither had enough time nor even the energy to help a hungry wolf in wait.

"Are you sure you want to stay here? Why don't we go to a better place where there is good company?"

"With these cheap clothes you wear, they will make fools of us," I answered.

"What's wrong with them? They are brand new and very expensive too."

"The colors, the design … many things."

Masoud sat down; his feelings were not hurt. Clearly, he had a gift and a keen desire to rise.

"Today, I was browsing the net and was very surprised."

"Why were you?" I asked, my voice ringing with sarcasm.

"I discovered a blog called religion.newsblog.com."

"So?" I was actually eager to hear more.

"Can you believe it? They are allowed to use the Net freely and defend those infidels who renounced Islam and nobody cares. It seems to me the government has a hand in this."

"Why? Nobody speaks about the thousands of Muslims who preach Islam in the West?" I nearly snapped.

Masoud swallowed and shifted in his seat. "Anyway … nobody can imagine that a Muslim can renounce his religion and follow *shirk* (polytheism)."

"You are wrong. Many are becoming followers of Jesus. If they let people free, this country will become Christian in two decades."

"I don't believe you. For what? Money? Visa? women? Unbelievable!" He shook his head in indignation.

I wanted to say that the one who read about Jesus, even if he were as skeptical as me, could not help but get infatuated with that divine entity. Only the blind could not see the greatness of that son of man. But too good to be true, I thought.

"They say thousands are changing their faith every day — Egypt, Iran, even Saudi Arabia." I said.

"You speak as if you were one of them."

The remark caught me unprepared. Was I a Christian after all? Or had I no master yet? On reflection, if Christianity meant to read the Bible every night and love that entity named Jesus with every bit of one's might, then yes, I was a Christian.

"Christianity has never been part of our culture," Masoud pointed out.

"I do not understand what you mean," I said.

"I mean, we had only Jews in Algeria and families of Jewish origin. They had lived for thousands of years here. They kept to their synagogues and we kept to our mosques."

"There had also been so many Christian families before the advent of Muslim *Fath*, conquest. Actually, only the Berbers in the south remained pagans. Saint Augustine was one of them, remember?" I pointed out.

"Yes, but where are they now?"

"Killed, or driven away by the first invading Muslims. Don't forget Mohammed's famous order to oust all Christians from every conquered land."

"*Fath* is not an invasion," he defended, a slight irritation in his voice. Then he thought, and a smirk went over his face for a moment. I feared he would bring that futile argument advocated by Ahmadi Muslims: That all wars waged by Muslims were defensive, that blood was never shed for loot or the spread of Mohammed ideology by force. Luckily, he was not poisoned by Qadiani garbage.

"The wars did not spread Islam at that time, the people did. People had no Internet; books were not available. The only way to save the world was through those futuh'at (invasions). It gave the opportunity for the people who lived in *dhulom'at* (layers of darkness) to discover the beauty and the freeing message of Islam."

"Why were Mohammed's soldiers the only people who kept invading and looting innocent, non-belligerent societies? Why did all other people of faith keep to themselves and never ..."

"Because the others had no divine mission ... they simply followed the wrong path of the *kaffir*," Masoud cut in, then drummed his fingers on the table nervously.

"You said Islam did not spread by the sword, so why did all the people become Muslims in an instant? I will tell you why. Because the vanquished natives had only two choices: either pay excessive tax and live in constant degradation, or embrace Islam and be a citizen of a second degree. Most Christians left, but Jews, persecuted everywhere, had no choice. Some of them accepted Islam, but most of them paid their taxes, and skillful as they were in business, had no need to worry about what they had to give as *jizya*, a per capita income tax levied on non-Muslim citizens."

"What you say does not make sense," Masoud countered. "We all know that Muslims treated Christians better than Jews. The Qur'an enjoins us to treat them fairly but to constantly be on our guard regarding 'the grandchildren of pigs and donkeys.' Yet there is no single genuine Algerian Christian family. The very few are either of European origin or are *arrivistes* (opportunists), who call themselves Christians, but still are Muslims at their very hearts."

"You know better than me that the Roman Empire reached the outskirts of Tebessa if not further. I even read an article some days ago speaking about the discovery of an old church in Kabyle, right in the heart of the Berber kingdom. Look at the remnants of churches built everywhere in Algeria. Do you think they were built for decoration? I will tell you a secret. When Jesus was taken to Golgotha, who was taking the cross on his back? It was Simon from Kairouan-a North African." I took a good sip from my cold espresso.

"Anyway, *tabshir* (evangelization) is a big threat. It gnaws at the fabric of our society. It threatens the interior peace and causes extra problems to any Muslim society."

"We live in the 21st century. Don't you believe in the freedom of religion? Do you think we can continue like this forever? Do you believe the U.N. will not interfere one day?" I asked.

Masoud looked straight at me, blinked warily and shook his head. "Let me tell you something," he began. "Our society is a Muslim one and it will remain so till the end of days. There are some exceptions, of course: homosexuals, atheists, people who call themselves Christians. And let us not forget the *jihadists*. But, all in all, we are a homogeneous society, a society that has its own rhythm, its own identity, you see what I mean?"

"No," I said, but smiled to show that I was only joking. Actually, I was not. It was so difficult for my simple mind to understand why we Muslims fought for slavery and isolation with every bit of our might.

"This is a serious threat, Jamal. If all the people of our society become, let's say, homosexuals or Christians or psychopaths … what would be the consequences?"

"No comment," I managed to say.

"I know you think my comparisons are far-fetched, but believe me, it's the same."

"The same?" I asked in disbelief.

"Yes. By Allah, every one of them represents a threat … psychopaths commit murder, homosexuals spread AIDS and Christians are the worst … they contaminate minds."

I saw with my third eye, Jesus the Lord of Hazem, smiling to his persecutors, blood oozing out from five parts of his body. Then an idea flashed through my mind from nowhere. The five-pointed star that hung upon all minarets represented the five wounds of Jesus. The *hil'al*, the crescent, facing the sky represented the two horns of Shaitan. A cold horror sliced through my heart.

"I think we should not let these people contaminate our serene and harmonious society," Masoud added, then paused to make effect. "Our society is roughly speaking peaceful …"

"Have you ever heard of a Christian who blew himself up?" I immediately asked then I continued "Of course not. The real threat is in these *jihadists* — the true Muslims, I believe — who still want to do *Fath* (conquest) and believe they have a divine mission."

"Most of these so called *jihadists* are kids — very poor kids" Masoud said.

"It is not poverty, my friend, and you know that!" I countered.

"I still believe it is poverty. When a young kid sees one of his peers driving a fancy car in the company of a beautiful girl and he is simply an observer, what do you think will happen? Hatred inside him will spread like a disease and then, at a certain point of time, he will do anything to give vent to that volcano inside. It's natural," Masoud said and shrugged his shoulders.

"You think it's poverty and you seem convinced ... *'bon appétit!'*"

"What do you mean?"

"The real problem is in Tawbah Surah (The Repentance), my friend. They have to abolish it from the Qur'an, if they want to make it right. Not only have the poor been part of *jihadist* massacres. Actually, most of them had good jobs: engineers, teachers, even businessmen. Bin Laden is a case in point. He was one of the richest men in Saudi Arabia."

"*Astaghfirullah,* I ask forgiveness from Allah. Are you aware of what you are saying now? And for what? For the sake of U.S.A.? I will tell you something — whatever you do they will always look askance at you ... always think you are a potential threat. Besides, when are you going to put this in your mind: They hate us."

In a way, Masoud was right but I was not ready to give in.

"I don't blame them. Actually, I think they are stupid and too lenient," I said almost to myself.

I could see the anger rising in his face and eyes, and to my stupefaction I saw with my third eye the beast inside him ready to get out and do me harm. Was that the beast foretold by the John I read about in Hazem's book? Or was I wrong after all? Whatever the answer might be, I was sure of only one thing: Islam and Mohammed were part and parcel of Saint John's prophecies.

At home I hurriedly ate my dinner and went to sleep. I was exhausted physically and spiritually. Even my mum did not venture to give me one of her lectures. When I woke up in the morning, I realized that it had been the first night I had spent without reading the Bible. A sword cut through my heart and I was stunned by my own reaction.

CHAPTER 57

I always hated Fridays, the best day of the week for Muslims. I ordered a cappuccino at the old shabby café in my neighborhood and lit up a cigarette before the drink was even ready. The short, balding man behind the counter was busy lecturing a small but avid crowd of customers about Iran.

"These people are crazy. Now they are making a film about Ibrahim (Abraham), the father of all prophets. There is a real actor who plays the role of our father; can you imagine it? A mortal who goes to toilet every day playing the role of the father of all prophets, peace be upon him."

"Next time, they will even put our prophet Mohammed in a film. They will make one of their stupid actors play his holy role. "*Astagfirullah*," I ask pardon from Allah," a middle-aged spectacled man exclaimed.

"*Astagfirullah*. If they do it, the whole world is going to burn — more than 1 billion Muslims around the globe will take up arms. No, my friend, they are not that stupid to play with fire."

"If the father of Mohammed, Ibrahim — peace be upon him — is already cast in a film, do you think they won't do it one day?" another skinny, tall young man said.

The waiter drummed his fingers on the counter and sighed. He looked at me through the corners of his eyes expecting me to say something.

"Is it ready … my cappuccino?" I asked. The man looked at me, took my ticket and turned to his old and rusty coffee machine. With a dexterous move of his right hand he kept on pushing the handle forward and soon the black, brewed coffee started dripping inside my cup.

"Iman Kalba'ni, their greatest sheikh, said in a *fatwa* (legal pronouncement) that it was alright to make one of the prophets appear on television," the waiter said while adding foamy milk to my cappuccino.

"Abraham was a human being like us whom God had chosen to represent him on Earth. I think making him appear on TV adds more humanity to his character," I said.

The men looked at each other and fell silent. There was a great deal of hatred in their eyes, but I had decided to speak my mind.

"Even our prophet should appear on television. There are famous *hadiths* (prophetic sayings) describing everything about him — his hair, his eyes, his brows, the way he walked, the way he sat, etc. Are we going to simply ignore these *hadiths* that describe to the least detail his features?"

I paused for effect; the silence became filled with murmurs and the fists transformed into balls.

"Of course not," I went on. "If the Saha'ba described him in that detailed way and even mother of the faithful, Aisha, described how he behaved in bed — think about it. Do you think it is too much to show him on television?"

I was expecting a strong fist hitting my face, but nothing happened. The people simply ignored me and the waiter served me coldly. I took my cappuccino and sat at a table outside. In times of such rare intellectual victories, I felt what it truly means to be free. It was as if one had wings and could fly.

What does a man feel when he knows that he doesn't have long to live? I recall that I held my destiny in my hand. I was in a twisted way happy, but I felt empty from inside. The story of Jesus gave hope, but unfortunately, I thought it was too good to be true.

True, I felt some anguish, but it was neither the anguish of Heidegger or Sartre. My anguish was simpler, but deeper. I feared the few seconds of pain that was necessary in every dying act, but it seemed to me it was better than writhing in pain for months in one's bed. The only difference is that the dying person still held hope in a miraculous healing, for example, but in my case it was a one-way trip.

On a deeper level, I feared the hereafter. What if the beautiful story of that holy entity named Emanuel was true? What if most scientists were wrong and the Bible's account was accurate? I reckon my second fear was stronger, for it involved hope and the possibility of redemption. As I was lost in those thoughts, Zied grabbed my arms.

"Where have you been, man? I went to your house twice this morning."

"I woke up early and decided to take a walk."

"You are a lucky man. You live like a king — I really envy you."

"Appearance versus reality … the famous Shakespearean dichotomy …" I said, my voice trailing off.

"Oh please, stop it. Say *al-hamdulillah* (thanks Allah). You are educated, you have a good job, you are lucky with women. What do you want more?"

I asked myself the same question but in a different way. If I had not lost my job and continued to live in a big fallacy called Islam, would I have been able to lead a happy life? I was not so sure, but sometimes doubt makes one's decision, however solid it might be in his eyes, seem frivolous and stupid.

"Sometimes it seems to me you do not listen at all, you treat everybody around you with a kind of cold antipathy." He continued.

Zied was becoming emotional, I thought. Was it because of his young brother who drowned last year in the Detroit of Gibraltar trying to cross illegally to Spain, or was he really in love with that fat girl who always wore the same black *hijab*.

"Are you still with that girl?"

"She eats a lot, Jamal. She needs a restaurant owner, not a poor man like me. When we went out last week, she ate her sandwich and then finished mine. By Allah, if I marry her I will die of starvation."

I laughed at the way he spoke about his fiancée and he laughed at his bad luck.

"Say, Zied, can you find me some stuff?"

"What stuff?" He asked quizzically.

"Pills," I forced out.

"By Allah, you are mad. You are a teacher, man. Do you want to be like those bumps in the neighborhood?"

"I need them," I said, swallowing hard.

"For what?" He asked with concern.

"You don't need to know." A smile of recognition beamed over Zied's face. "By Allah, those women of high birth ..."

"Will you help me?" I cut in.

"Okay, I will see what I can do."

I spent the whole day outside. I ate my lunch in a cheap restaurant, then I spent the rest of my evening roaming the streets of the most prestigious neighborhoods. I went to an expensive bar restaurant, the clients of which were either rich Algerians or expatriates. I tipped lavishly the waiters, the beautiful dancer who danced a special oriental dance on the top of my table. I do not remember how much money I slipped inside her bra each time she moved her waist so close. I still remember her snake death dance, the smoke of cigarettes, the sweat, and the looks of prostitutes who thought I was rich and carefree. Indeed, my farewell night was quite a night.

CHAPTER 58

That Friday night I decided to step into action at last. I hugged my mum for a long time.

"What is it, my dear?" she asked while both concern and happiness rang in her voice.

"Nothing, Mum, I just wanted to say how much I love you."

"You are drunk … don't you know we are in Shaban (the month of separation). Only two weeks before the coming of the holy month of Ramadan."

I hushed her with a finger and hugged her tight. I could feel the hot tears brimming in her eyes.

"I miss your father. I wish he was present at this moment," she said.

"I know. I'm sure he watches us now, smiling that smile of his," I comforted.

"I won't be able to sleep."

"Maybe I should stay with you for a while."

Mum's eyes brimmed with tears again. She could not help it. Whether happy or sad, her tears flowed abundantly. She sat on her chair and switched off the television. Once again, memory called at her. From time to time, when she was really happy and deeply moved, she would pour her heart and tell her story. Now and then, a smile would light her face; other times her face would crumble and tears would well in her eyes. But her story had to be told and I had to listen even though I knew what she would say next. I felt that it was like probing a sore tooth, but I had to listen as I had listened before to my late father telling the same story.

Each one of them had a slightly different version, but it was good, for I could compare and make a whole picture out of it.

Leila, my mother, was the sole daughter of a rich landlord, my grandfather, Sheikh Ahmed. They used to live in El Oued or Oued Souf, a city in El Oued Province, Algeria. The oasis town was watered by an underground river, hence its name. The river enables date palm cultivation and the rare use (for the desert) of brick construction for housing. As most roofs are domed, it is known as the "City of a Thousand Domes."

From age seven, Leila was destined to marry her uncle's son. My grandfather Ahmed was a strong man. One day, my mother once said, he choked an ox to death with his bare hands just to show his strength in front of a mesmerized crowd. Ahmed taught the Qur'an to young children in the mornings and made *hijabs* (amulets) for every type of pain and trouble in the evenings.

At night, he shook off the exhaustion of the day by listening to poetry or stories of ancient heroes such as Shanfara, Antara and Shater Hassan. He was the only educated person in that region. Grandfather Ahmed had studied in *zitouna*, Tunisia, the oldest theological institute in North Africa. Then his father had sent him to the prestigious El Azhar in Egypt, where he had spent two years. Mum said that my grandfather's voice was warm like a flute, and his mastery of the art of recitation was unparalleled.

My grandfather was a *salafist* (conservative) by conviction and thought the new Muslim brotherhood of that time too lenient and too political. He always doggedly repeated, "*Al halal bayen wa al haramo bayen,*" which meant what is religiously permitted is clear and what is forbidden is clear, too. He despised Sayed Kutb's modern exegesis of the Qur'an, ridiculed Ahmed Amine's novels and scoffed at every modernist heresy. He had spent most of his life fighting what he considered a degenerate way of embracing the *kaffirs'* (unbelievers') way of looking at life and things.

My grandfather loved my mum dearly, but he did not teach her how to read or write. He thought a perfect woman should be a good housewife and love her husband more than anything in the world.

Leila grew as attractive and resourceful as my grandfather expected. Each day she became more beautiful and riper for her maternal mission. She was a gift from God, and he had never weighed the option of getting married again to have a male heir. He raised her like a girl, but expected her to be strong like a boy. One thing was for sure, he loved her with every bit of his might. Consequently, Leila never felt the weakness of a woman nor was she devoid of deep feelings.

Mum told me once that she had never considered Ali — her cousin — as a man with whom she would one day live. He was like a brother to her, but she respected her father and had decided not to antagonize his resolve.

My father — Hedi — was from the capital, and even if he had not been a soldier in the French army, he had no chance to ask Leila's hand. At that time, only women of bad reputation married a man from another tribe. Leila was an exceptional pearl, and her chances of marrying a foreigner were, at the best, very low.

It all started one morning when she rode her favorite donkey towards the river. Normally one of the servants would take the jars and do the job of collecting water, but on that particular day the servants were busy, for my grandfather, Ahmed, was celebrating the circumcision of a group of orphans.

Hedi was sitting on a log near the river wearing his French uniform and looking as handsome as Jupiter. Their eyes met, and that was all — no words, no smiles, not even the least shred of doubt. It was love at first sight; they knew it, and they were both ready for the terrible challenge. When a man and a woman fall in love, they simply know everything important about the other person; my mum would usually point out.

Leila and Hedi kneeled to Cupid, the great Roman god, marveled at his baby smile and the sweetness of his arrows. They experienced that magic chemistry of sentimental nirvana. No power in the world could have hindered their desire to finish together the hard journey humans tend to euphemistically call life. The decision was made in an instant and all that followed was a response rather than a stimulus.

Sheikh Ahmed was an active member in the resistance of that time. Ahmed Ben Bella, who had volunteered for service in the French Army in 1935, was in Grandfather's eyes the intellectual son of the French Revolution. Ben Bella even had played center midfielder for 'Olympique de Marseille.' He was awarded '*la Croix de Guerre*' and '*la medaille militaire*' for bravery at Mont Cassino from Charles de Gaulle. For Sheikh Ahmed, Ben Bella embraced European enlightenment and was nothing but a *mona'fik* (hypocrite). However, he never considered him as an unbeliever.

Therefore, my grandfather was determined to help his next-of-kin against the spiteful outsider. He smuggled guns from Tunisia and Egypt, taught young soldiers sacred *jihad*, blessed the martyrs, and provided food and shelter to all the fell' *agas* (resistance fighters) in his region.

Sheikh Ahmed hated the French and, above all, the puppets that helped them hold the reins of their unjust colonization. He was educated and rich and assumed all the people were like him, free and able to decide.

My future father, Hedi, was uneducated and very poor. To avoid starvation he enlisted in the French Army. He never fired a bullet in North Africa or shot a Muslim, he had once said. He spent his whole military life as a foreigner fighting foreigners in a foreign land. The French trained him hard and then used him to fight first Hitler, then the communists in Indochina.

When Paris was occupied, most of the French kept drinking champagne and dancing at night. Most of them cherished the purple extravagance of the City of Lights and fought to remain alive and keep the show on. The French of the colonies fought bravely, but not the French of France. General Petain was not an exception; he, rather, represented the mood of that time —

the possible peaceful coexistence with the Germans under the second Reich. My late father always said that if Petain were to blame, then all the French were to blame.

People of the colonies feared neither Hitler nor the incomparable shrewdness of Rommel, the Desert Fox. They bravely fought for those who gave them food and shelter, and most of them died, and then what? They were soon forgotten with the first streaks of liberation, when the first American soldiers trod on the beach of Normandy, but that's another story and who cares, after all? Even history does not.

Sheikh Ahmed was cruel when things went against his wish, but my mother and father were deeply in love and were ready to die for their sacred bond. Leila told her beloved not to ask her hand. "You will get killed if you dare do this. Please, don't do it," she beseeched him, tears welling in her eyes.

My father was a soldier, and the only thing he had learned from wars was never to turn back or give up. "Don't worry. When it comes to death and danger, I'm always lucky," he comforted her. He had spent five years in Indochina — what would later be called Vietnam — and had returned home safe and sound, not even a wound or single scratch. Bullets feared him, for he was destined to die a normal death.

He came to Sheikh Ahmed's house wearing his French uniform and asked for Leila's hand. All the people of the tribe were waiting for a sign to pull the triggers of their guns, but Sheikh Ahmed admired his courage and ordered them not to fire. "If I or anyone of my tribe sees you here in my region again, then you will die the most horrible death. No mercy, am I clear?" Sheikh Ahmed warned.

"Crystal … I will not leave the region without your daughter, sir. I just wanted you to know this," he replied with respect and resolve.

"You have 24 hours to leave … I advise you to return from where you came."

Father saluted him like a soldier and left. As he was leaving the big house, their eyes met and the message was instantly transmitted. The next morning, with the first streak of dawn, Hedi and Leila met by the river and escaped. They went to Algiers and got married there. The French commander, a tall man who looked like Charles de Gaulle loved the story, signed their marriage act and wished them a happy life. After two weeks, Sheikh Ahmed died of a stroke and Leila never saw a member of her family again. My father had told me that she had wept silently for a while and then regained her sweet smile. My father had always felt guilt, but my mother had never regretted her decision, though she prayed every day for her father's salvation.

Leila, my mother, loved her husband more than she loved herself and endured with him times of real pain and also enjoyed times of real bliss. Though she was uneducated and born in a world that glorified hatred and darkness, my mother knew, by instinct, the magic power of love. She believed in its supremacy to transform life. Even if she did not have the right words to describe her feelings, she somehow bequeathed her legacy to me. Most probably, the raw diamond inside her son's heart needed polishing, but everything had a destiny, as the wise men said.

The *muezzin* cried *"Allah Akbar"* and my mother, like in *The Arabian Nights,* finished her story and rushed to the living room for her *fajr* (dawn prayer). She hummed her imploration for the prophet, *saha'ba* (prophet's companions) and all Muslims in the world. I waited for her to finish her prayers and then tucked her in bed.

CHAPTER 59

I said I had decided to carry out my suicide that night. I chose the easiest, cleanest and most painless way. I bought two tablets of Anafranil 75 from my neighbor.

After I put my mother to bed and waited until she snored, I closed the door of her room. In my room, I vent my feelings and wept silently for a long time, looking askance at Hazem's Bible. I thought that this time even Jesus would not be able to find me a way out.

I prayed for Allah, then for Buddha and finally for Hazem's God. I did not play a single card knowing that, after all, nobody knows. I swallowed the pills and laid down on my bed. I opened the Bible and read: *'They will come from the east and the west, from the north and the south, and sit down in the kingdom of God. And indeed there are last who will be first, and there are first who will be last.'* Luke 13: 29

Sleep invaded my eyes and I was slowly losing consciousness. I was entering that euphoric state that one feels just before death occurs.

That night I saw Jesus hanging on a cross. I heard him say in broken Arabic, or so I thought: *'Eli Eli lama sabaktani.'* Then he finished parts of psalm 22:

1 Mt. 27.46Mk. 15.34
Why art thou so far from helping me, and from the words of my roaring?

2 O my God, I cry in the daytime, but thou hearest not;
and in the night season, and am not silent.

15 My strength is dried up like a potsherd;
and my tongue cleaveth to my jaws;
and thou hast brought me into the dust of death.

16 For dogs have compassed me:
the assembly of the wicked have inclosed me:
they pierced my hands and my feet.

17 I may tell all my bones:
they look and stare upon me.

18 They part my garments among them,
and cast lots upon my vesture.
Mt. 27.35 · Mk. 15.24 · Lk. 23.34 · Joh. 19.24

26 The meek shall eat and be satisfied:
they shall praise the LORD that seek him:
your heart shall live for ever.

Then I heard Him say *"Mowton la tamout, Haya'ton tahya."* (No, you are not going to die, you are going to live.) At that point He disappeared and I saw so many mountains that I had to climb. By my bedside, there was a snake captured inside a jar about to get loose and bite at my flesh. I saw the pain and the hardships ahead. And then I saw an olive tree full of light. I went to that tree hanging above me in the sky. I climbed and climbed upward, and suddenly the tree became rooted inside the palm of my hand and then I saw my hand on the screen of a television.

I opened my eyes and saw Mum smiling triumphantly, holding a letter in her hands.

"They finally sent you this," she said and waited for me to

read the news, though she knew by instinct it was good. I opened the letter and read: 'Dear Sir. You are appointed as a teacher in the secondary school of … ' My mum uttered trilling cries of joy and my heart lost a beat.

I had no doubt that the Messiah had visited me that night. Only one thing that bothered me was why He did not speak good Arabic? I did my research and discovered a stunning truth. Aramaic was so close to Arabic and that is why he had seemed to me unable to master good Arabic.

That day I became a Christian. I have never been to a church, never have been baptized or helped spiritually in this exciting journey I have just begun. The Lord had put in my path people who had helped me break the shackles of Islam. Now I am sure the Lord will send his angels very soon. At home, after a hard working day at school, I would open my television on TBN, Church Channel and Daystar. Sometimes I would watch *al Hayat* channel or *The Truth*. I would watch and learn and feel anointed.

For the first time in my life I felt safe and full of hope. Slowly, the terrifying image of God that I held in my imagination due to long years of indoctrination and misinformation disappeared and in its place was the warm and loving image of the father. Slowly but steadily I cleared my heart and mind from all the poisons I had taken since my early childhood. My confidence increased as I I discovered a new God after the so many years of being devoured by locusts. My third eye or let me say now the Holy Spirit tells me the harvest will exceed even my wildest expectations. The blessings and the prosperity will be miraculous. One day, very soon, I will write another book that specifically enumerates what the Lord had done for me. I know that all these good things are going to happen for this Jesus that I have come to know is so real, so powerful and so great. All in all, I do not have anything to worry about, for I have the King of Kings by my side.

I have no doubt that Jesus is the embodiment of God in the flesh — the Lord of Lords. The hope and light. He is everything and everything is in Him — Hallelujah!

CPSIA information can be obtained at www.ICGtesting.com
Printed in the USA
BVOW031853301112

306853BV00003B/15/P

9 781938 388019